# THROUGH THE YEAR WITH
# JOYCE HUGGETT

Alan William Garrett,
on the occasion of his
confirmation by.
I am, Bishop of Lewes,
on
7th June, 1995
at Storum Parish Church.

Ken Lewes

# THROUGH THE YEAR WITH JOYCE HUGGETT

Edited by
Teresa de Bertodano
and
Derek Wood

eagle
Guildford, Surrey

Typeset by Falcon Typographic Art Ltd, Fife, Scotland.
Printed in the UK by HarperCollins Manufacturing, Glasgow.

# Introduction

From time to time I have had the privilege of speaking to groups of people whose understanding of English is limited or non-existent. I recall, with gratitude, the interpreters who have formed the bridge on which my audience and I have met.

The relationship between an author and an editor is not unlike the speaker-interpreter partnership and as I look back over the years I have been writing, I realise that I have been particularly privileged to be partnered by some superb editors.

To the first I owe so much. Derek Wood encouraged me to write before I ever became aware that I could write. Without his encouragement I would never have completed my first book and without his patient and persistent editing, that book would not have been read by engaged and married couples all over the world. So I was delighted when Derek – now ex-editor and special friend – agreed to take part in the compilation of this book.

Teresa de Bertodano came into my life only comparatively recently, first through a mutual friend and fellow author, next through visiting me when I was a patient in a London hospital and then through editing the book I wrote about the way God met me while I was a patient in that hospital. I think it is true to say that Teresa is the most ruthless of all my editors and I appreciate her so much for that. She is to my writing what the best interpreters are to my speaking: interpreting not merely my words but the unexpressed nuances which are sometimes so hard to communicate. Like Derek, she has given me endless encouragement and affirmation and helped me to grow.

When David Wavre, Managing Director of Eagle, friend and editor, suggested that we publish a book entitled *Through the Year with Joyce Huggett* and when, eventually, I agreed to the proposition, my mind went immediately to Teresa. Would she take on the task of reading most of my books and magazine articles? Could she make the time to listen to tapes of talks and sermons I have preached? Having waded through all this material, would she be able to sift and sort out enough quotations to fill a book which provided readers with a page a day for a whole year? She did. And I am not only deeply touched that she was prepared to undertake the task in the first place but full of admiration for the way she performed it.

In recent years I have enjoyed, not only the co-operation of fine editors, but also the partnership of three talented artists. The first to illustrate my work was Sr. Theresa Margaret CHN – friend and fellow retreat-giver. She spent part of her own retreat reading the excerpts Teresa had selected and illustrating the twelve sections of the book accordingly. As always, when I saw her drawings, I was both moved and excited.

They are meditations in themselves and will enhance the text accordingly. And the photograph on the front cover is a favourite of mine. It was taken by another friend, Gerry O'Mahoney who readily and generously gave me permission to make it available to others in this way. It is also available, in card form from Loyola Hall, Warrington Road, Rainhill, Prescot, Merseyside L35 6NZ.

And so the six of us: Derek and Teresa, Gerry and Theresa Margaret and David and I, together with the other authors I have quoted, offer the reader a thought for each day of the year. Different readers will handle the book differently. Some may want to work their way through it systematically. Others will want to 'dip' just occasionally. Yet others may prefer to forget about the dates and simply look up a section when the need arises – at Christmas time, for example, or when relationships become strained. Some will read a whole page at one sitting. Others may apply the principles of slow reading to a particular page: reading until a phrase or a concept, a word or a sentence draws them to itself, then pausing and pondering, letting their musings give birth to a prayer or a resolve or further meditation.

One of my books is called 'Open to God' and my prayer is that those who journey through these pages may do so in a spirit of openness and with the readiness to receive riches from the God who loves to lavish good gifts on those who will accept them.

Joyce Huggett

# Bibliography

Approaching Christmas, Lion Publishing, Oxford, 1987
Approaching Easter, Lion Publishing, Oxford, 1987
Bible Reading Fellowship Notes, BRF, Oxford, 1990
Conflict, Friend or Foe, Kingsway, Eastbourne, 1984
God's Springtime (book), Bible Reading Fellowship, Oxford, 1992
God's Springtime (cassette), Eagle, Guildford, 1992
Growing into Love, InterVarsity Press, Leicester, 1982
Just Good Friends, InterVarsity Press, Leicester, 1986
Living Free, InterVarsity Press, Leicester, 1986
Listening to God, Hodder & Stoughton, London, 1986
Open to God, Hodder & Stoughton, London, 1989
Marriage Matters, Eagle, Guildford, 1991
Prayer Journal, Marshall Pickering, London, 1990
The Smile of Love, Hodder & Stoughton, London, 1990
Two into One, InterVarsity Press, Leicester, 1981
Under the Caring Eye of God, Eagle, Guildford, 1991

# Late have I Loved You

*Faith, hope and love abide; these three but*
*the greatest of these is love*
**1 Corinthians 13:13**

St Augustine's yearning for God echoes down the centuries

I was so slow to love you, Lord,
your age-old beauty is still as new to me:
I was so slow to love you!
You were within me,
yet I stayed outside
seeking you there;
in my ugliness I grabbed at
the beautiful things of your creation.
Already you were with me,
but I was still far from you.
The things of this world kept me away: I did
not know then
that if they had not existed through you
they would not have existed at all.
Then you called me
and your cry overcame my blindness;
you surrounded me with your fragrance
and I breathed it in,
so that now I yearn for more of you;
I tasted you
and now I am hungry and thirsty for you;
you touched me,
and now I burn with longing for your peace.[1]

(Taken from the Smile of Love, p 120)

# The Joy of Giving

*On coming to the house, they saw the child
with Mary, and they bowed down and
worshipped him. Then they opened their
treasures and presented him with gifts of gold
and of incense and of myrrh.*
Matthew 2:11

True worship always results in reckless giving. One way to
learn how to love in this self-sacrificing way is to observe
the generosity of others and to receive inspiration from it.

Ask the Holy Spirit to create in you a similar desire to be generous;
the ability and willingness to imitate the Father, the Son and the
Magi. Ask him to show you where you have been less than generous
and to show you how he feels about stinginess. Beg him to change
you: to show you what you can give and to whom; to give you the
courage to abandon your entire self to him as a love offering.

Recall the faces of refugees you have seen on television or the
figures of people who are down and out:

We are all God's children.
I have knocked at your door
I have called to your heart
because I dream of a soft bed
because I am eager for a well lighted house.
Why do you drive me away?
Open to me, brother!

Why do you question me
About the shape of my nose
The thickness of my lips
The colour of my skin
The name of my gods?
Open to me, brother![2]

(Taken from Open to God, pp 152, 154)

# Surrendered to the Father

## *On the eighth day . . . it was time to circumcise him . . .*
### Luke 2:21

J esus is just eight days old when we first observe him surrendering himself to his Father and humanity:

By submitting himself to the ritual of circumcision he was publicly identifying himself with the sinful state in which every human being is born. Yet he was sinless. Perfect. The spotless Son of God. He was also identifying fully, in racial terms, with the Jews. If he had refused to take this step, he would not have been recognised by the Jewish authorities as a son of David nor acknowledged, later in life, as a teacher in Israel. Rather, he would have been dismissed as an uncircumcised Gentile. A dog. Yet he was the Messiah, the Son of God. As an unknown writer has put it:

He was circumcised for the same reason that he was born, for the same reason that he suffered. He did nothing for himself, but all for his chosen ones. He was neither born in sin, nor circumcised from sin, nor did he die for his own sin: but it was all for our crimes . . . to be Saviour is his very nature.[3]

(Taken from Open to God pp 141, 142)

# Star of Bethlehem

*'The star they had seen in the east went
ahead of them until it stopped over the place
where the child was'*
Matthew 2:9

John Chrysostom offers a fascinating suggestion about the
nature of the star. He insists that it could not have been
an ordinary star for a number of reasons. First, because it
moved from the east to the south ('for so Palestine lies in
relation to Persia'), second, because it was visible not only by night
like any other star but also 'in the full light of day, which is not
within the nature of any star, nor even the moon'. Third, because
it seems to play hide and seek: 'after they had entered Jerusalem, it
hid itself; and when they had left Herod it showed itself once more'.
Fourth, because this star appears not to have followed a course of
its own. Rather, 'when the Magi travelled, it travelled with them.
When they halted, it likewise halted, as the pillar of cloud in the
desert, (Ex. 13:21). And fifth, when it beamed its light over the
place where Jesus lived, 'it accomplished this, not by remaining on
high, but by coming low, which indicates, not the action of a star,
but of some rational power'. He concludes that 'this star was but the
sign of invisible power, revealing itself in this form'.

(Taken from Open to God, pp 122–123)

# Simeon

*Simeon said: 'This child is destined to cause the falling and rising of many in Israel, and to be a sign that will be spoken against, so that the thoughts of many hearts will be revealed. And a sword will pierce your own soul too.'*
. Luke 2:35

When Jesus was born, hopes of the coming of the Messiah ran high. Most people believed he would come with pomp and ceremony to rescue Israel from its enemies. But a few thought differently. These were known as 'The Quiet in the Land'. They did not dream of violence or power or armies. Rather, they devoted themselves to a life of quiet prayer and constant watchfulness and waited patiently for the time when God would send the promised Saviour. Among these praying people was Simeon.

Simeon predicts that Jesus' life will demand a response from people. They will either be for him or against him. And he tells Mary the privilege of being God's mother will prove to be a costly one.

*Lord Jesus, I marvel at the prayerfulness of
Simeon which brought him into the kind of
stillness where your voice is clearly heard And
I marvel at the quiet trust displayed by Mary
as, step by step, your will for her Son was
revealed. As this new year unfolds, grant to me
that quiet trust which is prepared to watch
and to wait, to listen and to believe in you at
all times and in all places.*

(Taken from Approaching Christmas, pp 84, 85)

# Who Made That?

*An Angel of the Lord appeared in a dream to Joseph in Egypt and said, 'Get up, take the child and his mother with you and go back to the land of Israel.'*
Mathew 2:19–20

Meditating on the return of Mary, Joseph and Jesus from their exile in Egypt, I imagined that I was travelling with them from Egypt to Nazareth. I was sitting astride a donkey with the Christ-child on my lap, playing with him to help to while away the time.

We were playing a game called, 'Who made that . . . ?' The child would ask me, 'Who made oranges?' And I would reply, 'God did'. He would giggle with glee before asking, 'Who made lemons?' and my reply would always be the same: 'God did'.

We had been playing this imaginary game for some time before the realisation dawned that, in fact, the child who was riding between the donkey's neck and me had made the oranges, the lemons, the blue sky and the warm sun. I was on holiday at the time and spent the rest of the day in a daze. I felt full of awe and wonder, seeing the sun shimmering on the sea through very different eyes. The next day, the same thing happened: 'While I walked, I saw creation through the eyes of my Creator: the star-like grasses, the filigree-fragrance of the almond blossom. I knew that I wanted to walk through his world seeing things (creation and pain) through *his* eyes – having his perspective. I did. And as I did so, I kept gasping at the sheer beauty by which I was surrounded. I saw that my Creator is an artist and an author, a musician and a sculptor who has made all things well.'

(Taken from Smile of Love, p 38)

# Friendship with Jesus

*'You will not be left alone; I will come back*
*to you'*
John 14.18 (GNB)

F
riendship with Jesus is intimacy. It is availability. And it is constancy. Jesus' offer of friendship means that we shall never, ever, be alone again. We may *feel* alone but our feelings mislead us. Jesus is at pains to assure us of this fact. Other friends may depart. He will not.

This means, that whenever the storm of loneliness threatens to drown us, we can place our hand in the hand of the God who dwells within: the constant, caring companion Jesus. For Jesus' involvement in our lives is likened, in the New Testament, to the commitment of marriage. Jesus is the heavenly bridegroom. We are his bride. He wants us to relate to him in the confidence that his love is faithful, unending, permanent.

We see this in nature. In spring, if you walk through a field where lambs and sheep graze side by side, you will find that the very sight of a person will send the lambs scampering to their mother. They will snuggle into her, suckle and stay close to her side until the danger has passed. The friendship Jesus offers is similar though even more secure. When loneliness bears down on us, he is our hiding place. There is no safer refuge in the universe than sheltering under the shadow of his wings.

(Taken from Just Good Friends, pp 147, 148)

# Confess and Forgive

## *Love is always patient and kind*
### 1 Corinthians 13:4

Friendship Jesus-style is characterized by unfailing forgiveness. When a friend has failed you, hurt you yet again, don't brush it under the carpet, pretending it hasn't happened. Acknowledge the hurt. Feel the full force of the pain. Then, in prayer, stand with your friend at the foot of Christ's cross. Look them in the eye. Say that it really hurts, but let your love extend beyond the pain. Forgive freely. This is forgiveness Jesus-style: love embracing the hurt *and* the one who caused the injury; love continuing to express itself actively and with compassion.

Such love is slow to apportion blame, as Paul reminds us in 1 Corinthians 13:4–7; it is, however, quick to admit personal culpability. The reason why fractures in friendship often fester is that one or both parties refuse to admit that even a portion of the blame might be theirs. This is tragic. Admit your own failure before God. Don't grovel. Do confess – first to God, then to your friend. Having acknowledged your own failure, perhaps with that powerful little word-trio, *I am sorry*, ask your friend a direct question, 'Will you forgive me?' I have on my desk a card from a friend to whom I put that question recently. Her warm response '*Of course*, I'll forgive you' brings healing to some very grazed places inside of me and motivates me to work towards lasting reconciliation.

(Taken from Creative Conflict, pp 55, 56)

# Choose Wisely

## *You did not choose me, no I chose you*
John 15:16

J esus chose his friends (John 15:16). The element of controlled choice is important. Jesus did not open himself to everyone he happened to meet. Neither did he unveil his innermost secrets to all those who would have befriended him. He was careful: selective. From the multitude, he selected seventy. From the seventy he selected twelve with whom he lived and talked and walked and shared, with whom he enjoyed intimacy.

We read that before calling the disciples he retreated to the hills for a whole night of communion with God. Did he ask the Father a specific question? 'Father, who are to be the men who will live and work with me?' The prayer, if he prayed it, is not recorded but we read that, immediately after that prayer-time, Jesus chose the twelve. Out of this group of twelve, he made a further selection of three: Peter, James and John. And from the three emerged one: John, the beloved.

If we seek intimacy, we must follow the example of Jesus and let our choosing arise from our prayer.

(Taken from Just Good Friends, pp 22, 23)

# Friendship Jesus-style

*Many of his followers said 'This is intolerable.*
*How could anyone accept it?'*
John 6:60

Jesus' friendships were sometimes stormy but he refused to withdraw into a hedgehog ball. Instead, as John shows, he set himself up for more rejection and hurt (Jn 6:60–70). When Jesus watched his disciples take offence at his teaching and abandon him, he turned to the twelve with the question, 'You do not want to leave too, do you?' Peter vowed loyalty at that moment only to stab him with the knife-wound of rejection later.

If we would offer friendship Jesus-style, even when the going is tough and former friends have deserted us, we must be prepared to take the risk: to reach out to offer continued friendship fully recognizing that this might be flung back in our face. This is the commitment Jesus models to us.

(Taken from Creative Conflict, pp 56–57)

# Closeness

*Her tears fell on his feet and (she) he wiped*
*them away with her hair; then she covered his*
*feet with kisses*
Luke 7:38

J esus was unafraid to express affection. His love was an intimate
love. It was expressed through touch: we find a woman of
dubious reputation smothering him with tears and kisses (see
Luke 7:36–38) and we see John leaning his head on Jesus'
bosom at the Last Supper. These demonstrations of affection were
warm, innocent, but deep. If we would be like Jesus, at ease with our
own sexual make-up, as he was, we must learn the delicate art of
appropriate touch.

'Touch? I've never touched anyone in my life!' This protestation
from a thirty-year-old simply highlighted his need for healing. He
was terrified of touch because he had never experienced the joy of
demonstrative love during his childhood. As Jim Bigelow observes,
'Infants and children who grow up in a "non-touch" culture become
adults with all manner of fears and hang-ups where affection and
intimacy are concerned.'4 Jesus had no such inhibitions and the
Holy Spirit's work is to free us from ours: to free us *for* intimacy.
It sometimes makes me sad that some Christians are not more free
in this area. Jesus did not create us to be wooden-tops but warm,
flesh and blood.

(Taken from Living Free, p 103)

# Warmth and Touch

*In his love and pity . . . he lifted them up and*
*carried them*
Isiah 63.9

We all need touch, warmth and affection. This was highlighted during the war by nurses who were working in an emergency hospital ward. To this ward were admitted the babies whose parents had been killed. The babies were given adequate food and clothing. But the mortality rate was alarmingly high. This continued until some of the nurses started to cuddle the babies. Every day they would hold them, coo over them, look down on them lovingly, just as their mothers might have done if they had lived. These infants, starved of love and hungry for touch, responded and thrived. Food and clothing are not sufficient. Babies need to *feel* the warmth of a loving human being if they are to survive and what is true for babies is also true for adolescents and adults. We need to feel the warmth of another's care and concern and tenderness. Where such intimacy is not communicated, a vital part of us disintegrates. We strive to build bridges which span the gulf between the island of our existence and the islands where others exist.

(Taken from Just Good Friends, p 17)

# The Little Prince

*I am the Lord your God*
*I grasp you by your right hand*
*I tell you do not be afraid*
*I shall help you*
Isiah 41:13

In Antoine de Saint-Exupery's *The Little Prince* the child and the fox discover the wonder of closeness. Yearning for intimacy, the fox asks the little prince, who is a visitor from another planet, to tame him.

'What does that mean — "tame"?'

'It is an act too often neglected,' said the fox. 'It means to establish ties.'

'To establish ties?'

'Just that,' said the fox . . . 'If you tame me, then we shall need each other. To me, you will be unique in all the world. To you, I shall be unique in all the world.'

'What must I do to tame you?' asked the little prince.

'You must be very patient,' replied the fox. 'First you will sit down a little distance from me — like that — in the grass. I shall look at you out of the corner of my eye, and you will say nothing . . . But you will sit a little closer to me every day . . .'

The next day the little prince came back.

They sat a little closer to one another every day so that when it was time for the little prince to leave and return to his own country, a great sorrow seized both of them. They had learned, little by little and bit by bit, that they mattered to one another.

(Taken from Marriage Matters, pp 39,40)

# God of Stillness

## *Be still and know that I am God*
### Psalm 46:10

Silence is vital for a number of reasons. Silence is the context in which God most readily reveals himself, in which his voice is most clearly heard and where he rains on us the riches of his love. Silence is the language of lovers. It is therefore the language God delights to use to woo us to himself and the vocabulary we choose to express our response to his love. Silence before God has little to do with achieving but a great deal to do with receiving. In silence, we gather energy, receive guidance, gain God's perspective, discern his priorities and find refreshment. It is essential to the person of prayer that they learn how to drop into this re-creative stillness which is so manifestly enriching:

In silence we come face to face with ourselves. So often, while claiming, believing and singing that 'Jesus is Lord', our lives centre, not around him, but around 'number one'. Self. When we are still, this inconsistency is high-lighted, and we become aware of our need to de-throne self and enthrone Christ afresh.'5

(Taken from Open to God, pp 31, 32)

# Sacrificial Love

*Christ loved the Church and sacrificed himself*
*for her to make her holy. He made her clean*
*by washing her in water with a form of words*
*,so that when he took her to himself she would*
*be glorious, with no speck or wrinkle or*
*anything like that, but holy and faultless:*
Ephesians 5:25–27

True love cares little about receiving; it always rates giving higher than getting. Indeed, not to give would be painful. The model for this kind of sacrificial love is the love Jesus bears for his bride, the church. His love is not so much a feeling as an orientation, a faculty, a series of choices which guarantees the well-being of his bride.

Giving love is caring love. It requires sensitivity, understanding and insight. This intuitive oneness with the loved one not only senses his/her need; it is the propellant thrusting you into the activity which meets that need. To care for someone in this way is costly. And yet, as the Lord demonstrates, sacrificial, caring love is not impoverishment, being cheated of one's rights. It is a sign of inner strength. Erich Fromm puts it well:

'Giving is the highest expression of potency. In the very act of giving, I experience my strength, my wealth, my power. This experience of heightened vitality and potency fills me with joy. I experience myself as overflowing, spending, alive, hence joyous. Giving is more joyous than receiving, not because it is a deprivation, but because in the act of giving lies the expression of my aliveness . . . Whoever is capable of giving themselves is rich.'[6]

(Taken from Growing Into Love, pp 102,103)

# Real Love

## *Courage. It is me, do not be afraid*
### Mark 6:50

'The most important thing that happens between God and the human soul is to love and be loved.'

Kallistos Ware

Real love, God's love, knows when to affirm and when to challenge, when to intervene and when to hold back. God sees the end from the beginning and never loses sight of love's purpose: to promote the *long-term* well-being of the loved one. He understands our frailty, and hurts when we hurt. He is also capable of healing, providing, protecting, but when he sees that we will benefit more in the long-run from working through pain rather than being released from it, he sustains us in the storm instead of sending the storm away.

(Taken from The Smile of Love, pp 13,27)

# Everyday Loving

*It is by your love for one another that
everyone will recognise you as my disciples*
John 13:35

My parents incarnated the love of Christ to the chimney sweep, the window cleaner, the insurance agent, the grocer and the butcher, the greengrocer, the newsagent, the coalman, the policeman, the nurse and the housewives who lived, cheek by jowl with them. They were not plaster saints. They were ordinary working-class people struggling to make a living and, at the same time, trying to live a Christ-like life in the only home they could afford: a rented two up, two down, back-to-back terraced house in a run-down area of Exeter.

If anyone had told them that they were reflecting the love of God to the people in our street or that they had a ministry of helping, they would have made light of such labels. Yet this was what they were doing. And in doing it they were making their own response to the great commission of Christ in which Jesus commands his followers to love as he loved, to care as he cared, to hurt when others hurt. Such love, he said, is the hallmark of the Christian. And such love is one of the basic requirements of anyone who would seek to stretch out a helping hand to others in the middle of life's crises.

(Taken from Listening to Others, p 31)

# The Heart and the Word

*Let it be the hidden disposition of the heart with the imperishable jewel of a gentle and quiet spirit which in God's sight is very precious*
1 Peter 3:4

Every Christian is indwelt by God in their innermost being. The same Spirit of God who has taken up residence in the temple of our soul also energises God's Word which comes to us from outside.

'From the very outset there exists an affinity between the Word from outside, awakening us, and the Spirit watching and waiting in our sleeping heart . . . When the Word of God accosts our heart, then suddenly and quite unexpectedly the one may recognise the other, thanks to the one Spirit who is present in both. A bridge is made, as it were, between our heart and the Word. From heart to Word a spark is transmitted. Between the Spirit lying dormant deep within our heart and the Spirit who is active in the Word a fruitful and vitalising dialogue begins.'[7]

(Taken from the introduction to Praying with the New Testament, p ix)

# The Peace of Jesus

*'Peace is what I leave with you; it is my own peace that I give you'*
John 14:27

The peace which is spoken of here is the ability to remain calm, tranquil and serene in every circumstance because we entrust our life and loved ones to the wisdom, sovereignty and protective care of God. It is the kind of quality of life which the Dutch Christian Betsie ten Boom demonstrated in the concentration camp at Ravensbruck. Although her father had been tortured and murdered and although she and her sister endured intolerable conditions in the camp, peace so controlled her that she was able to bring comfort and joy to the women who were fellow-prisoners with her. Peace so pervaded her spirit that she transformed the foul cell which she shared with crowds of other women.

'The straw pallets were rolled instead of piled in a heap, standing like pillars along the walls, each with a lady's hat atop it. A headscarf had somehow been hung along the wall. The contents of several food packages were arranged on a small shelf . . . Even the coats hanging on their hooks were part of the welcome of that room, each sleeve draped over the shoulder of the coat next to it like a row of dancing children.'[8]

(Taken from Reflections for Lent, p 54)

# 'God With Skin On'

### 'Stay with us, Lord, the day is almost over and it is getting dark'
### Luke 24:29

Most of us, from time to time, find that we are rather like the small boy who, for a special treat, went on holiday with his father. Lying in the dark and in that strange bed, he felt alone and frightened. His father, sensing the fear, attempted to reassure him with the comforting thought that there was no need to be afraid because he was not by himself. God was with him. 'Yes,' replied the boy. 'But just for tonight I would like to have a God with skin on.'

People who incarnate the love of Christ become those much needed 'Gods with skin on' which provide us with the props that are essential to our well-being when we are heavy hearted. The kind of people I have in mind are those who so respect the bruised and bleeding of this world that even in the midst of their own pain they offer them warmth, sensitivity, understanding, concern, unconditional love and Christ-like compassion. These are the kind of people of whom it is often said as it was of the scientist and priest Teilhard de Chardin, 'Just to speak to him made you feel better; you knew that he was listening to you and that he understood you.' These are the people who bestow, even on the broken-hearted, a sense of their full worth as children of God.

(Taken from Listening to Others, pp 234, 235)

# Fisherman's Hook

## *The love of Christ controls us*
### 2 Corinthians 5:14

When God loves us he loves us forever: 'Love is like the hook on a fisherman's line; the fish must take the hook or the fisherman can never catch him. After the hook is once in his mouth, the fish may swim about and even swim away from the shore, but the fisherman is sure finally to land him. And this I compare with love. Whoever is caught by love is held perfectly fast, and yet in a sweet captivity. Whoever has received the gift of Divine love, obtains from it more freedom from base natural tendencies than by practising all possible penances and austerities. He it is that can most sweetly endure all misfortunes that happen to him or threaten to overwhelm him; he is the one who most readily forgives all the injuries that can be inflicted on him. Nothing brings thee nearer to God; nothing makes God so much thy own, as the sweet bond of love. Whosoever is caught by this hook is so entirely captive, that feet, hands, mouth, eyes and heart — everything that is himself — becomes God's own.'9

# New Growth

*The Kingdom of God is like a man scattering seed upon the ground. Night and day while he sleeps and when he is awake the seed is sprouting and growing he knows not how.*
Mark 4: 26–27

Gardens speak of hope. They remind us of the value of co-operation and they show us the rewards of hard work.
On a Derbyshire hillside, half hidden by towering pine trees there is an undulating expanse of land which was once waste ground.

Now, if you go there in spring, you will find a landscaped garden ablaze with flamboyant colour – crimsons, reds, pinks, vermilions, purples, oranges, greens, browns and pure white. Wander along the paths between the matured rhododendron bushes and you will see primulas, narcissi and alpine rock plants.

A plaque explains how the miracle came about:

> Beginning in 1935, at the age of 68, John Marsden-Smedley transformed this one-time quarry into the sheltered garden needed for rhododendrons. The making of this garden gave him and others many happy hours during the remaining 24 years of his life.

Those who co-operate with a re-creative God find relationships flourishing in the same way as flowers blossom on waste ground.

(Taken from *Two into One*, p 127)

# 'The Baptised Imagination'

*The day shall dawn upon us from on high to*
*give light to those who sit in darkness*
Luke 1: 78–79

I had prepared a bowl of potting compost, buried a hyacinth bulb in it and thrust it into a deep, dark cupboard. While I was attempting to pray later that day, God seemed to give me a glimpse of the activity which would soon cause that bulb to change: the white roots which would push their way out of the shrivelled up bulb and into the nourishing soil; the green poker-like shoot which would nudge its way above the surface of the earth; the tiny flowers which would unfold and, in bursting open, would fill my study with fragrance.

The voice which I was learning to recognise as God's whispered, 'This is what the darkness of depression will do for you; it will result, eventually, in prolific growth and wholeness,' I felt strangely comforted. When depression did its worst, it was to this visual promise that I clung.

It has never worried me that this kind of meditation leans heavily on the use of the imagination. I came across a phrase which C. S. Lewis uses, 'the baptised imagination', and this encouraged me to believe that when our imagination is soaked in the living waters of the Holy Spirit, God can use it. Similarly, John Powell makes the claim: 'God has access to us through the power of imagination.'[10]

(Taken from Listening to God, pp 124, 125)

# Pray for me, Lord

*The man and his wife heard the sound of the
LORD GOD as he was walking in the garden
in the cool of the day, the LORD GOD called to
the man, 'Where are you?'*
Genesis 3:8–9

Jesus calls us into his felt presence before we decide to come to
him. The initiative is his.

Thank him that he calls, watches, waits, and yearns for
you to come. Be aware of anything which keeps you apart.
Be ready to allow him to remove that barrier: an attitude, a grudge,
an obsession, a friendship. Allow him to do what he will. Allow him
to express his love for you in any way he chooses.

Recall that Jesus is praying for you. I find it helps to have that
written up in my study where I spend much of my day. 'Jesus
is praying for me now.' My prayer depends, not so much on my
technique as on him and his ceaseless activity before the throne of
grace. Trust God to interpret accurately all the sighs, groans, and
tears which may express what you want to say more adequately than
words. Be open to the re-creative love of God which is at work within
you, like yeast in the dough.

(Taken from Living Free, pp 59, 60, 61)

# Discerning the Spirit

*Test everything. Hold fast to what is good*
1 Thessalonians 5:21

Jean Darnall showed me that dreams and visions and voices and thoughts come from three possible sources:

* the Holy Spirit
* my own spirit
* the Evil One.

'If you believe God has told you to do something,' she advised, 'ask him to confirm it to you three times: through his word, through circumstances, and through other people who may know nothing of the situation.'

I became far more cautious about listening to God and testing the ground in the way Jean suggested. And I was grateful for the apprenticeship, which enabled me to grow in confidence.

I now realise that we can never be one hundred per cent certain that the picture we see or the voice we hear or the prophecy we speak out is winged to us from God. That is why listening to God is hard, why speaking out in the name of God is costly and leaves us feeling vulnerable.

If the voice is truly from God, it will have an ice-cutting quality about it. Someone will hear it and say, 'Oh yes! I see!' If the voice comes from our own hurt spirit or over-anxious or over-loving spirit, no lasting harm will be done so we need not worry. But we shall be able to tell the difference between this and God's voice because there will be a lack of authority and dynamism about what is shared. The word or picture will probably fall flat on its face like a badly told joke.

(Taken from Listening to God, pp 140, 141)

# His Banner over Me is Love

*I sleep but my heart is awake,*
*I hear my love knocking,*
*Open to me my sister my beloved*
Song of Songs 5:2

One night I dreamt that I was in a quiet public place like a library. Sitting next to me was a man who began to tell me that he loved me and asked me to go away with him. I protested that I had no time. It was essential that I returned home to my work. He seemed disappointed but accepted my refusal.

When I woke up and thought about the dream, describing it in my journal, the realisation gradually dawned that the stranger in my dream was Jesus – but like the disciples on the road to Emmaus on Easter Day, I had failed to recognise him. Jesus had been trying, once again, to convince me that he loved me and I had sent him away. As I recalled that the reason I had sent him away was because I was busy, I reflected on the number of times I had done that in real life in recent months. I begged him to come back. He did, through another dream. He showed no signs of rejection – only of accepting love.

This time, instead of sending him away, I responded. In my journal I tried to capture some of the deep-down joy: 'Everything has changed'. I was '. . . filled with delight; with pure, deep joy and with consolation. I really can say with deep understanding and meaning: "I am my Beloved's and he is mine and his banner over me is love."'

(Taken from *The Smile of Love*, pp 153–154)

# Saved

*The only thing I can boast about is the cross
of our Lord Jesus*
Galatians 6:14 (J.B.)

A man called Ron once told me why he boasts about Christ's cross. Ron was a paratrooper in the Second World War. On New Year's Eve, 1944, his battalion stayed in an Abbey in France and one of the monks gave him a metal crucifix. On the morning of 24 March 1945, Ron pushed this crucifix in his battledress pocket as he rushed for reveille. That day his battalion crossed the Rhine by plane and were then commanded to jump. Even as he landed, Ron's parachute was punctured by a burst of bullets and his body was spun round by the force of the fire. But he was able to run, unhurt, and shelter in a trench. He found bullet holes in his smock, his battledress and his shirt — but it was two days later, as he stripped for a bath in a military hospital, that he discovered why he had escaped injury.

Embedded in his clothes he found the spent bullet which had cut holes in his clothes. He also drew out of his pocket the metal crucifix which was now broken in two and he realized that this cross had taken the full impact of the bullet and had protected his body from being punctured like his parachute. That was over forty years ago but Ron still thanks God every day for a life which might have ended in 1945.

(Taken from Reflections for Lent, p 67)

# Chosen People

*You did not choose me, but I chose you*
John 15:16

C hristians are chosen people. 'You are a chosen people, a royal priesthood, a holy nation, a people belonging to God' (1 Peter 2:9). 'We know that he has chosen you' (1 Thessalonians 1:4). Christians therefore carry huge responsibilities: 'I chose you to go and bear fruit — fruit that will last' (John 15:16). 'You are a chosen people . . . that you may declare the praises of him who called you out of darkness into his wonderful light' (1 Peter 2:9). We are chosen for obedience: 'Why do you call me, "Lord, Lord," and do not do what I say?' (Luke 6:46). 'Not everyone who says to me, "Lord, Lord," will enter the kingdom of heaven, but only he who does the will of my Father who is in heaven' (Matthew 7:21). Clearly, the Christian is one of whom sacrifice and one-hundred-per-cent loyalty is expected.

All this presents few problems and a whole galaxy of joys until our wills clash with God's will. Then there are tears and tantrums, rebellion and the flat refusal to believe that God not only knows what is best for us but actually has our best interests at heart.

(Taken from Just Good Friends, pp 109, 110)

# The Need for Silence

*Your salvation lies in conversion and
tranquility
Your strength in serenity and trust*
Isaiah 30:15

The more I give, not only to my husband, my children and my friends but to people in need as well, the more I pant for times of solitude with God. Catherine de Hueck Doherty's observation is particularly relevant:

'If we are to witness to Christ in today's market places, where there are constant demands on our whole person, we need silence. If we are to be always available, not only physically, but by empathy, sympathy, friendship, understanding and boundless *caritas*, we need silence. To be able to give joyous, unflagging hospitality, not only of house and food, but of mind, heart, body and soul, we need silence.'[11]

(Taken from Listening to Others, pp 125, 126)

# Beside the Still Water

*The Lord makes me lie down in green*
*pastures*
*He leads me beside still waters*
Psalm 23:2

F.B. Meyers' commentary on the Twenty-Third Psalm is an unfailing source of nourishment.

'WE ALL NEED REST. There must be pauses and parentheses in all our lives. The hand cannot ever be plying its toils. The brain cannot always be elaborating trains of thought. The faculties and senses cannot always be on the strain. To work without rest is like over-winding a watch; the main spring snaps, and the machinery stands still. There must be a pause frequently interposed in life's busy rush wherein we may recuperate exhausted nerves and lowered vitality . . . Be at rest! . . . In all moments of peril and dread, softly murmur His name, Jesus! Jesus! and He will at once comfort thee by His presence and by His voice, which all the sheep know; and this shall be His assurance: "My sheep shall never perish, neither shall any man pluck them out of My hand."'[12]

(Taken from Listening to Others, pp 49, 50)

# Time to be Still

*Be still and know that I am God*
**Psalm 43:10**

The value of a prolonged period of stillness is that we find ourselves viewing life through God's eyes.

The story of three bereaved brothers illustrates this powerfully.

When their mother died, one of the brothers announced, 'I'm going off to look after the sick. The cities teem with them. I will take them healing and love.'

The second brother was equally concerned to be useful. He decided to become one of the world's peacemakers: 'Everywhere I go I see people at loggerheads. I'm going to bring them peace.' The third brother announced, quite calmly: 'I'm staying here.' Two years later, the brothers met for the first time. The first one sighed in despair: 'It's useless. There are so many sick people in the world that I can't possibly cope with them all.' The second brother was equally despondent: 'It's impossible. I feel torn into tiny shreds. Far from bringing peace to others, I've lost the peace I once had.' The third brother went to the river and brought back a bowl of muddy water which he stood in the centre of the floor.

They watched. And they noticed that gradually the silt sank to the bottom of the bowl leaving the water quite clear. That is what happens when people 'steal away to Jesus'. The silt of their busyness sinks. Their perspective clears. And they hear the still, small voice of God.

(Taken from *Open to God*, p 70)

# Samuel

## *Speak, Lord, Your Servant is Listening,*
### 1 Samuel 3:10

Gods's call to listen is highlighted most movingly in the history of the youth Samuel:

The Lord called Samuel a third time, and Samuel got up and went to Eli and said, 'Here I am; you called me.' Then Eli realised that the Lord was calling the boy. So Eli told Samuel, 'Go and lie down, and if he calls you say, "Speak, Lord, for your servant is listening."' So Samuel went and lay down in his place. The Lord came and stood there, calling as at the other times, 'Samuel! Samuel!' Then Samuel said, 'Speak, for your servant is listening' (1 Sam. 3:8–10).

Samuel's short prayer frequently finds an echo on my lips.

(Taken from Listening to God, p 85)

# Plugged in to God

*This is my Son, whom I love; with him I am
well pleased.* Listen to him!
Matthew 17:5, emphasis mine

I looked at this verse long and hard and found it difficult to believe that it does not say, 'This is my dear Son, talk to him.' Nor does it read, 'This is my dear Son, ask him for things.' Neither does it encourage, 'This is my dear Son, tell him your diagnosis when someone is sick.' No. It reads, 'This is my Son . . . *Listen to him.*'

The same command to listen throbs through the early chapters of the book of Revelation like a persistent drumbeat:

If you have ears, then, *listen* to what the Spirit says (2:7)
If you have ears, then, *listen* to what the Spirit says (2:11)
If you have ears, then, *listen* to what the Spirit says (2:17)
If you have ears, then, *listen* to what the Spirit says (2:29)
If you have ears, then, *listen* to what the Spirit says (3:6)

Men and women in the Bible remind me of my milkman who does his entire round tuned in to a voice other than his own. In the pocket of his overalls he carries a radio. Into his ears he tucks the headphones and his face, indeed, sometimes his whole body, responds to a sound which is not audible to anyone else. Men and women in the Bible seemed similarly plugged into and responsive to God. When they listened and responded obediently to the will of God, their lives ran smoothly.

(Taken from Listening to God, pp 85, 86, 87)

# A Heart that Listens

*Give your servant a heart to understand how*
*to discern between good and evil, for who*
*could govern this people of yours that is so*
*great?*
1 Kings 3:9 (JB)

Listening to people is not so much a technique as an attitude
and listening to God is an attitude of heart every would-be
helper needs to cultivate. Solomon summed the situation up
right at the beginning of his reign when he prayed: 'Give me, O
Lord, a heart that listens.'

That is an amazing prayer in the light of the invitation God had
given him: to ask for whatever he wanted. This verse (1 Kgs. 3:9)
has been variously translated: an attentive heart, an intelligent heart,
a heart full of judgement, a heart full of understanding, a wise heart,
a discerning heart. The prayer seems to include all these shades of
meaning and many more besides for Solomon was not simply asking
for the gift of wisdom which would have boosted his own ego and
therefore been a personal enrichment and gain. What he did was to
ask for 'that openness of heart which is a preparation for the reception
of wisdom'; a soul which listened out for every appeal and whisper
from God, which was constantly on the watch for every breath of
the Spirit and which so opened itself to people that it offered them
'an interior welcome at a deep level'[13] and a silence so impregnated
with love that it tuned in accurately to the groans of sufferers.

(Taken from Listening to Others, pp 126, 127)

# Listening to God

*Father make me quick to listen but slow to*
*speak*
**James 1:19**

C harismatics need no persuading that God is at work today, changing people's lives in a supernatural way.

But this very enthusiasm can be their greatest handicap. Spontaneity can be the greatest obstacle they bring to the work of listening to God. For God says, in effect, 'Shut up!' 'Listen!' And shutting up is a discipline in which they do not excel!

The charismatic Christian whose hunger to hear God is real can learn from the contemplative to stop talking, stop clapping, stop praising for a while. And listen. In the stillness all that is phoney is stripped away. In this stillness authentic adoration is born which can later be expressed in exuberant praise. In this stillness the desire for the spectacular is replaced by a deeper desire to know God for himself alone, not for anything he can do.

And charismatics, like contemplatives, must follow the example of Jesus and steep themselves in scripture. They need to sharpen their thinking or they risk finding themselves making pronouncements in the name of Christ which run counter to the Word of God. To do so is serious. God cannot contradict himself. If we are to speak out in the name of God, we must make it our responsibility to know what the word of God contains.

(Taken from Listening to God, p 217)

# Speak Lord

## *Coasts and islands listen to me; pay attention.*
Isaiah 49:1

I f you are an evangelical, and are thirsting to hear God's voice more adequately, the first thing to do is to be grateful for the tools which your background has, in all probability, placed at your disposal already: a thorough working knowledge of and love of the Bible.

Evangelicals must learn that listening to God involves much more than cerebral activity. It demands a living response: obedience. And it demands attentiveness to God at many levels: intellectual, emotional, spiritual. In other words, the challenge to the evangelical may well be to tune into God with the emotions, the will and the spirit as well as with the mind. As Jesus put it, love for God involves a whole-hearted dedication of heart, mind, soul and strength. Until we give this, we miss the very heart of the gospel and tune out much of what God is attempting to say.

The evangelical Christian who is anxious to listen to God more attentively may have other disciplines to master. Evangelical Christians are not very experienced in keeping quiet. They have to *learn* to 'be still', to know that God is God. They have to learn 'to be' and not necessarily to achieve. They may even need to be persuaded that God is prepared to speak to them in unexpected ways, through nature, other people, the imagination, as well as through his revealed Word, the Bible.

(Taken from Listening to God, pp 218, 219)

# Common Sense or Nonsense?

### 'Can I tell the good from the bad?'
### 2 Samuel 19:35

Listening to God can be the most sublime and joy-filled privilege in the world

True listening prayer, operates when we are in the pits, needing to be rescued by God, and it is operative, too, when we soar to unexpected spiritual peaks. And, of course, God goes on speaking in the ordinary, in-between days when life seems mundane, even monotonous. He not only speaks, he woos us, calling us to receive him into our lives, persuading us to fix our gaze on him.

Listening prayer can however, become the most absurd exercise we ever embark on.

For sheer absurdity, I have never encountered an example which surpasses the one quoted by Jim Packer:

'There was once a woman who sincerely wanted to listen to God about the details of her life. Each morning, having consecrated the day to the Lord as she woke, she would then ask whether she was to get up or not. She would not stir until the still, small voice told her to dress. As she put on each article she asked the Lord whether she was to put it on. Very often the Lord would tell her to put her right shoe on but to leave the other off. Sometimes she was to put on both stockings but no shoes and sometimes both shoes and no stockings. And thus listening to God she would deal with every article of dress in turn.'[14]

(Taken from Listening to God, pp 139, 62)

# Listening to God

*After the fire there was a light murmuring*
*sound when Elijah heard this . . . he went out*
*and stood at the entrance of the cave. Then a*
*voice came to him*
1 Kings 19:13

Whenever I close my eyes in an attempt to listen attentively to the sounds around, I am amazed at the mixture of noises which I had failed to hear until that moment: the humming of the fly, the hoot of the owl, the final faint song of the chaffinch, the creak of a chair. Similarly, whenever I tune into God's still, small voice the medley of experiences he gives astounds me. I can never anticipate beforehand what he will say or how he will act. What I can foretell is that whatever he gives will be worthwhile.

Early on in my prayer pilgrimage, I discovered that listening to God did not necessarily result in mystical experiences. Often, it was not other-worldly at all. Rather, it was a deeply practical affair.

I remember an occasion when the concept of listening to God seemed strange and new. While I was praying, the words, 'Ring Valerie' kept pounding through my brain. Valerie was a close friend who lived eighty miles from my home. Feeling rather foolish, I telephoned. Valerie gasped when she heard my voice. We had not made contact for several months. 'What made you ring tonight?' she asked. 'Pam's here with me. Her husband died suddenly last night and I don't know what to say to her. She's just been saying, "I'd love to talk to Joyce." Will you speak to her?'

Pam was a mutual friend. She had expressed care for me after my father died. Now God gave me the privilege of drawing alongside her in her bereavement.

(Taken from Listening to God, pp 205, 206)

# God's Healing Love

*Beloved, if God so loved us we also ought to
love one another*
1 John 4:11

Two people can become very close when one of them is
sharing confidences and the other is attempting to listen
in an attentive, caring way. Such intimacy need not be
inappropriate or wrong. It can be healing. But it is Gods' love which
heals not mine. Indeed if all I offer to a person is the paucity of my
human warmth and acceptance, the person might feel supported,
affirmed and valued, but the transformation we are both looking for
will not take place. What is needed is not simply that I should feel
for and with a person in pain nor that I should be able to express
this concern. What I must always remember is so to open myself to
the love of God that I simply become the embodiment of his love
to that person. Agnes Sanford underlined this for me in her book
*Sealed Orders*:

"'Love heals", people say. I do not find that necessarily so.
God's love heals, yes. But our own love, if too emotional, may
even stand in the way of that great flow of God's love which is
an energy rather than an emotion . . . I learned to put Christ
between me and the person for whom I was praying, to send
my love to Christ and let him do with it what he would.
Thus people felt from me or through me, power rather than
affection.'[15]

(Taken from Listening to Others, pp 117, 118)

# Receiving the Other

### *'Hear my prayer and give ear to my cry'*
#### Psalm 39:12

Myra Chave-Jones underlines that listening is like receiving a priceless gift.

I learned to ask myself, from time to time, whether I was unwrapping a person's gift eagerly or grudgingly, with the kind of care I would finger something fragile or in a cavalier fashion. I learned, too, to detect the kind of person whose gift I could scarcely handle because I failed to identify with them and I discovered the value of asking myself why I found it so hard to stay alongside that particular person and others like them.

'Recognise any particular fears and phobias you harbour – like death or cancer', I was once told. 'And any bees in your bonnet which might affect the way you listen – like, "I must press everyone I meet to make a decision for Jesus."'

Asking myself such questions, I found, helped me to grow in self-awareness and this, in turn, seemed to make the ministry of listening to others more effective.

As David Augsburger puts it: 'If I am to hear you I must also hear me.'[16]

# Don't Interrupt

*'So now Lord please take my life for I might*
*as well be dead as go on living.' The Lord*
*replied: 'Are you right to be angry?'*
Jonah 4:3–4

G ood listeners have a good reason for any question they ask; they do not ask questions out of idle curiosity but only out of the desire to promote growth. 'Can you tell me more about that?' 'How did that feel?'

Despite years of practice, I still find myself interrupting inappropriately from time to time and I take comfort from John Powell when he writes:

'Most of us, when we are in the listener's role, feel compelled to be speakers. We feel a compulsive inner urgency to interrupt others as soon as they start to reveal themselves. We feel a strange obligation to advise them, and to support our advice with a few chapters from our autobiographies. We jump in at the first pause, and go on nonstop unless we are exhausted and the other person is near despair. Regrettably, I have done this to others. I have also had this done to me. I have experienced the sadness of not being heard because someone had not cared enough to listen to my sharing and to learn who I really am.'[17]

# Hitchhiking with the Listener

## *'Listen I have something important to tell you'*
### Proverbs 8:6

John Powell tells us that 'the listener should offer only suggestions and never directions'.[18]

'I sometimes have to work at stifling my old urge to turn into a computer printer spitting out all kinds of interpretations and advice. I have personally been working on the technique of the well-placed question. It goes something like this: "Gee, I don't know what you should do. What do you think? In your judgement, what are the possibilities?" Sometimes a suggestion can be successfully floated into the conversation by way of a question. "Say, did you ever think of going back to school and getting a degree?"'[19]

He goes on to explain that the reason for this is that if adults are to behave as adults and not overgrown children they must assume personal responsibility for their behaviour and their lives. They must therefore be allowed to have their own thoughts and to make their own choices. The listener who insists on telling another what they should or should not do runs the risk of hindering a person's growth: 'The one sure way not to grow up is to hitchhike on the mind and will of someone else.'[20]

(Taken from Listening to Others, pp 110, 111)

# Other Centred

### *Blessed, whoever listens*
Proverbs 8:34

Why do I want to listen to people? Is it because I enjoy having people confide their troubles in me? If so, why? Is it because this boosts my morale; makes me feel important? Is it because I am curious about the troubles others face? Is it because I need to be needed? Or am I, perhaps, feeding on these people emotionally – using people in need as a substitute for the mutuality of friendship?

The reality is that in pouring out love to others, I must expect nothing from them in return. When I listen to a person in need I listen for the sake of their well-being, not because I have a need for closeness with others; my real and legitimate needs for friendship and intimacy must be met through the mutuality of supportive friendships – in my relationship with my husband, in the fellowship of Christ's people and through the support of a soul-friend who will listen to me in a caring attentive way.

(Taken from Listening to Others, pp 131, 132, 119)

# Thank You

## *I thank my God whenever I think of you*
### Philippians 1:3

When we listen to people it can be important to thank them for giving us the privilege of being the one to hear and handle their innermost thoughts and feelings. John Powell reminds us that it is risky and frightening to put our most sensitive confidences in the hands of another, to examine our failures or to reveal our vulnerability. 'Consequently, we should practise the habit of thanking others for their self-disclosure and for their trust in us.'[21]

I remember the overwhelming sense of privilege and gratitude which swept over me when I first said to someone: 'Many people would have counted it a privilege to listen to you in the way you have allowed me to do today. Thank you for your trust – for entrusting yourself to *me*.' This took the person completely by surprise. But I could see that at the same time he felt valued because of what had been said.

(Taken from Listening to Others, p 117)

# Let Go and Let God

*One man's offence brought condemnation on all humanity*
**Romans 5:18**

God has engraved the word obedience on my heart. For this reason I have studied the salutary warnings the Bible gives to the disobedient. I have combed the pages of the Bible in an attempt to discover what God requires of me in certain situations: as a wife, a mother, a friend, a business woman; as a sexual being, a female and one entrusted with Christian leadership. I know that disobedience can lock and bolt the door against God's still, small voice. Even so, I find it easier to write about obedience, read about obedience and preach about obedience than to obey. I know how to leap this hurdle: simply discover God's will and do it. But I find it hard.

The same stubbornness characterises my current attitude to stillness. I love it. I benefit from it. Yet I neglect it because I persuade myself that the pressures on me do not allow it space. I know the way out of the problem: respond to the wooing of God.

The joy of surrendering to him is usually sweet. A privilege. And being found, held, and loved by God all over again and receiving his activity deep into the inner recesses of my being fills me with fresh awe and wonder and praise. The encounter is usually so powerful that it leaves me asking the question: '*Why* don't I make more time for this more often?'

(Taken from Listening to God, p 169)

# God's Will. My Will

*My aim is to do not my own will but the will of
him who sent me*
John 5:30 (JB)

'Obedience' seems to be a dirty word these days. Christians don't like to hear it mentioned. Not so Jesus. He knew his Father well enough to know that God had his best interests at heart. Instead of resenting the call to obedience, he embraced it willingly — even when it hurt him to do so.

Jesus became man because it was his Father's will. And he says of himself that to obey his Father is his 'meat', his nourishment. The Holy Spirit's task is to work in us in such a way that we become more Christ-like; more obedient. And just as certain skills like carpentry and cookery can be improved by watching master craftsmen at work, so we can be inspired to obey by observing the obedience of Jesus.

(Taken from Open to God, p 140.)

# Cleaning the Clutter

*If you obey the commandments of the Lord
your God . . . you will live*
**Deuteronomy 20:16**

Once God faced me with an inevitable choice — my way *or* his — I squealed. For months I was so full of self-will that I heard little from the still, small voice of God. Bible meditation ceased, Bible study stopped. I would dip into the Bible from time to time but it communicated nothing. This was hardly surprising. I had not yet learned that God's Word is not simply to be studied, read or personalised. It has to be obeyed. But as William Barclay warns: 'There are people into whose minds [and emotions] the word has no more chance of gaining an entry than the seed has of settling into the ground that has been beaten hard by many feet.'22

There are many things which can close a person's mind. Disobedience is the most effective. As has been aptly said: 'The one who truly listens is also the one who truly obeys.'

Eventually, God showed me what had to be done. A load of rubble had to be tipped out on the dumping ground of the cross where Jesus would take responsibility for it. Slowly and thoughtfully I made a reappraisal of my life: where I was going, what I was wanting, what God was asking of me. Anything which obstructed the path would have to go. Equally slowly, but quite deliberately, I cleared out the clutter which had kept me from Christ.

(Taken from Listening to God, pp 167, 168)

# Yellow Eye

## *Jonah set about running away from the Lord*
### Jonah 1:3

We changed our car recently. This new model boasts an economy gear and a yellow light winks when the car decides the driver should change gear for the sake of economy. This little yellow eye irritates me intensely. I know it is irrational but there are times when I would like to speak to it quite firmly. 'Look here! I've been driving cars for over twenty years. I don't need you to give me the wink every time I should change gear. I'm well able to make my own decisions.' Some of us bring that sort of intransigence into our relationship with God. When the light of his Word reminds us to change gear, we rebel.

(Taken from Living Free, p 163)

# The Harvest of the Spirit

### *Be imitators of me as I am of Christ*
### 1 Corinthians 11:1

Jesus' personality and ministry were magnetic. His love for God was demonstrated in his willingness to obey him in everything – even in dying on Calvary's Cross. His love and trust were so complete that his chief joy was his relationship with the Father. And toward other people Jesus was kind, generous, reliable and forgiving.

Paul exhorts us to live like that. He explains that the task is not as impossible as it sounds. If the Holy Spirit indwells us like a root, this spiritual fruit must ripen. As Jesus expressed it: 'Every tree bears good fruit' (Matthew 7:7). Or as William Temple put it:

'It is no good giving me a play like Hamlet or King Lear, and telling me to write a play like that. Shakespeare could do it; I can't. And it is no good showing me a life like the life of Jesus and telling me to live a life like that. Jesus could do it; I can't. But if the genius of Shakespeare could come and live in me, then I could write plays like that. And if the Spirit of Jesus could come and live in me, I could live like that.'

# Open Sesame

### *If you love me, you will obey what I command*
John 14:15

Those who are in rebellion against God, who set out to thwart his authority, and defy his laws, make no progress in prayer. Only those who are serious in their desire to be transformed by the truth will appreciate the beauty of prayer, endure its refining pain and submit to the hand of love which is also the hand which disciplines.

A quick visit from someone you love can raise your spirits and, keep you going for days. Through prayer, Bible study and the indwelling Holy Spirit we have a similar spiritual life-line: one of the tragedies of today is that Christians have ceased to think of prayer and Bible reading as valuable assets, the privileged 'open sesame' to God. We shall never experience Christian growth until we commit ourselves to the twin delights of prayer and Bible reading.

(Taken from Living Free, pp 63, 64)

# Tough Love

*'You must go to all to whom I send you and say whatever I command you'*
Jeremiah 1:7

L ove sometimes hurts. Even the love of God. Love challenges the status quo. And in becoming imitators of God's love, we may find ourselves in situations where we, too, must ask uncomfortable questions or confront for the sake of Christ's Kingdom. Like Jesus, we must know when to be tender and when to challenge; when to go to hurting people and when to protest against the social injustices which infiltrate every society on earth. If we fail to do this, we are not imitating Christ; by our silence, we are colluding with injustice. And this Jesus never did.

But we will never have the wisdom and insight to know when to speak and when to keep silent unless we have allowed God to do *in* us what he wants to do *through* us. This simply means that, in opening ourselves to his love, we must be prepared to be consoled by Christ and to be challenged by his uncompromising, pure, confrontational love. We must expect him to ask *us* soul-searching questions, cause us to sift our motives and bring us face to face with our own self-centredness. We need to reconcile ourselves to the fact that discipline and rebuke, questioning and confrontation can be just as much signs of God's love as comfort and consolation.

(Taken from The Smile of Love, p 29)

# Love or Hate

*Trouble and distress will come to everyone who does evil; honour and peace will come to everyone who does good*
**Romans 2:9,10**

The dividing line between love and hate is wafer thin. Just as I have been trained to live for number one, to feed her desires, so my husband, my children and my brothers and sisters in Christ are equally egocentric, expressing their desires just as fiercely. The result, very often, is an inevitable clash of personality. As Christians we are learning to die to the sin-biased self that prevents us from becoming Christlike, but this dying is never instant. On the contrary, it is a long-drawn-out process. When my brother or sister presses on an open sore in my life, leaving me frightened or in despair, or when someone seems wilfully to deprive me of something I felt I needed, I am not above wounding them.

We twentieth-century Christians need the self-awareness and integrity of Paul to acknowledge that much of the failure in relationships resides in our own sin-pocked personalities. We need the humility to come regularly to God and to plead, 'Lord, deliver me from the prison of my selfhood' (Thomas Merton's phrase).

(Taken from Creative Conflict, pp 17, 18)

# Sacrificial Love

*Love is ready to endure whatever comes*
1 Corinthians 13:7

Dustbin tipping is essential to our emotional health: 'People have a right to ventilate their feelings, however dark or negative they may be.' Such propaganda persuades us that what we *feel* is objective truth. In other words, if I feel you have let me down, this proves that you have let me down. Such a philosophy, of course, is nonsense. But many of us imbibe this teaching unquestioningly. So if I feel my friend has betrayed me, I accuse. I even believe it is my right to do so. By labelling him with a name like 'traitor', I not only confine him to a restrictive pigeon-hole, I withdraw my trust; and worse, I pour onto him the full force of my wrath. And I wonder why the friendship-boat lies on the rocks, wrecked.

This self-centred, uncontrolled behaviour is un-Christlike and unbiblical. Yet such worldly philosophy has become the life-principle of some Christians. They have ignored the fact that the Christian should take as a yardstick only the behavioural standards that are consistent with life in the kingdom of God: the kingdom of love. They have ignored the fact that, if Jesus is Lord, feelings must never be given permission to dominate a person's life. They have ignored the fact that love takes responsibility for others, never thinks primarily of its own needs, however urgent they may be, never demands its own way. They have ignored Paul's teaching: Love 'is not irritable or touchy. It does not hold grudges and will hardly even notice when others do it wrong . . . If you love someone you will be loyal to him no matter what the cost' (1 Corinthians 13:5, 7, LB).

(Taken from Creative Conflict, pp 60, 61)

# Creative Conflict

*My grace is sufficient for you; for my power is
made perfect in weakness*
**2 Corinthians 12:9**

Christians who confront conflict creatively need never fear the incoming tide of tension. Though the waves rush against their relationships, those relationships cannot be smashed to pieces. Even the fiercest waves do no more than wash away unsightly angularities, thus making the relationships smoother.

Some years ago, friends of mine bought a derelict farmhouse which, when I first visited it, seemed little more than a heap of rubble. That building now houses a community of forty people who have committed their lives to one another, to Christ and to a common purpose: to create a loving community that will nurture each community member, minister to a needy world and bring glory to God. When Christians – couples, friends, households, communities – prayerfully take conflict on board, God continually performs a similar miracle: from the rubble of wrecked relationships he raises renewed and renewable love.

(Taken from Creative Conflict, p 192)

# Spiritual Aerobics

*Put yourselves to the test . . . examine*
*yourselves*
2 Corinthians 13:5

Originally, Lent was kept as a pre-Easter retreat: a prolonged period of time when Christians would 'tone up' spiritually. Their spiritual aerobics were not unlike the intensive training an athlete undergoes before an important race or the strict diet a person goes on in order to lose weight for medical or cosmetic purposes.

The reason why Christians took Lent so seriously from the days of the Early Church onwards is that Easter Day was the highlight of their year. On this day, like us, they celebrated the amazing fact that Jesus' body was not left in the grave to decay. He rose from the dead. But on this day they also welcomed converts to Christianity into the full fellowship of the church and welcomed back people who had once believed in God but whose faith in him had grown dim and whose love for him had grown cold. Throughout Lent, these people would prepare for Easter by becoming familiar with the basic teaching essential to an understanding of Christianity. They would be encouraged to repent of past failures and be shown how to live life God's way. Committed Christians did not escape the rigours of the Lenten season. They, too, took Lent seriously and used it as a time to examine their life-style, to turn their backs on the sin that so easily creeps into our lives and to re-dedicate their lives to God.

(Taken from Reflections for Lent, pp 5–6)

# God with Us

*You should pray like this: 'Our Father in heaven, may your name be held holy . . .'*
Matthew 6:9

When I read that verse, my mind often goes to Israel where I once travelled on an over-crowded bus away from the Sea of Galilee to a small town in the hills. On the seat near where I stood, a little Jewish boy was sitting on his father's knee. I watched him look into his father's face, stroke his cheek and whisper, 'Abba' before snuggling into his father's arms where he fell asleep. There, on that bus, I sensed I understood that one reason Jesus invited us to call God, 'Abba', 'Daddy', was that he wanted us to enjoy the kind of intimacy with God this small boy was enjoying with his father – the kind of closeness Jesus enjoyed with God.

*Father,*
*teach me to relate to you as Jesus did*
*as one who knows they can enjoy intimacy with you.*

# The Glory of the Lord

*Jesus took Peter, John, and James with him and went up a hill to pray. While he was praying, his face changed its appearance, and his clothes became dazzling white . . .*
Luke 9:28, 29

I once climbed the Mount of Transfiguration where I meditated on this miraculous moment in Jesus' life. As I sat on the grassy plateau at the top of the mountain, I could almost see the cloud descending, hear the Father affirming the innate value of his Son and sense the nearness of the Father, Son and Holy Spirit. Others, too, were filled with awe. As I worshipped with them in a service of Holy Communion in the church on the mountain, I contemplated the transfigured Jesus: his body shot through with the brilliance of God, his face radiating his Father's glory and his clothing gleaming with a whiteness the human eye could scarcely tolerate.

I am grateful that, during Lent, we are encouraged to relive this moment – to relish its mysteries: the mystery of God's greatness and the twin mystery of Jesus' humility in stripping himself of his glory to clothe himself in human flesh.

*Transfigured Lord,*
*As I contemplate you afresh,*
*may I be filled with wonder*
*love*
*and overflowing praise.*

# Racing to the Rescue

## *Deliver us from evil*
### Matthew 6:13

Satan employs one temptation only: the temptation to rate self-gratification more highly than pleasing God. This temptation comes with many faces and a variety of disguises. But it is the same temptation. The way we handle it affects every choice we make.

A young mother may be tempted to believe the feminist cry, 'You must discover yourself. Never mind about your marriage, your husband, your children.' A wealthy bachelor may be tempted to furnish his new home with priceless antiques. 'Never mind that Christians in the Third World are starving; that our missionaries on furlough are feeling the pinch.' A young man is tempted to make sexual conquests. 'Never mind about trivializing the sacred sex act; abusing another's body.' Temptation comes in many disguises. The root is the same: making self supreme.

When we accept Jesus as Lord, he may allow us to be sorely tempted so that our resolve may be strengthened. Every time we endorse our decision, every time we resist the temptation to put self first, sin's stranglehold is weakened. Temptation is then the gateway to triumph; the place where the Holy Spirit races to rescue us like red blood corpuscles fighting an infection.

(Taken from Living Free, pp 146, 147)

# Lead Us Not into Temptation

*Your enemy the devil is prowling round like a roaring lion, looking for someone to eat*
1 Peter 5:8

S atan tests us through our feelings. On the days when we cannot feel God's presence he tries to persuade us that God has abandoned us; that he is a God who is more absent than present. He would even tempt us to doubt God's trustworthiness. These lies are to be rejected.

The tempter is also capable of using our innermost thoughts and desires to bring about our downfall. He launches his attack against our mind, our will and our passions so that even though we know that a certain course of action is not permissible for the Christian, we do it; even though we know that a certain place is riddled with temptation, we go there.

At times Satan confuses us so much that we don't know whether we want to obey God or not. Michel Quoist expressed this confusion powerfully:

I'm at the end of my tether, Lord.
I am shattered,
I am broken.
Since this morning I have been struggling to escape temptation,
    which, now subtle, now persuasive, now tender, now sensuous,
        dances before me like a glamour girl at a fair.
I don't know what to do.
I don't know where to go.
It spies on me, follows me, engulfs me.
When I leave a room I find it seated and waiting for me in the
    next . . .[23]

(Taken from Reflections for Lent, pp 28, 29)

# Sin Stains

*For freedom Christ has set us free . . . do not*
*submit again to a yoke of slavery*
Galatians 5:1

S in stains. It stains our clean robe of righteousness with grime. It stains our consciences with guilt. It stains our reputation before God. And it separates us from the fellowship with God we once enjoyed. One Christian put the situation quite simply when he said: 'Sin is like slapping Jesus in the face. You see him hanging on the tree. You look at his dying form and say: "You died for me. You bore my sin. But I simply do not care."'

Thomas Merton writes, 'A sinner is a drowning man, a sinking ship. The waters are bursting into him on all sides. He is falling apart under the pressure of the storm that has been breaking up his will, and now the waters rush into the hold and he is dragged down. They are closing over his head, and he cries out to God: "The waters are come in even unto my soul." The sinner is a person who knows his soul to be "logged with these icy waters".'[24]
(Taken from Living Free, pp 162, 163)

# Tipping out the Debris

*We do not know what we ought to pray,*
*but the Spirit himself intercedes for us with*
*groans that words cannot express. And he*
*who searches our hearts knows the mind of*
*the Spirit*
**Romans 8:26–27**

Confession is telling God the whole sordid story as we perceive it, tipping all the debris of our lives at the foot of the cross, withholding nothing from a merciful God.

For some people, it seems sufficient to pour out the whole sad story to God on their own, and receive his forgiveness. However some sin, and particularly sexual sin scars the mind, the memory, the imagination and the body. James' suggestion then is: 'Confess your sins to each other and pray for each other so that you may be healed' (James 5:16).

I am not suggesting that we unveil our innermost secrets before the assembled fellowship group or Bible study group. But if we have confessed privately and still feel confused, weighed down by the burden of past misdemeanours, or lack peace with God, it is worth seeking a discerning, wise, prayerful person who is capable of keeping confidences. In the presence of this trusted person, pour your pain into the lap of God remembering that he is well able to interpret words, sighs, groans, tears and silence.

(Taken from Just Good Friends, pp 193, 194)

# Penance and Healing

*Repent and believe in the good news*
Mark 1:15

M y own first taste of confession and penance is a good example of the constructive contribution it can make to the spiritual growth of the Christian: I could have come away from the experience feeling condemned by God and my confidante. Instead this spiritual guide talked with me about the reason for my visit: he made no attempt to excuse my sin. What he did was to disentangle the sin from the need which had given birth to it: emotional wounds which would not stop bleeding. He explained that the sinful element had been dealt with through confession and Christ's forgiveness; the emotional need would be met in a different way. By inviting me to read the book, *The Cloud of Unknowing*, he believed that some of my confusion would be clarified and I would glean insights which were essential to this stage of the pilgrimage of prayer.

An experienced and wise soul friend can set us on our feet again after we have fallen. As an objective observer he can discern more clearly than oneself where God wants to purge and prune and where he wants to bind up and heal.

(Taken from Listening to God, pp 192, 193)

# Repent and be Healed

## *You must repent*
### Acts 2:38

Repentance is seeing our sin and turning from it.[25]
Repentance is positive; a re-orientation, a *metanoia*, the New Testament word for a complete and utter change of heart. Repentance is deliberately placing our body, mind, imagination, talents, friendships, emotions, intellect, time at God's disposal so that every part of our being becomes a weapon fighting in the holy war *against* sin.

The repentant person is humble and unafraid to request a special empowering of the Holy Spirit to help conquer temptation. The repentant person is not afraid to give God access to the hurts which prevent obedience. The repentant person allows the Holy Spirit to permeate the hidden recesses of the intellect, emotions and psyche so as to bring true freedom.

(Taken from Living Free, p 165)

# In the Furnace

*The genuiness of your faith, more precious*
*than gold . . . is tested by fire*
1 Peter 1:7

Toughness is a sign of love sentimentality. A silversmith in Greece demonstrated this to me once when I was browsing in his shop.

Out of the corner of my eye I saw him take a pair of iron tongs, blackened with soot and remove a silver chalice from a shelf. I stared, indignant in my ignorance, as he thrust the chalice into the furnace which blazed at the back of the shop. He seemed to sense my dismay for when the time came to withdraw the chalice from the flames, he beckoned me to come. With a soft cloth, he wiped the chalice clean. And even my inexperienced eye could see the improvement. The refined silver gleamed.

Life is about the refining which precedes radiance. The heavenly silversmith knows how long to hold us in the crucible of his love. As soon as we are free of dross, there is no more need for purging. We are free.

(Taken from Living Free, p 192)

# Barracks or Hospital?

*Let us lay aside every weight and sin . . . and
let us run with perseverance the race that is
set before us*
**Hebrews 12:1**

In *Spiritual Depression*, Dr Martyn Lloyd-Jones urges us to be tough with ourselves when confronted with temptation, sin and the need to repent. He suggests that Christianity is far too often presented as a palliative:

> Come to the clinic and we'll give you all the loving care and attention that you need to help you with your problems . . . In the Bible I find a barracks, not a hospital. It is not a doctor you need but a Sergeant-Major. Here we are on the parade ground slouching about. A doctor is no good; it is discipline we need. We need to listen to the Sergeant-Major — 'Yield not to temptation but yield yourselves to God.' This is the trouble with the Church today: there is too much of the hospital element: they have lost sight of the great battle.[26]

Some of us need to hear those strong words and take them to heart. Others *do* need a hospital. And as has been rightly said, 'God prepares a hospital for those he has to wound.' Only *you* know which you need.

(Taken from Living Free, p 167)

# Standing Before God

## *He would willingly have filled himself with the husks the pigs were eating.*
### Luke 15:16

We can learn a great deal about God, human nature and the grace of forgiveness from the parable of the prodigal son. If we use our imagination to 'become' the spendthrift son moping in the pigsty or the waiting father scouring the landscape for the faintest sign of the returning son, the unquenchable love of God will take root in our hearts and the parable will take on a wealth of new meaning. Our findings will not vie with or challenge the findings of the intellect. They will supplement and complement them in a life-changing way.

Theophane summed this up beautifully when he wrote: 'The principal thing is to stand before God with the intellect in the heart, and to go on standing before him unceasingly day and night, until the end of life.' Commenting on 'the intellect in the heart' Peter Toon observes:

> Standing *before God* suggests a personal relationship – of child and heavenly Father, of sinner and Saviour, and of servant and Master. Standing before him *in the heart* suggests an attitude of sincere openness in the very centre of our being, the place where Love creates love; further, the placing of the intellect (mind) in the heart means that there is no opposition between head and heart, for both are open to, and submitted to, the Lord God.[27]

(Taken from Open to God, pp 54–55)

# The Welcoming Father

*While he was still a long way off, his father
saw him and was moved with compassion. He
ran to the boy, clasped him in his arms and
kissed him.*
Luke 15:20

The home-coming of the prodigal son would have astonished the crowds who were listening to Jesus' story. In the Middle East, it is unthinkable for an elderly man to run. It is considered humiliating and undignified. Yet the father in Jesus' story expresses his longing to be united with his wayward son by gathering up his robes and racing down the road to the place the boy had reached.

The father not only ran, he substituted a warm embrace for the expected rebuke and kisses of total acceptance for the deserved punishment. Jesus' listeners would have known how to interpret these gestures. The word Jesus uses for 'kiss' means 'to kiss again and again.' In Middle Eastern countries, such kisses and embraces are signs of reconciliation and forgiveness.

The moving, jubilant picture painted by Jesus presents us with a father who hurt to see his son hurting and who was prepared to lay on one side cultural expectations in order to communicate to his son the only message that mattered: I love you enough to accept you just as you are.

# Total Forgiveness

*Christ died for us while we were still sinners*
**Romans 5:8**

God's forgiveness and love cannot be earned. It is always undeserved. Nevertheless it is to be received with humbleness and brokenness of spirit. It is to be relished. It is to be accepted with thanksgiving. It reflects the victory Jesus won at Calvary. It turns our disgrace into trophies of his grace.

Lord, I can scarcely drink in the good news. Can it be true that you have wiped the slate clean of *all* sin? Yes! With my mind I know it. May that word NOTHING echo through the labyrinths of my entire being. NO THING. Not one single thought. No fantasy. No lust. NOTHING! Zero! The score against me from the divine perspective is nought. What relief! What joy! I am free: free from the guilt, free from the stain, free from the power of the Evil One, free to say no to all his fiendish suggestions. For this miracle, my Lord and Master, my Saviour, I praise you. May I be a faithful steward of the mystery of this grace of forgiveness. May I be a faithful steward, too, of *your* gift of love.

(Taken from Listening to God, p 62)

# Don't Nurse a Grudge

### *How often must I forgive my brother?*
### Matthew 18:21

Tom was a black American who delivered newspapers every day to white men. One day, he was doing his newspaper round as usual when he felt an urgent need to go to the toilet. Tom knew the law of Alabama: blacks are not permitted to enter premises belonging to whites. But Tom was desperate. He went into the toilets reserved for white men.

Suddenly, he became aware of a white man towering over him. The white man's face flushed with anger when he saw a black boy 'polluting' territory reserved for whites. He seized Tom by the scruff of the neck and rubbed his face in his own urine before the terrified boy could escape.

Outside the toilet, Tom ran into the arms of a big black man. By this time he was sobbing uncontrollably. Between his sobs, he blurted out his story. The man he told was Martin Luther King.

When he had heard the whole sad saga, he helped Tom to understand that he was now faced with a choice. Either he could go home, tell all his friends and neighbours and relatives what had happened and thus perpetuate the hatred which already existed between blacks and whites, or he could forgive the man. Then Martin Luther King challenged the boy: 'Forgive him, Tom. You can't harbour hatred in your heart for ever.'

(Taken from Marriage Matters, pp 130, 131)

# Released

## *Go and Sin No More*
### John 8:11

J esus' ministry to a promiscuous and adulterous generation was authoritative, powerful and full of compassion. Take the woman caught committing adultery, for example. He seems to have accurately understood her feelings, her despair. He forgave, he healed, he released and he re-established her.

When Jesus forgives, he gives a new start. His forgiveness is accompanied by unconditional acceptance of the sinner. While Jesus never condones sin, he does love sinners. He is able to cut them free from the failure which so often seems to strangle every attempt to move. When he sets people free from the past, he sets them free to a life of usefulness.

Why, then, do some Christians today remain in bondage to the past while others are restored instantly through prayer?

I have no slick answer:

Healing, forgiveness, release and restoration are gifts from God. They are his to give as and when he chooses. Our eyes must always be on the giver, God, and not on the way he chooses to deliver his people. But, of course, if we come to God to ask for forgiveness, we must also be prepared to forgive ourselves. It is not permissible for us as Christians so to magnify our sinfulness that we minimize the grace of God. And if we really want healing, we have to be prepared to walk away from the past with its sin and its pain. We have to be prepared to move into partnership with God and to grow up.

Isn't this what Jesus was implying when he said to the woman caught in the act of adultery, 'Go and sin no more' (Jn. 8:11)?

(Taken from Growing into Love, pp 72, 75, 76)

# Let Them off the Hook

*Be generous to one another, forgiving each
other as readily as God forgave you*
Ephesians 4:32

We need to forgive others as readily and as generously as Jesus forgives us. Until we do this we are imprisoned.

If we allow negative, poisonous emotions like bitterness, hatred, resentment, anger or jealousy grow in us, we become their captives. They weaken our resilience and sometimes bite into our bodies in the form of ulcers, hernias, migraine and backache. And we are so consumed by the tangled feelings which cling to us that we are no longer free to receive from God the resources with which he wants to nourish us: love, joy, peace, wholeness.

When, with an act of the will, we take the plunge and ask God to cut us free from negative emotions, a miracle happens: the miracle of reconciliation. To forgive means 'to let go', 'to let someone off the hook'. When Jesus prayed on the cross, 'Father, forgive them,' he was saying: 'Father, set them free from every single sin they have ever committed and every sin they will commit in the future. Deal generously with them. Because of my death release them from sin's bondage.' In comparison with that prayer it is a small thing that he asks us; to let others of the hook when they hurt or offend us.

(Taken from Marriage Matters, pp 126, 127, 128)

# It's *His* Fault

*Why do you look at the speck of sawdust in your brother's eye and pay no attention to the plank in your own eye? How can you say to your brother, 'Let me take the speck out of your eye,' when all the time there is a plank in your own eye? You hypocrite, first take the plank out of your own eye, and then you will see clearly to remove the speck from your brother's eye*
Matthew 7:3–5

Whenever a crisis erupts the human reaction is to find someone to blame. 'It's that toad, Satan, again.' 'It's the pastor.' 'It's the elders.' 'It's the organist.' Jesus speaks right into this normal, understandable series of reactions with his challenge in Matthew 7.

If we are to live biblically, the critical spirit, boasting, subtle emotional swiping of another, inappropriate jealousy, rivalry, slander, must all go. They must be replaced by the humility of spirit that takes conflict seriously, desires reconciliation, and therefore asks 'Lord, show me where *I* have failed. Bring me to the place of repentance.'

To say sorry and to forgive is not easy, but it is essential. If we refuse to forgive, we shall be taken over by resentment, bitterness and fear. This indwelling hostility generates the energy for wrecking relationships. Like Jesus we must forgive, not just those we are fond of, but our persecutors also. Like Jesus we must hold into the reconciling love of God the unholy tangle that surrounds conflict. Like Jesus, we must trust that the whole of life is in God's hands so that we learn to bear the brunt of conflict without retaliation.

(Taken from Creative Conflict, pp 39, 40)

# Getting Your Own Back

### *Lord, how often must I forgive?*
#### Matthew 18:21

'I don't get mad. I just get even.' We smile when slogans like that greet us from the back window of people's cars. Yet such tit-for-tat thinking is part of the clutter which sometimes hinders our prayer because it is incompatible with Jesus' teaching on forgiveness.

To forgive means to let go of resentment and bitterness, hatred and anger. To forgive means to let the offending person off the hook. To forgive means to cancel the debt we feel they owe us. To forgive is therefore extremely costly. And it happens in stages.

Forgiveness begins by feeling the full brunt of the pain and recognising that we have every reason to feel hurt as well as every right to want to retaliate: to hit back; to hurt as we have been hurt. But forgiveness continues by making a deliberate choice to refuse to exercise that right. By engaging the will forgiveness drops any accusations we might wish to make and switches off the gas which has kept our anger simmering. Forgiveness even goes further. While refusing to deny that we have been hurt, it searches for acceptable and significant ways of serving the one who harmed us in the first place. This, at least, is forgiveness following the pattern of Jesus.

(Taken from Open to God, p 167)

# Accepting Forgiveness

## *The Lord has forgiven you; now you must do the same*
### Colossians 3:14

Introverts are good at confessing and bad at receiving forgiveness particularly if they come from an evangelical background. I am an introvert and an evangelical and these words of Thomas Merton never cease to amaze me.

> We are not permitted to nurse a sense of guilt: we must fully and completely accept and embrace his forgiveness and love. Guilt feeling and inferiority feeling before God are expressions of selfishness, of self-centredness: we give greater importance to our little sinful self than to his immense and never-ending love. We must surrender our guilt and our inferiority to him; *his goodness is greater than our badness. We must accept his joy in loving and forgiving us*. It is a healing grace to surrender our sinfulness to his mercy.[28]

(Taken from Listening to God, p 60)

# His Joy in Forgiveness

## *God is greater than our hearts*
### 1 John 3:20

'His goodness is greater than our badness.'
'We must accept his joy in forgiving us.'
I recorded in my prayer journal an occasion when God wormed these words into my realisation. My emotions were in turmoil at the time. The problem was that I was working with a male colleague whose warmth and gentleness, tenderness and spirituality I was growing to appreciate. He was eliciting from me a response which was equally warm and this resulted in a special closeness which seemed like a gift from God.

Whenever God entrusts us with something of value and beauty, Satan sets himself the task of destroying or distorting it. In this instance he tried to soil this friendship by bombarding my mind with day-dreams and suggestions, thoughts and fantasies which, if translated into practice would turn *philia*, warm, compassionate, tender love into *eros*, a romantic love which would threaten my marriage and my integrity as a person.

God disciplines those he loves. And he disciplined me. It was while I was sitting in church one Sunday morning that his voice reached me through the tangle of my emotions. 'You've lost your cutting edge', was all he said. And I knew that he was correct.

(Taken from Listening to God, pp 60, 61)

# You are Mine

### *Behold, I make all things new*
### Revelation 21:5

A friend of mine was married to a pastor but had indulged in an affair with a married man.

Having repented of the illicit love-affair, she wandered into the woods to think and to pray. As she continued to pour out the bitterness of her soul to God, she described her life to him as nothing more than fragments of her former self. While she stood, silent and still before God, into her mind came a picture of the fragments she had described: they littered the ground like so many pieces of red clay. As she gazed at the broken vessel representing her life, into the picture came Jesus. She saw the tenderness of his face and observed the sensitivity of his fingers as he stooped down and started to turn over those forlorn fragments. 'Suddenly, he started to piece them together,' she told me. 'He assured me that, though the vessel was a mess, every tiny piece of the pot was precious. I watched the skill with which he put the pieces together again. He re-created that vessel. He showed me that it would be even more beautiful than it had been before and much more useful. Then, he glazed it and held it up for me to see. I couldn't see a single sign of the joins where the cracked parts had been pressed back together.'

(Taken from Listening to God, p 98)

# Bury the Hatchet

## *God's love has been poured into our hearts*
### Romans 5:5

It was not easy for Jesus to forgive me, to forgive you. It cost him the agony of Gethsemane, the terror of the trial, the humiliation of Golgotha. But he did it. He triumphed. And so must we, no matter how much it costs us, no matter what people do to us. If you cannot forgive, go one step further back in your prayer. Ask God to pour his Spirit of love into your heart – the love that wants to let go of hatred.

When we have forgiven the person who caused the hurt, when we have forgiven those involved, then we are ready to move out of the pain and abandonment to live life, stripped of what might have been, but held within the all-supporting hand of God.

Forgiveness is confronting hostile emotions, owning them as part of our hurting, helpless self, acknowledging who it was who inflicted the injury, and forgiving the offender; setting them free.

(Taken from Creative Conflict)

# Be Filled with the Spirit

*He is our peace . . . and has broken down the*
*dividing wall of hostility*
Ephesians 2:14

Corrie ten Boom, who became a world-famous evangelist after her release from the Ravensbruck Concentration Camp, tells of an occasion when God transformed her attitude and behaviour. She was speaking at a meeting in Germany. One woman in the meeting seemed unable to look into Corrie's eyes. After a while, Corrie recognized her. She was the nurse who had treated Corrie's dying sister with great cruelty. Corrie admits: 'When I saw her, a feeling of bitterness, almost hatred, came into my heart. How my dying sister had suffered because of her!'

Corrie knew that her duty as a Christian was to forgive this woman. She struggled, but she could not do it. 'Lord, you know I cannot forgive her. My sister suffered too much because of her cruelties.'

At the suggestion of a friend, Corrie invited this nurse to attend the meeting the following night. 'During the entire meeting she looked into my eyes while I spoke. After the meeting, I had a talk with her. I told her that I had been bitter, but that God's Holy Spirit in me had brought His love instead of hatred and that now I loved her . . . I told her more and at the end of our talk that nurse accepted Jesus Christ as her personal Saviour and Lord.'29

Just as God, by his Spirit, changed Corrie ten Boom's bitterness into love, so he longs to cultivate within the life of each Christian the fruit of the Spirit.

(Taken from Reflections for Lent, p 58)

# The Self-Denial of Jesus

*Jesus fasted for forty days and forty nights,
after which he was very hungry.*
Matthew 4:2

When Moses the law-giver, King David, Queen Esther and countless others in the Old Testament wanted to focus fully on God in order to discern his will, they. fasted. In the wilderness, we see Jesus keeping up this tradition. Here he gave himself to prayer, listened intently to his Father's instruction and set himself the task of discovering precisely how he was to rescue mankind from the clutches of 'the Prince of this world' – Satan.

Jesus seems to assume that we will also fast: 'When you fast . . .' (Matthew 6:16) seems to be presented as the flip side of 'When you pray . . .' That is why, for generations, some Christians have practised self-denial during Lent – giving up a meal once a week, or all food for one day each week, denying themselves the pleasure of a particular television programme or sacrificing some sleep in order to deepen their relationship with God. Yet Richard Foster suggests that, in our affluent society, fasting might involve us in a greater sacrifice than giving money to God.

# Fasting

*The people of Nineveh believed in God: they
proclaimed a fast . . . and God relented*
Jonah 3:5–10

Richard Foster explains why fasting highlights huge inconsistencies or seedling sins germinating in our lives.

Fasting reveals the things that control us . . . We cover up what is inside us with food and other good things, but in fasting these things surface. If pride controls us, it will be revealed almost immediately . . . Anger, bitterness, jealousy, strife, fear – if they are within us, they will surface during fasting. At first we will rationalise that our anger is due to our hunger, then we know that we are angry because the spirit of anger is within us.[30]

Fasting not only exposes the large lumps of wax in my spiritual ears, it makes a positive contribution to listening prayer. It provides uncluttered, purposeful space for listening to God. When I fast, there are no meals to prepare and no clearing up, I can linger in my prayer corner and listen to God without having to keep an eye on the clock.

In one sense, fasting of itself does not aid my ability to concentrate on God in that I am often acutely aware of my rumbling tummy or the headache which often plagues me at such times or the occasional dizziness which reminds me that I have not eaten for several hours. But, in another sense, the discipline of the fast, with its non-verbal commitment to hear God's presence or voice, makes a major contribution to listening prayer. The physical symptoms remind me of the purpose of this fast: prayer and attentive listening to God.

(Taken from Listening to God, pp 193, 194)

# Jesus in the Wilderness

*All have sinned and fall short of the glory of God.*
**Romans 3:23**

When Paul said that, he did not simply mean that we have all done wrong things – snapped someone's head off when they have upset us, ignored the plight of the poor and so on. Paul's understanding of sin goes deeper than that. He reminds us that we are ingrained with selfishness.

Sin does not stem from acts of disobedience. It is far more subtle and serious than that. Sin places self at the centre of the universe instead of God. Sin revolves around self instead of around God. Sin seeks to promote self instead of God's Kingdom. And Paul claims that all of us, without exception, are guilty of saying yes to self and turning our back on God. There is even a sense in which we cannot help ourselves. That is why we need a Saviour.

On his forty-day retreat in the wilderness, Jesus was brought face to face with Satan. The Evil One tried to pull Jesus away from God with the seeming attractions of popularity and power, pleasure and possessions. But Jesus made it clear that he had come to earth for one reason – to live for God. His life's motto was: 'Not my will, but yours'.

Create in me a new, clean heart, O God,
filled with clean thoughts and right desires.
Restore to me again the joy of your salvation
and make me willing to obey you.

(Taken from God's Springtime tape)

# Subtle Suggestions

*Then leading him to a height, the devil
showed him in a moment of time all the
kingdoms of the world and said to him, 'I
will give you all this power and the glory of
these kingdoms, for it has been committed to
me and I give it to anyone I choose. Worship
me, then, and it shall all be yours.' But Jesus
answered him, 'Scripture says: "You must
worship the Lord your God, and serve him
alone."'*
Luke 4:5–8

Jesus had eaten nothing for six weeks. He was physically weak.
Satan chose this moment to take him up a mountain which
doubtless afforded them a breath-taking, panoramic view of
God's wonderful world and he whispered: 'Worship me and
I will give all of this to you. Your task will then be easy.'
'Compromise'. 'Strike a bargain with me.' 'Change the world by
becoming like the people who live in it. That's the way to make
them follow you in droves.'

In response, Jesus rounded on the Tempter and said with
an authority which transcended his weakness: 'Go away, Satan.'
Refusing to compromise, he rises to his full stature as the Son of God
and is strengthened. Refusing to become part of the world's darkness,
he penetrates earth's gloom with a sudden shaft of heavenly glory.

# The Pinnacle of the Temple

*The devil then took (Jesus) to the holy city
and made him stand on the parapet of the
Temple. 'If you are the Son of God' he said
'throw yourself down . . .' Jesus said to him
. . . 'You must not put the Lord your God to
the test.'*
Matthew 4:5–7

Jesus was standing on the pinnacle of the Temple, probably at the corner looking down to the valley below – a sheer drop of four hundred and fifty feet.

If he had leapt, like superman, from this pinnacle, his fame would have spread throughout Jerusalem. He would have won the applause and admiration of everyone. But Jesus refused to become a sensationalist by drawing attention to himself through the miracles he performed. He silenced the Enemy with the reminder from Scripture: 'Do not put the Lord your God to the test'. (Matt 4:7)

'He meant this: there is no good seeing how far you can go with God; there is no good putting yourself deliberately into a threatening situation, and doing it quite recklessly and needlessly, and then expecting God to rescue you from it . . . God's rescuing power is not something to be played with and experimented with, it is something to be quietly trusted in the life of every day.'[31]

(Taken from Reflections for Lent, p 24)

# Unconditional Love

*Mary brought in a pound of very costly*
*ointment, pure nard, and with it anointed the*
*feet of Jesus wiping them with her hair*
John 12:3 (JB)

Six days before the Passover Feast where Jesus was to inaugurate the Last Supper, a special public Sabbath-day supper seems to have been arranged in Bethany. The celebrity guest was Jesus. Did Mary of Bethany's intuition tell her that this was the last meal she would eat with the one she loved? We are not told. Putting together Matthew and John's description of this meal, we are told that while Jesus was eating, Mary came in clutching 'a bottle of very expensive perfume, and poured it over his head.' She then poured some of it on Jesus' feet and 'wiped them with her hair. The sweet smell of the perfume filled the whole house.' (John 12:3 and Matthew 26:7)

Mary's generous gesture met with a barrage of criticism from the disciples — especially Judas, who asked accusingly: 'Why wasn't this perfume sold for three hundred silver coins and the money given to the poor?' (John 12:5). Jesus, on the other hand, dismissed the criticism, and paid a memorable and most moving tribute to Mary's expressed love.

Jesus opened his heart to others and thereby gave them power over him: the power to accept or reject his love. When his self-gift was accepted by Mary Jesus was filled with joy and encouragement.

(Taken from God's Springtime, p 62, 63)

# Mary and Martha

*It is a fine and beautiful thing she has done*
*for me . . . What she did was to pour this*
*perfume on my body to prepare me for burial.*
Matthew 26:10,12

Mary seems to have been the one person who took these words of Jesus seriously which was why she anointed his body in anticipation of his death.

Jesus drew from Mary the ability so to listen to his anguish, loneliness and grief that when she served him, it was without fuss or desire to draw attention to herself. Her ministry had one aim: to bring pleasure and comfort to the one she loved so passionately.

There is a Martha and a Mary in each person of prayer: a me-centred, attention-seeking, independent person living alongside one whose deep-down desire is to become increasingly abandoned to the adoration and service of God. A person who is capable of contemplating Christ in the middle of pressure, and who needs to sit at his feet, soak up his love and listen. This listening strips our service of 'self' and it is as incisive as Martha's statement of faith, when she said 'I believe that you are the Christ, the Son of God.' (John 11:27) Like Mary, we need to be still at the feet of Jesus so that our action stems from contemplation, becomes contemplative and constantly drives us back into the still place with God: Father, Son and Holy Spirit. Only then will we cease to feel fragmented and enjoy the harmony which comes to those who have learned that Martha and Mary can co-exist in the same person.

(Taken from The Smile of Love, pp 181, 182)

# Donkeys

*Jesus sent two of his disciples, saying to them, 'Go to the village ahead of you, and just as you enter it, you will find a colt tied there, which no-one has ever ridden. Untie it and bring it here.'*
Mark 11:1,2

I n Margaret Gray's beautifully illustrated book *The Donkey's Tale* the donkey Jesus rode gives courage to a girl who felt helpless.

'Once upon a time there was a very ordinary girl. One day she heard a knock at the door. It was the world asking her for help. "Why me?" she asked. "What can I do to help? Why not someone with more sense who is more reliable? I always make mistakes . . . I'm just useless."

"You, too?" said a donkey . . . "I've got long funny ears, my legs are too short, and I'm often stubborn and moody. But a long time ago, in a faraway land, a man chose me. Not a dashing white horse, but funny old me. He was heavy and the road was long, but he always gave me the strength to get there. . . . He doesn't need another genius – he needs a few donkeys who know they have to depend on his strength – not theirs

his wisdom – not theirs

his words – not theirs."

"So it doesn't matter that I feel useless," said the girl. "He will show me what to do and will give me what I need to do it?"

"Yes," said the donkey.'[32]

# The Last Supper

*Then he took a loaf and after thanking God
he broke it and gave it to them with these
words, 'This is my body which is given for
you: do this in remembrance of me.' So too,
he gave them a cup after supper with the
words, 'This cup is the new agreement made
in my own blood which is shed for you.'*
Luke 22:19

At the Last Supper Jesus knew what the disciples did not yet know, that on the very next day, his body would literally be broken and his blood spilled. He was about to sacrifice his life as a once-and-for-all offering for sin. It was to be a kind of charter sealed with his own blood which would dwarf any other previous attempts to bring God and man together. *This* agreement, steeped as it was in sacrifice, would reconcile God and man for ever. *This* agreement would secure man's forgiveness from sin. *This* agreement proved that God's love for mankind was unquenchable.

Remove from me, dear Lord, the heart of stone that can contemplate these mysteries without awe, without wonder, and without a response of adoring love. Give me, instead, a heart that warms with gratitude whenever I reflect on the fact that you, the Son of God signed the agreement which reconciled me to a pure and holy God with your own life-blood, freely shed out of love for me.

(Taken from Reflections for Lent, pp 84, 85)

# The Last Supper

*Greater love has no-one than this, that he lay down his life for his friends*
John 15:13

On the day before he died, Jesus tried to explain to his disciples how deep and real this love is. He was eating supper with them. He knew it would be the last meal they would share together before his death. In the middle of the meal, he took a loaf of bread in his hands, blessed it, broke it in pieces and handed it to his friends saying:

'Take this and eat it. It is my body – given for you'.

Then he took the cup which would have been brimful with wine. Thanking God for it he said:

'Drink this, all of you, for it is my blood . . . shed to set many free from their sins.' (Matt 26:26–28)

He was trying to tell them just how deeply he loved them. He was trying to draw from them a response. And, knowing that the next few days would be traumatic for all of them, he was strengthening them for the journey.

Our hearts are cold;
Lord, warm them by your selfless love.
Our hearts are sinful;
cleanse them with your precious blood.
Our hearts are weak;
strengthen them with your joyous Spirit.
Our hearts are empty,
fill them with your divine presence.

Lord Jesus, our hearts are yours;
possess them always
and only
for yourself.

(Taken from God's Springtime tape)

# The Call of Peter

### *Jesus said to Simon 'Put out into deep water'*
### Luke 5:4

When Jesus asked if he might borrow Peter's boat, Peter rowed Jesus away from the shore and spent the day with this comparative stranger. The result of that day with Jesus was that, by the same evening, Peter was pulling his boat onto the shore and abandoning it for an entirely new way of life: to become a partner with Jesus in heralding God's Kingdom on earth.

What had they talked about during those few hours at sea? What was it about the presence and personality of Jesus which caused Peter to change the direction of his entire life? Was it those eyes which seemed to read the secrets of Peter's heart without condemning him? Was it Jesus' smile? Or was it the aura of authority which seemed to surround this man wherever he went?

(Taken from The Smile of Love, pp 24–25)

# Simon Peter

*Simon, son of John, do you love me more than these others do?*
John 21:15

Peter's call to accompany Jesus came in the form of an irresistible inner desire – a compulsion. Although the glory of Jesus was veiled, it was not long concealed from Peter. He discerned early on in his friendship with Jesus that he was 'the Christ', the Messiah. Peter was given the immense privilege of contemplating the Transfigured Christ, of hearing the Father's insistence, 'This is my Son, whom I love'. Consequently Peter resolved to do anything and to go anywhere for Jesus – but he crumbled when put to the test. On the night before Jesus died, in Caiaphas' courtyard, Peter was the one who denied that he had ever known Jesus, the Galilean (Mark 14:66–72).

In those agonising hours between the Crucifixion and the Resurrection, Peter must have felt that he had forfeited God's love. Jesus took the trouble to go to him after the Resurrection to assure him that he was forgiven. John shows us how Jesus drew Peter back into the circle of love with his persistent question, 'Do you love me?' Not until Peter had been wooed into the circle once more, and not until he was once again enjoying the mutuality of love he and Jesus had enjoyed for the previous three years, did Jesus give him a fresh commission: 'Feed my lambs . . . Feed my sheep' (John 21:15–17).

(Taken from The Smile of Love, pp 178, 180)

# You Will Deny Me

*Jesus said to them, 'This very night all of you
will run away and leave me.'*
Matthew 26:31 (GNB)

Being let down by friends is one of the most painful things
that can happen to anyone. It's hard enough when it happens
unexpectedly but it must have been doubly difficult for Jesus
because he knew in advance that when he needed his disciples most
one of them would betray him and the rest would desert him.

No wonder John remembers that Jesus became deeply troubled
during the Last Supper. There he was, taking bread in his hands,
breaking it, offering it to his closest friends, telling them that soon
his body would be broken for them and all the time he knew that
these same friends would throw his love back in his face.

In his film *Jesus of Nazareth*, Zefferalli suggests that they were wise
after the event. In the film, on Easter Sunday morning, we see Mary
Magdalene telling Peter, Andrew and John that she's seen the Lord.
That he is risen. At first the disciples make their scornful disbelief
very obvious. Mary is hurt. She goes away. Then Peter and John
admit that they actually believe her. Whereupon Andrew rounds on
his brother and asks how he can possibly be so gullible.

'I always believed him', Peter admits.

'But Peter, you denied him. You denied him three times.'

'Yes I denied him because I was a coward. We're all cowards.
We accused Judas of betraying him but we all betrayed him. We
all abandoned him,' Peter replies. 'We ate with him, we lived with
him, we knew he was the Christ and still we betrayed him.' If Peter
did make such a claim, he was correct. The disciples did betray and
deny Jesus. And they deserted him – the one who had poured out
his life searching for them and loving them.

Jesus, Lord,

I, too, have failed you.

Have mercy on me, a sinner.

(Taken from God's Springtime tape)

# The Route to Jerusalem

*Jesus took the twelve disciples aside and said
to them, 'Listen! We are going to Jerusalem
where everything the prophets wrote about
the Son of Man will come true. He will be
handed over to the Gentiles who will mock
him, insult him and spit on him. They will
whip him and kill him.'*
Mark 10:33, 34

J esus knew all along that it would not be easy to rescue us from
the clutches of Satan. He kept warning his disciples that the
final weeks of his life would be tough.

What made him do it? I kept asking myself that question one
Palm Sunday as I sat by the Sea of Galileee – that place Jesus loved
so much. What made him tear himself away from all this beauty and
stillness and warmth? What made him exchange it for the bustle and
chill of Jerusalem when he knew what would happen to him?

The answer came to me later that day. It was love. No nails could
have kept him on the cross. It was love which drove him there and
love which kept him there. Love for us.

Lord our God,
grant us grace to desire you with our whole heart;
that so desiring, we may seek and find you;
and so finding, may love you;
and so loving, may hate those sins
from which you have delivered us.[33]

# The Garden of Gethsemane

*Jesus . . . prayed. 'Father, if you are willing,*
*take this cup from me; yet not my will,*
*but yours be done.' An angel from heaven*
*appeared to him and strengthened him. And*
*being in anguish, he prayed more earnestly,*
*and his sweat was like drops of blood falling*
*to the ground*
Matthew 26:42–44

The writer to the Hebrews reminds us that, here in the Garden of Gethsemane, Jesus prayed 'with loud cries and tears.' (Hebrews 5:7) In these awesome moments, Peter and James and John caught a glimpse of the way their Master dealt with inner anguish and fear. He did not deny its existence, he descended into the abyss and found that, having fallen headlong to the bottom of the terrifying pit, underneath were his Father's everlasting arms. On this occasion, his Father sent an angel to strengthen him.

If we want truly to hear God's voice and sense his presence, we too, must be prepared to descend into our own abyss of loneliness or anxiety, fear of being unable to cope or grief. Only then will we feel those everlasting arms embracing us. Only then will we be able to rejoice with Jesus and the Psalmist:

'Praise the Lord, O my soul; . . .
who redeems your life from the pit
and crowns you with love and compassion.'

(Psalm 103:1, 3)

# Trumped-Up Evidence

*Prophesy for us, Messiah! Who hit you?*
Matthew 26:68

Flanked on each side by heavily-armed Roman soldiers, Jesus was marched from the Garden of Gethsemane to the big, double courtyard near the High Priest's home. There trumped-up charges were brought against him.

Caiaphas knew that it was illegal for a trial to take place at night. He also knew that a man could not be condemned on his own evidence. But Jesus' trial took place in the middle of the night and he was convicted of 'blasphemy' simply because he told the truth about himself, admitting that he was the promised Messiah. But being subjected to this humiliating trial was only the beginning of the insults and injuries which were to be inflicted on him:

He who clothes Himself in light
as in a garment,
stood naked at the judgement;
on His cheek
He received blows
from the hands which He had formed.[34]

# Peter's Denial

## *'I don't know what you are talking about'*
### Luke 22:60

A fire had been lit in the centre of the courtyard and Peter joined those who were sitting round it. When one of the servant-girls saw him sitting there at the fire, she looked straight at him and said, 'This man too was with Jesus!' But Peter denied it. 'Woman, I don't even know him!' After a little while a man noticed Peter and said, 'You are one of them too!' But Peter answered, 'Man, I am not!' And about an hour later another man insisted strongly, 'There isn't any doubt that this man was with Jesus, because he also is a Galilean!' But Peter answered, 'Man, I don't know what you are talking about!' At once, while he was still speaking, a cock crowed. The Lord turned and looked straight at Peter, and Peter remembered that the Lord had said to him, 'Before the cock crows tonight, you will say three times that you do not know me.' Peter went out and wept bitterly. (Luke 22:55–62)

Being let down by friends is one of the most painful things that can happen to anyone. It is hard enough when it happens unexpectedly but it must have been doubly difficult for Jesus because he knew in advance that when he needed his disciples most one of them would betray him and the rest would desert him.

While he was being arrested in the Garden of Gethsemane, all his friends disappeared into the night leaving Jesus to face his captors, the trial before Caiaphas and the scourging alone. To add insult to injury, he witnessed Peter's denial. Yet he continued to love these fickle, frightened friends. On Easter Day, Peter was one of the first people to see Jesus. (Luke 24:12 and 34) Eight days later, on the beach by the Sea of Galilee, Jesus gives him three opportunities to reaffirm his love and commitment.

(Taken from God's Springtime tape)

# Simon of Cyrene

*They came across a man from Cyrene . . .*
*and forced him to carry Jesus' cross*
Matthew 27:32

The armed soldiers and the centurion (who headed the procession on horse-back) would have controlled the crowd with their spears, but they could do nothing to control the body of Jesus. It would appear that he lost his balance, lurched forward and fell, unable to steady himself because his hands were still bound by the rope and burdened with the big beam. Neither could they compel Jesus to continue to carry his own cross. Strength had ebbed from him. He was powerless – like someone with a slipped disc whose body seems locked and full of pain. Instead, 'they came across a man from Cyrene'.

The Gospel writers do not actually give details of a fall, but it would seem probable that this was the reason why Simon of Cyrene was coerced into carrying Christ's cross. The Bible does describe how Jesus was probably feeling at this stage of the journey:

My strength has drained away like water,
and all my bones are out of joint.
My heart melts like wax;
my strength has dried up like sun-baked clay;
my tongue sticks to my mouth,
for you have laid me in the dust of death.

(Psalm 22:14,15)

Hold into the arms of the Christ who collapsed under the weight of the cross those who feel that they can't carry on – particularly those who stand by and watch loved ones suffer and die.

Think of occasions when you have felt as though you could not carry on, and ask God to touch and heal the memories.

(Taken from God's Springtime, pp 96, 97)

# Father Forgive Them

*It was the third hour when they crucified him*
Mark 15:25

Peter Green takes us into the scene:

'The Cross is laid on the ground. Jesus is stripped and thrown roughly onto the Cross. Nails are driven through each hand and foot. The Cross is jerked up, throwing the whole weight of the body upon the tortured hands and feet. Then with a sickening jar the Cross is dropped into the hole prepared for it, and wedges of wood are driven in to stay and support it, each blow of the hammer sending an agony through the whole of our Lord's Body. And he meets this with the often-repeated prayer: "Father, forgive them, for they know not what they do." For the Greek makes it quite plain that this word was not spoken once. The text should be translated 'Jesus kept on saying, "Father, forgive them, for they know not what they do."'[35]

The Greek word for 'forgive' is *aphesis*. Jesus uttered this word at the tomb of Lazarus when he invited the by-standers to 'loose him', to set him free from his restrictive grave clothes. Here on the cruel Cross he utters it again. He has not forgotten the events which have broken his heart; Judas' betrayal, Peter's denial, the disciples' desertion, the crowd's condemnation: 'Crucify!'. Yet he pleads with his Father: 'Abba, loose them, set them free to become the people you always intended them to be.'

# The Son of God

*The army officer who was standing there*
*in front of the cross saw how Jesus had*
*died. 'This man was really the Son of God!'*
*he said.*
Mark 15:39 (GNB)

An Archbishop of Paris once told his congregation the story of two small boys who were playing outside Notre Dame Cathedral. Seeing people enter the magnificent building to make their confession, they decided to play a trick on the priest whom they despised. One boy dared the other to think up the worst crimes imaginable and to go to the priest and pretend that he had committed all of these sins.

The small boy did as he was dared. When he had completed his confession, the priest invited him to go to the back of the Cathedral where he would find a cross with a figure hanging on it – the figure of Jesus. 'Kneel at the foot of that Cross, gaze at that figure and say, "I know you died to save me from my sins but I couldn't care less."'

The lad knelt at the cross but instead of mocking the Crucified One, he found himself overwhelmed by the forgiveness and undeserved love which poured from the man on the cross.

'I know that that story is true', the Archbishop concluded 'because that small boy was me.'

Like the army officer on the first Good Friday, the mischievous school boy discovered in an unforgettable way that the man on the Cross was the Son of God.

We adore you, O Christ, and we bless you, because by your holy cross you have redeemed the world.[36]

# Between Two Thieves

*Remember me, Jesus when you come as King*
Luke 23:42

One of the criminals hanging there hurled insults at him: 'Aren't you the Messiah? Save yourself and us!' The other one, however, rebuked him, saying, 'Don't you fear God? You received the same sentence he did. Ours, however, is only right, because we are getting what we deserve for what we did; but he has done no wrong.' And he said to Jesus, 'Remember me, Jesus, when you come as King!' Jesus said to him, 'I promise you that today you will be in Paradise with me.' (Luke 23:39–43)

The penitent thief knew nothing about the meaning of Jesus' death yet, instinctively, he begged for forgiveness and experienced the joy of sins forgiven. Just as Jesus set this man free, so to-day, he continues to meet with convicted criminals. Brian Greenaway explains how this happened to him when he was serving his sentence in Dartmoor prison. He was reading *Run Baby Run* by Nicky Cruz.

'Where could I find this Jesus who came so suddenly into Nicky's life, taking away the nightmares and allowing him to sleep soundly again? I needed so much to understand . . .

Then I remembered the yellow book lying beside me – the Living Bible . . . I didn't know one end of it from the other. I simply opened it and read . . . As I lay on my bed facing the door I knew that Jesus had his arms opened out towards me. He was saying, 'All you've got to do is ask me and I will change your life.' I wanted it more than anything I had ever wanted. Out loud I asked him to do for me what he had done for Nicky – to change my life, taking away all that was rotten, making it worth living.

At that instant I began to feel all the pus and poison in me drain away through my feet. All the frustration and anger that had held me a prisoner for most of my life just flowed away. At the same time it was as though a hole opened up in my head and God's love began pouring in. For the first time ever I was experiencing real love and it was God's pure love. In tears of joy I cracked up and fell to my knees on the floor, thanking God for bringing us together. After that, I slept a dreamless sleep – at peace with God.'[37]

# Joseph of Arimathea

## *A secret disciple of Jesus*
### John 19:38

J oseph of Arimathea, who had been a secret disciple of Jesus for fear of the Jewish leaders, boldly asked Pilate for permission to take Jesus' body down; and Pilate told him to go ahead. So he came and took it away. Nicodemus, the man who had come to Jesus at night, came too, bringing a hundred pounds of embalming ointment made from myrrh and aloes. Together they wrapped Jesus' body in a long linen cloth saturated with the spices, as is the Jewish custom of burial. The place of crucifixion was near a grove of trees, where there was a new tomb, never used before. And so, because of the need for haste before the Sabbath, and because the tomb was close at hand, they laid him there. (John 19:38–42 LB)

Jesus
buried in the tomb,
Jesus in burial bands,
you are life
and the source of life;
you are the seed in the earth,
the secret of the Eternal Spring;
you are the wonder of Heaven
and love's unending flowering.

Grant to us all,
Lord Jesus,
that in the soul's long winters
we may patiently
grow imperceptibly,
in the rhythms and seasons
of your love
and so enter into your peace.[38]

# A Day of Preparation

*As the body was taken away, the women
from Galilee followed and saw it carried
into the tomb. Then they went home and
prepared spices and ointments to embalm
him; but by the time they were finished it was
the Sabbath, so they rested all that day as
required by the Jewish law.*
Luke 23:55,56

What did the women and the disciples do on that Saturday? Did they sit huddled behind locked doors for fear of recrimination from Jesus' enemies? Did they weep and mourn as they re-lived the last agonizing moments of Jesus' life? Did they give voice to the pain which separation from their master must have inflicted on them? Were they restless or frustrated because they could not visit the scene of Jesus' burial earlier? Did they suffer that intolerable emptiness the bereaved person experiences when they have lost a loved one? We are not told. What we do know is that they spent part of the day in preparation. Luke hints at this when he shows that all their preparations were completed before the crack of dawn

O happy fault, O necessary sin of Adam,
which gained for us so great a Redeemer!
Most blessed of all nights, chosen by God
to see Christ rising from the dead! . . .
The power of this holy night
dispels all evil, washes guilt away,
restores lost innocence, brings mourners joy;
it casts out hatred, brings us peace, and humbles earthly pride.
(The Roman Missal)

(Taken from Reflections for Lent, pp 88, 91)

# My Redeemer Lives

### *Dying, behold we live*
2 Corinthians: 6:9

Archbishop Anthony Bloom reminds us:

The joy of the Resurrection is something we . . . must learn to experience, but we can experience it only if we first learn the tragedy of the Cross. To rise again we must die. Die to our hampering selfishness, die to our fears, die to everything which makes the world so narrow, so cold, so poor, so cruel. Die so that our souls may live, may rejoice, may discover the spring of life. If we do this then the Resurrection of Christ will have come down to us also . . . the Resurrection which is joy, the joy of life recovered, the joy of the life that no-one can take away any more! The joy of a life which is superabundant, which, like a stream runs down the hills, carrying with it heaven itself reflected in its sparkling waters . . . It is not only with our hearts but with the totality of our experience that we know the risen Christ. We can know him day after day as the Apostles knew him. Not the Christ of the flesh . . . but the everliving Christ . . . Christ, once risen, is ever alive, and each of us can know him personally. Unless we know him personally we have not yet learnt what it means to be a Christian.[39]

# Christ is Risen

## *Mary of Magdala went and told the disciples*
### John 20:18

I recall an evening when I was meditating on the resurrection of Jesus. John's gospel lay open on the floor at my feet. I read chapter 20 as slowly as I could, applying my senses to the unfolding scene. I watched Mary steal to the sepulchre in the grey darkness of pre-dawn. I sensed her dismay as she saw, not the sealed tomb, but a yawning hole where the stone should have been. I heard her run to alert Peter and John, observed their race to the grave and, in my imagination, I went with Peter into the belly of the rock. I, too, saw the strips of linen lying there, 'the burial cloth that had been around Jesus's head. The cloth was folded up by itself, separate from the linen' (John 20:7).

And I gazed from the neat piles of linen to John who had crept quietly into the sepulchre. As wonder spread across his face and as he worshipped, my heart leapt with joy. I fell on my face and worshipped the resurrected Lord, not from any sense of duty, but with well-springs of praise which rose from somewhere deep inside me.

(Taken from Listening to God, p 207)

# Know the Lord

## *'Mary' . . . 'Rabboni'*
### John 20:16

Jesus has a wonderful way of making his presence known to all kinds of personality types and to people from a variety of backgrounds.

Early in the morning, on the first Easter Day, Jesus appeared to Mary around whose neck we might hang the label 'contemplative', or 'introvert' while Mary wept out her grief at the mouth of the empty tomb. He gave her the luxury her heart pined for: a long, leisurely opportunity to gaze at the Master she adored; the opportunity to drink in the Lord's one loving word to her, 'Mary', her own name.

Think of the disciples who tramped the road which stretches from Jerusalem to Emmaus. Perhaps these two were extroverts: thinking types. As Jesus drew alongside them in their grief, his approach was quite different from his meeting with Mary. He appealed, not to their emotions, but to their minds. He expounded the scriptures, opened the eyes of their understanding, and rebuked them for neglecting to use their thinking powers. And by the end of the journey they heard him. In meeting them in their need he had used a language they could understand.

(Taken from Listening to God, pp 224, 225)

# The End of the Beginning

*Jesus came up and walked by their side but*
*something prevented them from recognising*
*him*
Luke 24:15

In *How to Be a People Helper*[40] Gary Collins explains how, in Luke 24:14, 15, we watch Jesus draw alongside the travellers who, from the way they turn the events of the past three nightmarish days over and over in their minds, still seem to be suffering from shock. Jesus takes the initiative and the trouble to establish a rapport with them so that they trust him.

Having built up a relationship, Jesus goes on to explore with them the nature of their problem. Why were they so discouraged? Why were they so stunned? He seems to have listened attentively as they poured out their perplexing tale, giving them ample opportunity to ventilate their frustrations, doubts and disappointments, and having penetrated to the heart of the problem and understood it Jesus decides on a course of action.

With a skilful use of questions and suggestions, Jesus sorts out the confusion by challenging their thinking and encouraging them to think differently about the string of curious events which has precipitated their crisis of faith.

But far from keeping himself detached or aloof, he comes close to his fellow-travellers and joins them for a meal. This fraternising was not an invitation to become dependent on him, however. On the contrary, we read that, quite literally, Jesus vanishes from their sight. This disappearing act seems to have spurred them into action and, on their own initiative, the travellers head back for Jerusalem where they become encouragers of others.

(Taken from Listening to Others, pp 112, 113)

# My Lord and My God

*Ask and you will receive, and your joy will be
complete*
John 16:24

If we are to find ourselves in harmony with joy, we must learn
to lay aside our self preoccupation.

This is one of the lessons the risen Christ seems to be trying
to drum into the minds of the disciples on the road to Emmaus.
In his encounter with them, Jesus' first task was to strip them of
the prejudices and presuppositions which clouded their perception
so that, eventually, their hearts were ready to receive Christ with
joy. He deals similarly with Thomas's doubts. When these have
been removed the scales fall from his eyes and with joy he cries:
'My Lord and my God.' And, perhaps most movingly of all, we are
permitted to eavesdrop as Jesus stands on the shore of the Sea of
Galilee and converses with the great deserter, Peter; the one who,
that very morning, had resolved to return to his former lifestyle:
fishing in the Sea of Galilee. And Jesus takes from his mind the
sting of the memory of that night in Caiaphas' palace when Peter
denied all acquaintance with Jesus and, in its place, he puts joy: the
joy of the awareness that he is still loved and capable of loving; that
he is not only usable but recommissioned.

(Taken from Listening to Others, pp 242, 243)

# Ascended into Heaven

### *He was carried up to heaven*
### Luke 24:51

Imagine that you have been allowed the privilege of walking with the eleven, out of Jerusalem to the Mount of Ascension.
Stay behind them as you leave the noise and clutter and the stifling heat of Jerusalem behind.

Feel the heat warming your body as you start the steep climb.

Feel the warm dust creeping into your sandals.

What can you see . . . ?

What can you hear . . . ?

What can you smell . . . ?

Take time to picture the whole scene as vividly as possible.

How do you feel?

Look at your companions, the eleven disciples.

What sort of people are they?

How are they dressed?

What are they talking about?

Is there anything you'd like to ask them — or say to them?

How does it feel to be about to meet him?

And now — there he is — standing in front of you!

Take a good look at Jesus —

at those hands still bearing the wounds of love

at those hands hovering over you to bless you.

What do you want to say to Jesus?

Watch carefully. He is leaving you now, being lifted out of sight. Soon he will be hidden by the cloud of God's presence.

Is there anything you want to do?

Anything you want to say?

Try to drink in what you have seen and heard.

Thank God for it.

(Taken from Listening to God, pp 155, 156)

# Lion of Judah

*Judah is a lion's whelp*
*a mighty lion; who dares rouse him*
Genesis 49:9

C.S. Lewis gives a unique insight into Gospel relationships:
'Oh, Aslan!' cried the children, staring up at him . . .
'Aren't you dead then, dear Aslan?' said Lucy.
'Not now,' said Aslan . . .

'Oh, you're real, you're real! Oh, Aslan!' cried Lucy and both girls flung themselves upon him and covered him with kisses . . .

'Oh, children,' said the Lion, 'I feel my strength coming back to me. Oh, children, catch me if you can!' He stood for a second, his eyes very bright, his limbs quivering, lashing himself with his tail. Then he made a leap high over their heads and landed on the other side of the Table. Laughing, though she didn't know why, Lucy scrambled over to reach him. Aslan leaped again. A mad chase began. Round and round the hill-top he led them, now hopelessly out of their reach, now letting them almost catch his tail, now diving between them, now tossing them in the air with his huge and beautifully velveted paws, and catching them again, and now stopping unexpectedly so that all three of them rolled over together in a happy laughing heap of fun and arms and legs. It was such a romp as no one ever had except in Narnia; and whether it was more like playing with a thunderstorm or playing with a kitten Lucy could never make up her mind.[41]

# The Second Coming

*Be on your guard, stay awake, because you never know when the time will come*
Mark 13:33

'Supposing Jesus returned *now*? What would he think of our life-style?

Most of us convince ourselves that Jesus will not come tonight nor even within the next five years and so we carry on, careless and complacent. But if we are serious about our Christian commitment, dare we watch the years roll by and continue leading mediocre Christian lives? Archbishop Anthony Bloom thinks not. Prayer and commitment to Christ, he claims, bring new responsibilities:

> We must learn to behave in the presence of the invisible
> Lord as we would in the presence of the Lord made visible
> to us. This implies primarily an attitude of mind and then its
> reflection upon the body. If Christ was here, before us, and we
> stood completely transparent to his gaze, in mind as well as in
> body, we would feel reverence, the fear of God, adoration, or
> else perhaps terror but *we should not be so easy in our behaviour
> as we are.*[42]

Add to this apt challenge a solemn question from Jesus: '"Why do you call me 'Lord, Lord,' and not do what I tell you?"' (Luke 6:46).

(Taken from Just Good Friends, p 60)

# Come, Lord Jesus

*The nations of the earth will wring their
hands as they see the Son of Man coming
on the clouds of the sky in power and great
splendour*
Matthew 24:30

One evening, while I was on holiday in Cyprus, I sat on the shore of a salt lake and watched the sun set. For nearly an hour, the sun was reflected like a golden ball, in the tranquil lake. As I watched, a black line divided the sun-ball in half. This apparent fissure deepened as the black mountains gradually swallowed up the now-red ball.

An hour later, back at the flat, I was still thinking about the splendour of that sunset. Suddenly, there was a loud bang. The flat began to shudder and the entire neighbourhood was plunged into darkness. An earthquake was shaking the little port. High-rise blocks of flats were swaying like trees in a breeze and countless people were struck with terror.

My mind flashed back to the sunset. And certain prophecies concerning Jesus' return immediately came to mind. 'Perhaps Jesus is about to return – *now*', I thought.

These strange happenings served to underline, for me, the truth that one day he will come back, not clothed in poverty and humility, as in his first appearance, but resplendent in glory and majesty. He will come in triumph. And everyone will see him.

(Taken from Approaching Christmas, p 43)

# Anointed by the Spirit

*In the last days, God says,*
*I will pour out my Spirit on all people.*
*Your sons and daughters will prophesy,*
*your young men will see visions,*
*your old men will dream dreams.*
*Even on my servants, both men and women,*
*I will pour out my Spirit in those days,*
*and they will prophesy*
Acts 2:17

The prophetic word is not only a word of love; it is also a timely word in the sense that it is necessary for that person or that group of people at that particular time. It is also an accurate word. Its accuracy survives the test of time. If it originates in God, the minutest details will be fulfilled.

Christians who open themselves to the Holy Spirit of God will, as occasion demands, be entrusted with the supernatural gifts of wisdom and knowledge, prophecy and visions. Like David Watson, I recognise that these gifts are 'tremendously important for every age'. They are 'not made redundant by the completion of the God-given revelation in the scriptures.'[43] Rather, they are made available for us by God through the anointing of his Holy Spirit.

(Taken from Listening to God, pp 135, 136)

# He is Risen Indeed

*Many shall come from the east and the west
and sit at table in the kingdom of heaven*
Matthew 8:11

Several years ago in Yugoslavia. I sustained head and back injuries in a car crash. Strangers had driven me to the nearest hospital and after the doctor had stitched up my head, I was wheeled into a ward of women who clearly spoke no English.

After supper, the patients prepared for bed. The woman in the next bed shuffled over to me, patted my hand and smiled before gently stooping down to kiss the small part of my forehead that was not covered in bandages. The other four followed her example. Those five smiles brought the warmth of a comfort and care which makes physical pain bearable. It was Good Friday.

On Easter Sunday morning, when the woman in the next bed came over carrying a picture of the empty tomb with her now-familiar smile and reassuring kiss, I showed her a simple card. She began to clap with excitement and the others crowded round her. When they saw the card, they too grinned from ear to ear, clapped and cried out 'Christus, Christus', pointing at me as though surprised that, like them, I believed in the Resurrection. I smiled back, relishing the fact that not only had we met on common ground, we had gone further and experienced an unspoken oneness in Christ. And all through a card and some smiles. It was the most memorable Easter gift I have ever been given.

(Taken from the Smile of Love, pp 14, 15, 16)

# Sacrament of the Present Moment

*Now is the acceptable time, now is the day of salvation*
2 Corinthians 6:2

'God's clocks keep perfect time' was a favourite saying of Dutch prisoner-of-war, Corrie ten Boom. For those who jet around the world carrying 'organisers', pocket year planners, portable computers and cordless telephones, a clock which moves one tick at a time seems frustratingly slow. We easily forget the supreme value, 'the now', or, as Pierre de Caussade, preferred to call it, 'the sacrament of the present moment'. Such forgetfulness and frustration hinder our prayer.

(Taken from Open to God, p 175)

# Even When Doubting

*Lord, I believe. Help my unbelief*
Mark 9:24

A group of young people was once asked the question: 'Do you think God understands radar?' Almost all of them instinctively said 'no'. They then laughed as their conscious minds realised the absurdity of their answer and recognised that, subconsciously, they believed in a God whose ability to cope with a technological age was inadequate. But as J. B. Phillips reminds us: 'We can never have too big a conception of God, and the more scientific knowledge (in whatever field) advances, the greater becomes our idea of His vast and complicated wisdom.'[44]

Even so, most of us struggle truly to believe in this all-powerful God we worship. Real faith sets reservations, doubts and misgivings on one side and takes God at his word when he says that he loves us. Real faith goes further. It stakes its life on the trustworthiness and promises of God. And real faith affects not just the mind. Real faith leaves no area of our life untouched.

Is it any wonder that people of real faith are few and far between; that when God discerns one he applauds and honours that person?

But such is God's love for us that he woos not just those who expect that he really will fulfil all his promises; God also draws to himself the doubters; those whose faith is no bigger than a mustard seed.

(Taken from Open to God, p 97)

# The Love of Jesus

### *He loved me and gave himself for me*
#### Galatians 2:20

A young angel was being shown round the splendours and glories of the universe by a more experienced angel. The little angel was shown whirling galaxies and blazing suns, infinite distances in interstellar space and, finally, the galaxy of which our own planetary system is a part. As the two of them drew near to the star which we call our sun and to its circling planets, the senior angel pointed to planet Earth. To the little angel whose mind was still full of the grandeur and glory he'd just seen, this planet looked as dull and dirty as a tennis ball.

'What's special about that one?' he asked.

'That,' replied his senior solemnly, 'is the Visited Planet. That ball, which to you looks so insignificant, has been visited by the Prince of Glory.'

'Do you mean to say,' queried the younger one, 'that our great and glorious Prince, with all these wonders and splendours of his creation, and millions more that I'm sure I haven't seen yet, went down in person to this fifth-rate little ball? Why should he do a thing like that?'

'He did it because he loves the people there,' replied the senior angel. 'He went down to visit them so that he could lift them up to become like him.'

(Taken from Reflections for Lent, p 60)

# Jesus and His Church

*Always be prepared to give an account to anyone about the hope that is in you*
1 Peter 3:15

Christian ministry is effective when it takes place where we work. It is at work that we are asked to be Christ's representatives, his ambassadors. It is there we must live out his likeness.

Jim Wallis underlines the importance of this dimension of Christian service.

When I was a university student, I was unsuccessfully evangelised by almost every Christian group on campus. My basic response to their preaching was, 'How can I believe when I look at the way the church lives?' They answered, 'Don't look at the church – look at Jesus.'

I now believe that statement is one of the saddest in the history of the church. It puts Jesus on a pedestal apart from the people who name his name. Belief in him becomes an abstraction removed from any demonstration of its meaning to the world. Such thinking is a denial of what is most basic to the gospel: incarnation. People should be able to look at the way we live and begin to understand what the gospel is about. Our life must tell them who Jesus is and what he cares about.[45]

(Taken from Living Free, p 176)

# Patience

## *The fruit of the Spirit is . . . patience*
### Galatians 5:22

The patience mentioned here is the endurance we need in our relationships with people – the quality of love which was modelled to us most perfectly by Jesus.

When he needed them most, his friends failed him. One betrayed him with a kiss. Another denied that he had ever known him. The rest ran in the opposite direction when Jesus was seized by his captors. And the crowd who cried 'Hosanna' on Palm Sunday became the mob who clamoured 'Crucify Him' on Good Friday.

Injured, insulted, hurt, rejected, Jesus could have taken revenge. He chose not to. Instead he continued to offer generous, undeserved, forgiving love to those who were bruising him. That is patience. And Jesus assures us over and over again that his love for us is so patient, it will never disappear.

# Perfect Timing

*For all who are led by the Spirit of God are*
*children of God*
**Romans 8:14**

One Sunday night, I prayed for a young man whose spirits had sunk very low. Early on Monday morning, I woke with this young man's need weighing heavy on my heart. As I prayed for him, I decided to telephone before he left for work to assure him of my continued prayer. 'I'll ring at eight,' I decided, and started to work on a book I was writing. At 7.45 a.m. a voice broke in on my concentration: 'Ring now!' I looked at my watch and decided there was no hurry. But the voice repeated: 'Ring now.' I rang. The young man thanked me for ringing when I told him the purpose of the call. 'Perfect timing too!' he teased. 'Why? When do you leave for work?' I asked. 'Oh! In two minutes' time,' he said. When I heard this, I offered silent praise to the God who, I believe, prompted me to act in time.

(Taken from Listening to God, p 108)

# Christ in Us

*The grace of the Lord Jesus Christ and the
love of God and the fellowship of the Holy
Spirit be with you all*
2 Corinthians 13:14

Within each broken Christian, God the Father, God the Son and God the Holy Spirit have taken up residence. To use the language of St Paul the mystery, the hope of glory, is that Christ is *in us*. We are indwelt by the three members of the Trinity. But we are also assured that we are *in* Christ. In God. So every damaged personality (and that is each of us) is enfolded in the Trinity and indwelt by the Trinity. Every Christian is also a part of a whole bevy of fellow believers: the body of Christ. My dream is that each member of the body of Christ should discover their gift and use it to the full.

(Taken from Listening to Others, pp 230, 231)

# Keep the Pipes Clear

*Tend the flock of God that is in your charge
. . . being examples to the flock*
**1 Peter 5:2, 3**

S.D. Gordon tells the story of a sleepy village in Colorado which was dependent on seasonal rainfall for its water-supply. One day, some enterprising young men ran pipes from the village to the clear lake in the hills. The village then boasted a plentiful and pure supply of water.

One morning, however, the housewives turned on their taps to find, not gushing water, but spluttering drops – and then nothing. The men climbed the hill. The lake was as full as ever. There were no breaks in the pipe. They were mystified.

People began to move away from the now prosperous village. It began to resume its sleepy-hollow existence.

One day, an official of the town found a note on his door-step. It was badly written but it bore an important message. 'If you'll jes pull the plug out of the pipe about eight inches from the top you'll get all the water you want.'

They found the plug. It was not very big, but big enough to fill the pipe and cut off the water-supply. When the plug was pulled out, the water ran freely.

Just as the water in a large reservoir can be held back by a small obstruction in a pipe, so the Holy Spirit's energy can be clogged by sin. Those of us who serve others must keep the connecting pipes clear.[46]

(Taken from Living Free, pp 183, 184)

# One with You

*Those who come to me shall not hunger and those who believe in me shall never thirst*
John 6:35

*Jesus, may all that is you flow into me.*
*May your body and blood be my food and drink*
*May your passion and death be my strength and life*
*Jesus, with you by my side enough has been given.*
*May the shelter I seek be the shadow of your cross*
*Let me not run from the love which you offer,*
*But hold me safe from the forces of evil.*
*On each of my dyings shed your light and love*
*Keep calling to me until that day comes*
*When, with your saints, I may praise you forever.*

(Taken from Open to God, p 105)

# Change me, Lord

### *I have engraved you on the palms of my hands*
Isaiah 49:16

A relationship between friends grows when they relax together. We need to learn to relax with Jesus; not to rush in and out of his presence with a nod and a mere 'Good Morning, God', but to be still before him. As the Psalmist put it, 'Be still, and know that I am God'. (Psalm 46:10) Sit or kneel. Allow your body to express openness. Unclench your hands. Unwind in the presence of God. Remind yourself that he wants you more than you want him and reflect on the amazing fact that Jesus is present with you. Your name is graven on the palms of his hands. You are never out of his mind. His eye of love is always on you. He cares for you. He is the vine, you are a branch. You dwell in him and he dwells in you. His life is in you like sap rising to feed and renew the branch. He loves you better than you love yourself.

He accepts you as you are. He is using your prayer to change you into his own likeness.

(Taken from Living Free, pp 58, 59)

# Clothed in Christ

## *Get up and pray*
### Luke 22:46

George Sinker writes: It is Jesus who comes and wakes you, by whatever means He uses, and invites you to spend the first moments of the day with Him. Why? From His point of view, because He loves you and desires your company. From your point of view, because He knows it will be another tiring day and He wants to pour into you the strength and courage, the patience and peace to face each test the day will bring.[47]

George Sinker also suggests that when we wash we turn our mind to Jesus and the man at the Pool of Siloam (John 9:7). 'Go, wash', Jesus said to this man. And he adds:

Jesus bids us wash. But washing to him always signified the sacrament of a clean heart. Washing in the Bible is a double action, bodily and spiritual. If we were to form that habit of thought, we would come consciously into His presence every time we washed, receiving the cleansing of His forgiveness and reunion with Him.[48]

And we would use the prayer of the Psalmist: 'Wash me and I shall be whiter than snow' (Ps. 51:7).

Dressing is another activity which can so easily be combined with prayer.

To be clothed with Christ means to be clothed with 'His beauty, His strength, His love, His understanding, His patience, His peace, His joy. There is no end to the glory of this garment which He offers you to put on first thing every day.'[49]

(Taken from Open to God, pp 28, 29)

# Launching into Prayer

*Each day with one heart they regularly went
to the temple*
Acts 2:46

God is always more anxious to speak than we are to listen. Christians who are serious in their desire to listen to God embark on a journey. It is full of surprises which make of it an adventure. But it is an ascent, a climb, hard work. Most of us can reserve a chair in a corner as a prayer place if we are disciplined. Most of us can carve out five minutes each day for God if we are disciplined. Most of us can learn to weave prayer into our chores if we are disciplined. Many of us *can* fast and even manage a Quiet Day if we are disciplined. And without discipline we shall never learn to listen.

(Taken from Listening to God, p 226)

# Prayer Place

*When you pray, go to your private room and,*
*when you have shut your door, pray to your*
*Father who is in that secret place*
Matthew 6:6

People who are serious about learning to pray hold two things
in tension: the fact that it is possible to pray at any time and
in any place and the fact that there is great value in heeding
Jesus' advice and ear-marking a certain place for regular prayer. That
place might be a corner of the bedroom, a certain chair in the study,
a quiet room in the house, a church or a particular walk or spot in
the garden. We know that when we retreat to that place it is for one
purpose only: the serious business of prayer.

Prayer, essentially, is developing a relationship with God. Friends
find time and places to meet. If we are serious about forging a
friendship with God, we will do what he says: prepare a meeting
place where the friendship can grow and deepen. The more we meet
God in the silence of this specific place of prayer, the more we shall
learn to recognize his presence elsewhere: in nature, while walking
or driving, ironing, gardening or talking to friends and neighbours.

(Taken from Reflections for Lent, p 32)

# Five Minutes for God

## *Pray at all times in the Spirit*
### Ephesians 6:18

Guarantee God a certain time each day: five minutes in the morning, perhaps, and five minutes in the evening. Don't set your sights too high. You can always give God *more* time than you promised initially but if you earmark half an hour and manage only five minutes your listening will be drowned by guilt feelings.

The most unselfish prayer is the prayer you pray when you least feel like it. Then you pray out of love for God, not because it appears to benefit you.

The crucial time is when we are not formally praying at all. True prayer must be integrated into our life. There is something phoney about the person who 'lives' in church but has a very bitter tongue.

(Taken from Listening to God, p 198, 199)

# Prayer Under Difficulties

## *Peter went up on the housetop to pray*
### Acts 10:9

The Christians I met in Singapore were superb examples of the need to find a particular place to pray. Many live in overcrowded high-rise apartments. Most share a bedroom with at least one other member of the family, often a Buddhist. Yet such is their zeal for the Lord and for prayer that these Christians find a place: a spot under a tree in one of Singapore's public parks; the office, before work begins; a patch of grass on the way to the bus stop. We, too, must use our imagination and find a place. The place may be a corner of the bedroom, a chair in the study, a quiet room in the house. We know when we retreat to that place that it is for one purpose only: the serious business of prayer. That is not to say that we cannot pray anywhere and everywhere. Of course we can. God is not limited by our prayer-places. But it does mean that our rhythm of prayer is aided by establishing a particular prayer spot to which we retreat regularly. Christians who are married or who share a house with others need this quite as much as others. As one young wife put it to me recently, 'When I'm sitting in that chair my husband knows why I'm there. He protects my privacy with God and doesn't disturb me.'

(Taken from Living Free, pp 72, 73)

# Pools of Silence

*I shall be with you all days*
Matthew 28:20

W hen taking paper out of my typewriter or making myself a cup of coffee or waiting at traffic lights, I turn my mind God-wards quite deliberately. Often God communicates his presence to me in some felt way.

Catherine de Hueck Doherty speaks of the 'little pools of silence' which punctuate one's day and goes on to demonstrate how prayer might feature in these so that the desert experiences of our life might be irrigated constantly. Whilst washing up, ironing, hoovering, dusting, gardening, walking to the post, driving to the shops, or travelling by public transport, try to listen to God as intently as in your place of prayer. It works. I was once caught in a sudden, heavy snowstorm which caused traffic chaos. It took me four hours to drive along a route which normally takes half an hour: That day I learned the truth of Catherine of Siena's claim: 'Every time and every place is a time and place for prayer. As I work, a Loved Presence over my shoulder, as I drive a Loved Passenger beside me. In my reading, cooking, studying, whilst teaching, nursing, accounting: in the maelstrom of the supermarket or waiting for the bus or train – ever the loving sense of a Presence – always that nostalgia for my Creator.'[50]

(Taken from Listening to God, pp 171, 173)

# Constant Prayer

*I praise you, Father, Lord of heaven and
earth, because you have hidden these things
from the wise and learned, and revealed them
to little children*
Matthew 11:25

O ne day, in the middle of talking to his disciples, Jesus
suddenly broke off the conversation and started to talk
aloud to his Father, as we read above.

In this way, even surrounded by people in need, Jesus kept in
close touch with his Father. It is not difficult for us to do the
same; to find God coming to us in the middle of our activities
as we turn our hearts and minds towards him.

We find many such prayers recorded in the Bible. These
can become a part of our vocabulary of prayer:

'Lord, save us. We're going to drown!'
(Jesus' disciples in a storm on the Sea of Galilee)

'Praise the Lord, O my soul and all that is within me
praise his holy name.'
Psalm 103:1

(Taken from Approaching Christmas, p 44)

# Arrow Prayers

### *Your will, not mine, be done*
#### *(Jesus, in the Garden of Gethsemane)*
Matthew 26:39

### *Away from me, Satan*
Matthew 4:10

W hen we call out these short prayers to our Father in heaven, we are so lifted above earthly things that we become conscious of being upheld by God. And when we school ourselves to pray like this on and off during the day, our special times of quiet take on a new significance. Because the mind and the heart have not been allowed to wander too far from God, when we are able to come before him in prolonged stillness, we relax in him with ease, tune into his presence with gratitude and are guided by him afresh as we learn to seek his will and his way in the practicalities of life.

> Breathe through the heats of our desire
> Thy coolness and thy balm;
> Let sense be dumb, let flesh retire;
> Speak through the earthquake, wind, and fire,
> O still small voice of calm!
> (John Greenleaf Whittier)

> *Oh, come to us, abide with us,*
> *Our Lord Emmanuel.*

(Taken from Approaching Christmas, p 45)

# Friendship with Jesus

### *I have loved you*
### John 13:34

Is it possible to develop a relationship with someone whose essential nature is truth? Indeed it is. One of the emancipating things about God's Word is that it assures us that God desires to forge a friendship with us no matter how sinful, struggling or worthless we may feel ourselves to be. When friends spend time together, they grow to be alike. It is as we spend time with the truth that we learn to shed the imaginations and desires and deeds of sin's underworld. Instead we delight in the truth and all that he stands for. This is why friendship with Jesus is a life-changing encounter, a transforming friendship.

We need never think of the truth as a formidable foe, the prefect who watches and waits for us to put a foot wrong. On the contrary, Jesus, who is the truth, is also love. 'God is love.'

Jesus underlined the fact of his love time and time again, especially in the hours leading up to his death. He proclaimed the message in simple terms: 'I loved you' (John 15:9); 'I am coming back to you' (John 14:28).

We must never lose sight of the fact that Christian commitment is two-way. I commit myself to Jesus because he has already committed himself to me. His commitment is total.

(Taken from Living Free, pp 55, 56)

# Prayer Plan

*At the hour of incense all the people were*
*outside, praying*
Luke 1:10

One way of checking whether our life is balanced is to draw up a proposed prayer plan and to plot on it a daily, a weekly, a monthly and an annual prayer pattern. Here we record our aims: when we plan to sit at Jesus' feet alone and when we plan to go there with others; when we propose to 'be' and when to 'do'; when to seek solitude and when and how to serve.

Certain questions help us to establish such a prayer pattern. 'How much time for personal stillness can I earmark day-by-day? Is it possible to carve out an extra hour for prayer and meditation at the weekends, or one evening a week? Would a monthly Quiet Morning, Quiet Evening or Quiet Day be possible? Might an annual forty-eight-hour retreat, or six- or eight-day retreat, be possible? Where do services of Holy Communion fit? And how will prayer spill over into the rest of my life so that others are enriched by it?'

(Taken from the Smile of Love, p 184)

# Help Me to Help You

*Present your bodies as a living sacrifice . . .*
*which is your spiritual worship*
**Romans 12:1**

S triking the right balance between action and contemplation
rarely comes easily, surrounded as we are by the kind of
need George Appleton highlights in one of his memorable
prayers:

> O Lord, so many sick, so many starving,
> so many deprived, so many sad,
> so many bitter, so many fearful.
> When I look at them
> my heart fails.
> When I look at You
> I hope again.
> Help me to help You
> to reduce the world's pain
> O God of infinite compassion
> O ceaseless energy of love.[51]

(Taken from The Smile of Love, p 184)

# Requests

## *Teach me your way O Lord*
### Psalm 27:11

I like to keep a resumé of the way God answers my prayers. Sometimes his answers have been so prompt and practical that I have been overwhelmed by his love. At other times I have to search my heart to discover what he is wanting to teach me. Sometimes I see that my request was inappropriate. Often he reminds me that some lessons can only be learnt in the school of waiting. And frequently he has to remind me that my ways are not his ways: and that his ways are mysterious and so much purer than my own.

(Taken from my Prayer Journal)

# Prayer Journal

*Blessed be God the Father of Our Lord Jesus Christ who has blessed us with all the spiritual blessings of Christ in heaven*
**Ephesians 1:3**

As I look back on some of my 'letters to God' I realise that it is all too easy to write one letter of complaint after another and to omit to thank God for his over-flowing generosity. It is also possible to become so absorbed in pouring out personal pain that the pressing problems overwhelming others and our world are over-looked and omitted from our prayer.

I now have a Prayer Journal with sections for Thanksgiving. Recollection, Requests and Reflections. It has restored a healthy objectivity and transformed my Prayer Life.

(Taken from my Prayer Journal)

# The Food of Love

## *Praise him with lyre and harp*
### Psalm 150:3

One of the ways God speaks is through music. In church, if I am battered emotionally for any reason, music is the ointment the Holy Spirit applies to the inner wounds. If I come to my place of prayer fraught by the pressures of the day, music woos me into the stillness where God's presence is most powerfully felt. Through meditative music, God seems to speak: of his longing to invade my spirit with the Spirit, of his consoling love, of his agony on the cross, of his gift of forgiveness. Some music causes a stirring in my heart and sets a fountain of praise playing inside me. It is as though the many layers of my personality respond to God in different ways. Music filters through to touch and communicate with the secret, hidden parts which rarely respond to words.

Music soothes weary brains and bodies. It melts hard hearts. And it reaches depths in a person into which words cannot trickle.

(Taken from Listening to God, pp 177, 178 and Open to God, p 33)

# Spiritual Welfare

### *Rest in the Lord*
Psalm 7.7

Quiet Days are occasions for resting in God. Although Evelyn Underhill wrote at the turn of the century before the days of motorways and ghetto blasters, no one has put the situation more persuasively:

Our so-called civilisation gets more and more complicated, more and more noisy. It is like one of those mills where the noise of the looms makes it impossible for the workers to hear each other speak. And if we go on at it long enough without a break we begin to think the looms are all that matter, and we are merely there to keep them going and must not bother about anything else. In other words, I am sure there is a real danger that Christian spirituality in its deepest and loveliest reaches will be killed out by the pressure and demands of the social machines and even of the ecclesiastical machine. People will get ever more utilitarian and this-worldly and will wholly forget their true relation to God . . . Even religion tends to become more and more pragmatic, utilitarian; more and more active, and less and less inward. To withdraw the worker from the clatter and pressure is to increase the quantity and quality of the work. So I sometimes think retreats should be regarded as a bit of spiritual welfare work; quite essential to the organisation of the Church, and specially to the efficiency of its ministers.[52]

(Taken from Open to God, p 71)

# Quiet Days

*I will give water from the well of life free to anybody who is thirsty*
**Revelation 21:6**

The Anglican convent near my home is a hiding place where I delight to spend a day in quietness. A large converted manor house, it stands in spacious grounds and overlooks acres of farmland. When I go there for a day, I accept this solitude as a gift of God's grace. To me the time and place are sacred.

What is the purpose of a Quiet Day? One of the desert fathers expressed it simply but powerfully. Into a jar he poured water and some sand. As he shook the jar, the water became murky, but as he allowed the jar to rest the sand settled to the bottom and the water became clear again. Using this visual aid, he taught his disciples that the pace people live their lives normally clouds their spiritual perspective. Those who dare to settle themselves into God's stillness find that the water of perception becomes clear again.

I value these sacred spaces more and more and know that my life and ministry are impoverished when I permit them to be elbowed out of my diary. The busier I am, the more I attempt to find God in everything, the more I need to stand in that still point with God where my looking becomes a beholding, my listening an attentive hearing, my touching a deep awareness, and my tasting a silent savouring.

(Taken from Listening to God, pp 184, 185)

# Taking your Spiritual Temperature

*He has made known to us . . . the mystery of his will*
**Ephesians 1:9**

hen I make a three or four day retreat, I bring to it four main aims:

* to realise more clearly the presence of God in the inner sanctuary of my being
* to assess the response I have been making to God's loving overtures since my last retreat
* to discern what God's will is for me in the here and now
* to readjust my life in the light that God gives.

In my prayer journal, I usually spell out my hopes and fears to God almost as soon as I arrive. Day by day I write to him and record his response. I often scribble quotations from my spiritual reading in this fat note-book. The fruit of my meditations is also captured there. At the end of the retreat, I keep a page called 'Retreat Resolves'. On this page, I write down God's re-commissioning for the coming months.

Several questions require examination and an honest answer during these times apart:

* Does anything in my life stand between God and me?
* Is anything preventing me from giving myself freely to fulfil God's plan for my life?
* What have I been doing for God?
* What am I doing for him at present?
* What ought I to be doing?

(Taken from Listening to God, pp 189, 190)

# Mundane not Mystical

*Look at the birds in the sky They do not
sow or reap or gather into barns: yet your
heavenly father feeds them*
Matthew 6:26

hen we are on retreat, much of our thinking and discovering will be mundane rather than mystical. Richard
Foster warns us to expect this:

Often meditation will yield insights that are deeply practical,
almost mundane. There will come instruction on how to relate to
your wife or husband, on how to deal with this sensitive problem
or that business situation. More than once I have received guidance
on what attitude to have when lecturing in a college classroom. It is
wonderful when a particular meditation leads to ecstasy, but it is far
more common to be given guidance in dealing with ordinary human
problems.[53]

(Taken from Open to God, p 81)

# Infernal Din

*There was silence in heaven for about half
an hour*
**Revelation 8:1**

To listen to God we need silence: internal silence and external silence. But our world is polluted by noise which, like a persistent drum-roll, drowns God's voice, or at least distorts it.

Screwtape, the senior devil in C.S. Lewis' book, *The Screwtape Letters*, divulges one of the reasons for this perpetual cacophony:

Music and silence — how I detest them both! . . . no square inch of infernal space and no moment of infernal time has been surrendered to either of those abominable forces, but all has been occupied by Noise — Noise, the grand dynamism, the audible expression of all that is exultant, ruthless and virile . . . We will make the whole universe a noise in the end. We have already made great strides in this direction as regards the Earth. The melodies and silences of Heaven will be shouted down in the end.[54]

There are times when the external noises in my own home banish the still, small voice of God. Ordinary, domestic noises — the sound of the radio, the shriek of the telephone, the songs my husband sings in the mornings — can prevent me from putting up the shutters of the senses to drop deep into the silence of God.

(Taken from Listening to God, pp 183, 184)

# Scriptural Warranty

### *These Scriptures testify to me*
### John 5:39

Jesus assumed his followers would possess a thorough working knowledge of the scriptures. When lack of biblical insight blinded their eyes, Jesus rebuked them. On the road to Emmaus, he found fault with his ignorant companions: 'How foolish you are, and how slow of heart to believe all that the prophets have spoken! Did not the Christ have to suffer these things and then enter his glory? And beginning with Moses and all the prophets, he explained to them what was said in all the Scriptures concerning himself' (Luke 24:25–27).

In the view of Jesus, it seems, the written Word contained in scripture is the Word of God. Jesus expresses this dramatically when, in the desert, he confronts Satan face to face. With authority and poise, he withstands the Enemy with one economical phrase: 'It is written . . .' (Luke 4:4,8).

For Jesus, as Jim Packer reminds us, 'It is written' was the end of the argument. 'There could be no appeal against the verdict of scripture for that would be to appeal against the judgement of God himself.'[55] For Jesus, the Old Testament taught and expressed God's mind and will.

(Taken from Listening to God, p 148)

# Letter From Home

*Everyday they studied the Scriptures to
discover whether it was true*
Acts 17:11

I f we are truly to open ourselves to God we must discover how
to open ourselves to his Word, the Bible. That is not because
as Christians we are bibliolators, people who worship a book,
but because we worship the God who speaks and the Bible contains
the truths which he has revealed for all time. In the words of
St Augustine, the Bible is our 'letter from home'. Or, to use Martin
Luther's parables: the Bible is the cradle that bears the Christ to us;
this book is like the swaddling clothes in which the infant Jesus was
laid: 'Poor and mean are the swaddling clothes, but precious is the
Treasure, Christ, that lives therein.'[56]

(Taken from Open to God, p 49)

# The True Meaning

### *In me you may have peace*
### John 16:33

I f we expect the Bible to speak to us, we must be prepared for hard work. We must ask questions, 'What does this passage or book really mean? Why did the writer express it in that way? Why did he choose that particular word? What was he intending to convey? What would it have communicated to the original readers? What does it imply for today's Christian? What is God saying to me?'

In coming to terms with some of these questions, we need to reach for commentaries, concordances, and Bible dictionaries. This kind of Bible exploration is illuminating and challenging. It is also time-consuming. Try to ear-mark at least an hour a week for this essential spade-work. Set yourself goals. For example, if you are to live biblically, you must know what the Bible teaches about key areas of life: marriage, sexuality, money, ambition, giving, to mention a few.

Take a recurring theme, like 'Peace' for example. Discover where that word is used, what it means, so that Jesus' words, 'In me you may have peace' (John 16:33) cease to be a vague promise you cling to when the going is tough but instead become consoling and strengthening words which you understand and apply.

(Taken from Living Free, pp 50, 51)

# What is Real Love

*Dear friends! Let us love one another, for love comes from God. Whoever loves is a child of God and knows God. Whoever does not love does not know God, because God is love*
1 John 4 7–8

The word 'love' has been so trivialised by the media that we need to ask ourselves certain questions before we can begin to claim that we understand the biblical use of the word. We can do this by looking up the word 'love' in a concordance and asking ourselves a series of pertinent questions: What does the Bible mean by love? What is entailed in the practice of love? Why does Jesus exhort us to love one another as he loves us? What is the value of this kind of love? How might I begin to love like that? What aids are there to help me to become more loving? Who are the people in the Bible, in history and in contemporary society who will model this dimension of love to me?[57]

# Three In One

*Before the world was created, the Word
already existed, he was with God and he was
the same as God . . . Through him God made
all things; not one thing in all creation was
made without him*
John 1:1, 3

The Bible gives us occasional glimpses of the relationship which existed between the Father, the Son and the Holy Spirit before the foundation of the world. John 17:5 is one example of this. Here we eavesdrop on a conversation between Jesus and his Father. 'And now, Father, glorify me in your presence with the glory I had with you before the world began.' John I is another example.

Before the beginning of creation relationship existed, a relationship between three co-equal persons which was characterized by co-operation, communication and love. 'Then God said, "Let us make man in our image, in our likeness"' (Genesis 1:26). It follows, therefore, that we are born capable of and needing relationship.

(Taken from Living Free, p 99, 100)

# Bible Priggery

*Be doers of the word and not hearers only*
James 1:22

There are perils attached to Bible reading. The chief peril is spiritual pride; or as C.S. Lewis puts it, 'priggery'. The spiritual prig pleads, 'Give us more teaching.' But the abundance of Bible knowledge, instead of providing a firm rule for life, inflates with the know-all pride the Lord so loathed in the Pharisees. The spiritual prig boasts about the number of Bible verses learnt by heart but pays no attention to a number of Bible commands. I am not knocking a genuine thirst for Bible teaching, nor pouring scorn on committing Scripture to memory. But it is wise to examine your motives. Let these disciplines be for one purpose only – that you may humbly obey the whole will of God.

(Taken from Living Free, p 49)

# A Two-Edged Sword

*The word of God is living and active. Sharper*
*than any two-edged sword*
Hebrews 4:12

The Word penetrates to the very depths of our being in an almost uncanny way. And it generates new life in us.

J.B. Phillips discovered the truth of this claim when he set himself the task of translating the New Testament into modern English:

I did my best to keep an emotional detachment. Yet I found that, again and again, the material under my hands was strangely alive. It spoke to my condition in a most uncanny way. I use the word uncanny for want of a better word. But it was a very strange experience to sense the living quality of these rather strangely assorted books.[58]

The longer he pored over the New Testament, the more he was gripped by the realisation that these living words were inspired. He confesses that no other work made a similar impact on him. No other work he encountered seemed similarly in-breathed by God.

(Taken from the introduction to Praying with the New Testament)

# Who is God?

## *Wonderful Counsellor, mighty God, Eternal Father, Prince of Peace*
### Isaiah 9:5

Either carve out an hour or more to do this exercise in one sitting or spread it over several days.

* Start with a prayer such as: 'Lord, I believe; help my unbelief'.
* Read St Mark's Gospel, recording what Jesus shows us about the nature of the human person and the love of God. Recall that Jesus came to show us the Father.
* In the light of your reading, list some of the Father's characteristics, asking the Holy Spirit to bring these to the surface of your mind.
* Write a prayer, asking yourself, 'How do I want to address God?' 'What do I want to say to him in the light of what I have learned?'
* Allow God to respond so that your prayer becomes a two-way conversation. Remember that he can speak in a variety of ways: through verses of Scripture; with a still, small voice; through pictures, lines of hymns or dreams.

(Taken from The Smile of Love, p 162)

# Surrender

*In every place people should pray reverently*
*lifting their hands*
2 Timothy 2:8

You may like to experiment with this suggestion from Richard Foster.

'Place your hands palms down as a symbolic indication of your desire to turn over any concerns you may have to God. Inwardly you may pray "Lord, I give to You my anger toward John. I release my fear of my dentist appointment this morning. I surrender my anxiety over not having enough money to pay the bills this month. I release my frustration over trying to find a baby-sitter for tonight." Whatever it is that weighs on your mind or is a concern to you, just say, "palms down". Release it. You may even feel a certain sense of release in your hands. After several moments of surrender, turn your palms up as a symbol of your desire to receive from the Lord. Perhaps you will pray silently: "Lord, I would like to receive Your divine Love for John, Your peace about the dentist appointment, Your patience, Your joy." Whatever you need, you say, "palms up". Having centred down, spend the remaining moments in complete silence. Do not ask for anything. Allow the Lord to commune with your spirit, to love you. If impressions or directions come, fine; if not, fine.'59

(Taken from Open to God, p 37)

# Remember

*Remember how the Lord God has led you
. . . to humble you and to test you in order to
know what was in your heart*
**Deuteronomy 8:2**

T he command to 'remember' is a recurring one both in the Old
Testament and the New. 'Remember, I am coming soon!'
says Jesus from heaven (Rev. 22:7,12).

When we obey this command to remember, we have at our disposal
a great potential for openness to God. We all have memories. And
our memories work over-time. We play on the screen of our mind
the quarrel which upset us, the unkind words that were said about us
or the praise people regaled us with. In a similar way, we can harness
our memories to specific examples of God's expressed love for us.
The Psalmist seems to have done this regularly. He writes: 'I will
remember the deeds of the Lord; yes, I will remember your miracles
of long ago' (Ps. 77:11). And as we do the same, we discover how
easy it becomes to imitate the Psalmist in another way – by coming
into God's presence with thanksgiving. Stored memories of God's
love and tenderness also stir up in us a response of love, strengthen
us for the present moment and give rise to fresh hope.

(Taken from Open to God, pp 52, 53)

# Fruit of the Spirit

*The Spirit brings love, joy, peace, patience, kindness, goodness, trustfulness, gentleness and self-control*
Galatians 5:22

The love Paul describes is Jesus' love, the unselfish affection and orientation which always promotes the well-being of others. The joy Paul describes is Jesus' joy, the ability to rejoice in spite of irksome circumstances, trying people or persistent pain. The peace Paul describes is Jesus' peace, the heart-knowledge which entrusts all things to the wisdom, sovereignty and omniscience of God. Patience (long-suffering), the ability to keep on enduring that which one does not enjoy, is Christ-like. Gentleness, the ability to place oneself in another's shoes and identify with their feelings so that needless pain is not inflicted; the ability to dispense with rudeness, harshness or abrasiveness, is Christ-like. Goodness, the freedom to reject all that is not of God, is Christ-like. Faithfulness is the loyalty, reliability, dependability and commitment which never disappoints and never lets another down; it is the quality which can assure another, 'When I say I'll be your friend, I'll always be your friend' and it was modelled to us by Jesus. Self-control – the ability to hear the clamour of one's own rebel emotions and inner needs coupled with the skill to know which to discipline and which to meet – was patterned to us only by Jesus in whom body, mind and soul were in perfect working order.

(Taken from Living Free, pp 83, 84)

# The Dark Tunnel

*Jesus offered up prayer and entreaty with loud cries and tears to the one who was able to save*
**Hebrews 5:7**

'If only there was someone who would sit with me in the pain – not necessarily to say anything but just to hold my hand and receive my jumbled thoughts and feelings.' By far the best way we can help a person suffering from depression is simply to make ourselves available to stay alongside in this darkness, prove our love by our faithfulness even when this self-sacrifice is thrown back in our face, spurned or doubted, and by listening over and over again to the same sad tale of woe, the same angry outbursts, the same lack of confidence, the same dreary outlook on life and the same lack of self worth.

This requires patience, stamina, the ability to interpret for depressed people the sights and sounds of this foreign land through which they find themselves stumbling and the willingness to sit with them in this darkness until the end of the tunnel is reached, remembering that this could take a very long time.

(Taken from Listening to Others, p 222)

# The Indwelling Christ

## *When I am weak then I am strong*
### 2 Corinthians 12:10

Depression needs skilled and sensitive handling if the person is to emerge from the tunnel to enjoy the wholeness which is theirs, by right, in Christ. And though, from the desperation of their need and the longing for someone to find a quick solution to their pain, they may scream for any kind of prayer or counsel on offer, the wise helper will discern when to pray and when simply to listen, to love and give practical support. The wise helper knows that God, in his infinite wisdom and love, does not always remove our pain instantly. Sometimes he gives us the resources to grow through it, learn from it and thereby enjoy his gift of maturity.

The mystery is that, within each broken Christian, God the Father, God the Son and God the Holy Spirit have taken up residence. To use the language of St Paul the mystery, the hope of glory, is that Christ is *in us*. Or to quote the language of Jesus, we are indwelt by the three members of the Trinity. But we are also assured that we are *in* Christ. In God. So every damaged personality (and that is each of us) is enfolded in the Trinity and indwelt by the Trinity.

(Taken from Listening to Others, pp 231, 226)

# Availability

*Save me O God for the waters have come up*
*to my neck*
Psalm 69:1

A depressed person needs someone who will not tire of listening to their main topic of conversation: themselves. Someone who will assure them that, even though they, the listener, may have nothing useful to say, they are prepared to stay in the darkness with the person suffering from depression until they emerge eventually from the tunnel's end. David Augsburger describes this patient listening well:

When hearing is done as an act of caring, it is a healing process. The exact nature of this process will remain forever a mystery, a gift of grace for which we become profoundly grateful as we see it occurring, before which we are rightfully humble as we know we have, in small measure, participated in it ... In caring-hearing, the hurt is opened, the festering bitterness of resentful illusions, the burning of angry demands, the numb frozenness of grief, the staleness of depression are allowed to drain. The light is allowed to pour in, sterilizing the infections and stimulating cells of hope and trust to begin new growth.[60]

(Taken from Listening to Others, pp 214, 215)

# Cottage or Palace

*Unless the Lord builds the house, those who build it labour in vain*
**Psalm 127:1**

There are no quick cures for depression. And maybe we should not even seek for them because if the lessons are learned thoroughly, depression could be the best thing that ever happened. C.S. Lewis puts the position superbly:

Imagine yourself as a living house. God comes in to rebuild that house. At first, perhaps, you can understand what He is doing. He is getting the drains right and stopping the leaks in the roof and so on. You knew that those jobs needed doing and so you are not surprised. But presently He starts knocking the house about in a way that hurts abominably and does not seem to make sense. What on earth is He up to? The explanation is that He is building quite a different house from the one you thought of – throwing out a new wing here, putting an extra floor there, running up towers, making courtyards. You thought you were going to be made into a decent little cottage: but He is building a palace.[61]

While the rebuilding is in progress, the living stones of the depressed person's life need scaffolding to keep them from disintegrating. And no one helper can hope to form a structure secure enough to bear this heavy burden on their own. Others must be involved. To admit this is not a sign of weakness or failure but practical common sense.

(Taken from Listening to Others, p 222, 228)

# God and Elijah

*'Lord' said Elijah 'I have had enough. Take my life. I am no better than my ancestors.' Then he lay down and went to sleep. But an angel touched him and said 'Get up and eat.' He looked round and there at his head was a scone baked on hot stones and a jar of water.*
1 Kings 19 4–6 (J.B.)

W hen a person starts to send out distress signals and is unusually listless, irritable, anxious or weepy, or complains of being 'down in the dumps' – it is wise to take prompt action. I take as my model the way God coped with Elijah when he collapsed in the desert exhausted and depressed.

The first thing is to listen sensitively and attentively. And just as God gave Elijah the freedom to pour out his feelings, try to receive the gift of the person's anguish and anger, tears and turmoil or the frozenness which prevents them from feeling or expressing even a fraction of the inner emotional pain. I remember so well the gratitude and relief that I felt when people sacrificed for me in a selfless way.

And we can take another cue from God. Just as he demonstrated his love and acceptance in practical ways, so it is necessary to try to put ourselves in the skin of the depressed person and provide appropriate practical help. I have not forgotten the relief I felt when, on numerous occasions, members of our congregation arrived on my doorstep with a ready-made meat pie or a chocolate souffle which was just what was needed to save me doing what I seemed to have no energy to do: cook for the family.

(Taken from Listening to Others, pp 219, 220)

# Absorbing the Anger

*Now, Lord, please take my life for I might as
well be dead as go on living!*
Jonah 4:3

My husband recently reminded me that when I was depressed nothing would dissuade me from the view that he had been guilty of neglecting me or had been particularly insensitive. I needed someone else to confront me, albeit gently, and to help me to see this false belief for what it was. Error of judgement. And I needed someone else's help to discover how to replace falsehood with truth. When I am listening to someone's wrath I try to hear the underlay of terror, to receive the trapped feelings, to accept the person with their rage, to focus more on the hurt than the wrath. It often happens that the molten lava has to be poured out before fears and frustrations are discerned. But when the time is ripe, it is sometimes possible to explore whether there are other ways of viewing the situation and dealing with it: ways of using anger constructively and not destructively.

# Using Suffering

*Be merciful to me, O Lord, for I am in*
*distress;*
*my eyes grow weak with sorrow,*
*my soul and my body with grief.*
*My life is consumed by anguish*
*and my years by groaning;*
*my strength fails because of my affliction,*
*and my bones grow weak*
Psalm 31:9, 10

M any great men of God have been entrusted with that
mysterious sickness of the soul, depression. In addition
to Elijah, there was the Psalmist. Whenever I feel really
low it is to the Psalms that I turn.

Many of the world's geniuses suffered similarly: Isaac Newton,
Beethoven, Darwin, Van Gogh, Tolstoy, Spurgeon and Martin
Luther. Their inner turmoil did not block their creativity. On the
contrary, their suffering seemed to contribute to their greatness.
While J.B. Phillips was depressed he translated the whole of the
New Testament into a powerful paraphrase. While William Cowper
was depressed he wrote some of his best hymns and poems. And
while C.H. Spurgeon was depressed he preached some of his finest
sermons.

This teaches me that I must not waste suffering. Instead I must
learn to use it.

(Taken from Listening to Others, p 206, 207, 208)

# Save Me Lord

### Come quickly to my help,
### Lord my Saviour!
Psalm 38:22

Anger is a reflex action, a surge of emotion prompted by certain circumstances. It is biochemical in nature. The reaction of *itself* is not sinful.

Whether the reaction *becomes* a sin or a sharp sword in the Master's hand is determined by what we choose to do with it. The problem is that when anger rises within us like milk coming to the boil, it spills over before we can reach out to switch off the gas. The choice we make about what to do with our anger must be made in split-second timing. That is why anger often turns to sin. That is why many Christians fail far more through their reactions than through their carefully planned actions.

When we feel anger coming to the boil inside us, we must recognize that this is normal, natural, a part of being human. But we must also acknowledge to ourselves two more truths: that this anger need not spill over as sin; that if we are seeking to live biblically and to love others, it *must* not result in sin. If this is the case, what do we do with such powerful negative emotions?

The only safe place for hostile feelings – anger, guilt, hatred, the desire for revenge, the longing to retaliate, bitterness – is the cross of Christ. And the only place where healing flows into the hurts that underlie much of this hostility is the lap of God. This is the most appropriate tip for our emotional rubbish.

(Taken from Creative Conflict, pp 112, 113)

# Ventilating Anger

*The one who is slow to anger is better than*
*the mighty and he that ruleth his spirit better*
*than he that taketh a city*
Proverbs 16:32

'Pound a pillow, throw crockery against the wall, smash up some old furniture, get the anger out.' For some people this vicarious ventilation of anger seems to help. But the Christian must not take the next seemingly logical step: to give the offending person a 'piece of your mind', to tear strips off another while the angry feelings are still red-hot. Neither must the offending person's reputation be ruined through gossip and half-truths, responses to anger that occur all too often even in Christian circles. Far too many people have already been ground to powder by such inappropriate expressions of anger. We are to be angry, but not to sin (Eph 4:26).

When anger rages inside me like a caged animal, I try to go quickly to the cross and ventilate it there. Sometimes it is enough to express my anger verbally. On other occasions such is the strength of the violence, that it seems as though I hammer home the nails that pinned the Lord's body to the tree. On such occasions I am reminded that Jesus can take the full force of my wrath, that he understands, that he hung there for this purpose, to take away my sin. I know, too, that he will receive the mangled mess of my emotions, sift them, keep anything that is worth keeping – the shreds of love – and with the breath of compassion throw the rest away.

(Taken from Creative Conflict, p 113)

# To Comfort and to Challenge

*Remember this, my dear brothers: be quick
to listen but slow to speak and slow to rouse
your temper*
James 1:19

*Better an equable man than a hero,
a man master of himself than one who takes
a city*
Proverbs 16:32

Anger can plunge you into pain. The place for this pain is the lap of God. Tell him about the hurt. Ask him to heal it. Often it is helpful to talk to someone about the pain, to confess to hatred and anger so that you are not in the hole alone.

Look for someone who will both understand you and confront you: 'It must be very hard for you at the moment but have you thought of . . .'; someone who will face you with the need to forgive, someone who will hold before you a biblical standard; the need to resolve conflict, to settle disputes quickly, the need to refuse to let anger out indiscriminately, the need to refrain from the uncontrolled expression of anger that damages others.

Avoid the trap of looking for someone who will simply say what you want them to say.

(Taken from Creative Conflict, p 114)

# Jesus Cleanses the Temple

*They came into Jerusalem and Jesus went into the Temple and began to drive out those who were buying and selling there. He overturned the tables of the money-changers and the benches of the dove-sellers, and he would not allow people to carry their water-pots through the Temple.*
Mark 11:15–17

The Temple had been built as a house of prayer for all nations. But Gentiles were only allowed in one outer court which the Jews abused by using it as a thoroughfare and for trade. It was always thronging with people and it had become the scene of double-dealings which outraged Jesus. The money-changers whose booths dominated these outer precincts of the Temple fleeced pilgrims by placing a heavy surcharge on every transaction they made. And the dove-sellers were equally deceitful. They charged extortionate prices for their wares but rejected any doves bought elsewhere on the grounds that these were blemished and were therefore unfit offerings for God. With a ruthlessness that must have astonished all his onlookers, Jesus rid the Temple of these practices which could never co-exist with a holy God.

*Lord, your word reminds me that I, too, am a temple;*
*that your Spirit has taken up residence inside me.*

(Taken from Reflections for Lent, p 81)

# The Anger of Jesus

*My house shall be called a house of prayer for all nations. But you have turned it into a thieves kitchen*
**Mark 11:17**

J esus is our model for the effective use of anger. When he watched men defiling his Father's house, he was angry. He overturned the tables and evicted the money-lenders from the temple. He ventilated his anger, took action against those who wronged God, but he did not sin.

One way to make anger work for us is to ventilate it. When aggression is driven down inside it saps the energy needed to cope with crises. But when it is expressed, it earths feelings, releases tension and sheds light on the reason for these feelings. Repressed anger has physical consequences: high blood-pressure, hypertension, eczema, for example. There may be depression, insomnia or phobias of various kinds. 'Anger, like a baby, grows stronger when it is nursed.'[62] In its proper place it is a necessary and healthy part of human nature.

(Taken from Two Into One, pp 116, 117)

# Keep Me Safe, Lord

### *My refuge and my fortress*
Psalm 91:2

The enshrouding blackness
engulfs my being.
Alone. Afraid.
My mind a whirlpool
ever inwards
towards an eternity of intolerable pain.

I used to reach out a hand
into the black unknown in hope.
But my soul was torn from me,
and I hoped no more.

It was like a pit.
Unfathomable depth.
Tortuous grovelling
My tears the only sound
in the impenetrable darkness.

I had no hope,
but turning back along the path I came,
I see a gracious hand
and a loving smile.
I see a guiding light
and feel a protecting wing.

Nestling in your warmth
my cold heart has thawed.
The blackness of my soul
has blossomed into a million blooms.
My tears have turned to jewels,
and my bitterness to honey.

But I remember the pit.
Keep me, O Lord,
Safe in the refuge of your wings.[63]

# No Man Is An Island

### *It is not good for man to be alone*
Genesis 2:18

God did not intend us to 'go it alone'. God did not even create us equipped to operate solo, to live life in splendid isolation. Even in the perfection of Paradise, man could not cope with his existential loneliness. God created us with an ingrained need for others; for one other, for *an* other.

The disobedience problem had not yet polluted Paradise. God and Adam were still living in uninterrupted harmony. The fall had not yet fouled their fellowship. Even so, without human friendship, Adam suffered an intolerable loneliness.

It would appear, then, that God not only created mankind with a need to relate to others; he also created us with love-needs which he himself chose to meet not with his own presence and comfort, but through people; through a person. What Paul Simon describes in his pain-filled song *I am a Rock* is the antithesis of God's plan. 'I have no need of friendship, Friendship causes pain; Its laughter and its loving I disdain . . .'. John Donne's familiar 'No man is an island' is far more accurate. The truth is that friendship is one of the most precious gifts God entrusts to us. As Margaret Evening observes, 'Life without friendship is hardly life at all.'[64] Or as the writer of Ecclesiastes puts it, 'Two are better than one' (Ecclesiastes 4:9).

(Taken from Just Good Friends, p 14)

# Help Me, Jesus

### *Jesus fled back to the hills alone*
### John 6:15

Loneliness conveys the message that we need to be loved. We need the love of friends. We need the love of God.

If I feel abandoned, or rejected, or isolated, I am quickly persuaded that someone somewhere has cast me on one side, rejected me or neglected me. This may or may not be true of our human friends. But it certainly is *not* true of our heavenly Friend. The fact of the matter is that we are not *totally* abandoned, no matter what our feelings tell us. We are uniquely loved by God.

And we must always keep this in mind, however lonely we may feel. The solution to the loneliness problem is found only in friendship with Jesus. Look elsewhere and you run headlong into disappointment, if not despair.

(Taken from Just Good Friends, pp 143, 149, 150)

# The God of Today

*Surely the Lord is in this place and I was not aware of it*
Genesis 28:16

When God communicates with those he loves, it is he who takes the initiative, by preceding the person and providing them with an awareness of his presence or speaking in clear unmistakable ways. So the psalmist cried out in wonder, 'Thou, God, seest me.' Mary Magdalene heard that one, welcome, economical word at the tomb, 'Mary!' And the disciples on the road to Emmaus enjoyed the companionship of the stranger whose company and conversation caused their hearts to burn within them.

Several of Jesus's parables encourage us to expect God to take the initiative in this relationship of love. The father waits and watches for the return of the prodigal and gathers up his skirts so that he is free to run to greet the returning wanderer. The woman searches until she finds the coin she has lost. The good shepherd searches ceaselessly for the sheep who has wandered away.

As David Watson puts it: 'God did not finish speaking to us when the scriptures were completed . . . God is the living God, the God of today; and every day he wants us to enjoy a living relationship with him, involving a two-way conversation.'[65]

(Taken from Listening to God, pp 82, 83)

# Say It Straight

*Lord, do you not care that my sister has left
me to serve alone: tell her then to help me*
Luke 10:40

Good communication doesn't just happen, it has to be
learned. Good communication is the ability to convey
messages, emotions and attitudes to another person as
accurately and as lovingly as possible. It also includes the ability
to receive such messages from another person without filtering
those messages through the wire-mesh of our preconceived ideas.
It means checking out meanings rather than assuming that you have
understood correctly. 'Do you mean . . . ?' 'Are you saying . . . ?'
This dimension of communication is vital. When relationships
between two people break down you will often hear each one
say, 'I thought you felt . . .' 'I thought you said . . .' You can
avoid this kind of misunderstanding by clarifying 'Am I correct in
thinking . . . ?'

And we must spell out the situation as we see it. Say it straight.
'*I feel* angry because you forgot to tell me that the sermon was to
be fifteen minutes instead of half an hour.' '*I feel* hurt because you
failed to understand my anguish the other night.' 'I feel . . .' is a
much more loving and accurate prefix than 'You don't . . .', 'You
didn't . . .', 'You never . . .', 'You failed . . .'. Not: '*You didn't* tell
me that my sermon was to be fifteen minutes instead of half an
hour.' '*You failed* completely when it came to understanding me the
other night.'

(Taken from Creative Conflict, pp 36, 37)

# Lifeblood of Relationship

## *No one has ever spoken like this man*
### John 7:46

John Powell says of communication that it is 'the lifeblood and heartbeat of every relationship.' Indeed, it is 'the essential gift of love. All other gifts-jewellery, colognes, flowers, and neckties — are only tokens or symbols. The real gift of love is the gift of self.' He makes a further claim:

Communication is the most important of all the sources of happiness and health. Communication is the essential foundation of our happiness.[66]

When people begin to communicate effectively, a total change begins which ultimately affects all the areas of life. The senses seem to come alive. Color that was never noticed before is newly appreciated. Music that was not heard before becomes an accompaniment of life. Peace that was never before experienced begins to find its place in the human heart[67] . . . Communication [is] the beginning of all real change.[68]

# Papering Over the Cracks

*The Samaritan went up to him and*
*bandaged his wounds, pouring oil and wine*
*on them. He then lifted him onto his own*
*mount and took him to an inn and looked*
*after him*
Luke 10:33,34

Most of us work hard at papering over the cracks. We over-work to beguile the world and ourselves into believing that all is well. We flit from one superficial social engagement to another to give the impression that we are popular, though deep down we know that we are lonely. We clutter ourselves with spiritual paraphernalia and rush from this service to that rally, from this Bible study to that prayer meeting in an attempt to present to the watching world an image which, alas, does not stand the test of time. And the inner bleep of our loneliness refuses to be silenced. It brings us face to face with reality: not the personal success-story we project to the world, but the true situation: our inner poverty.

'Lord Jesus. You see where I am hurting inside. Thank you that my brokenness is not hidden from you but that you care about it. You care about me. Just as the Good Samaritan came to the wounded traveller and bound up his wounds, I ask that, by the gentle anointing of your Spirit, you would come to my inner hurts like that. Cleanse the sores. Anoint them. Bind them up. Then, would you pick me up so that I can begin living again, not in my own strength, but buoyed up with yours. I ask these things for my healing and for the glory of Jesus.'

(Taken from Just Good Friends, pp 143, 196)

# Loneliness or Solitude

*The Spirit drove him into the desert . . . and
the angels looked after him?*
Mark 1:12,13

How can 'aloneness' become the solitude, where we are
recreated? We need to carve out time when, like Mary
of Bethany, can 'just be' alone with Jesus. I am not talking
here about daily times of quiet with God, but recommending some
added extras: leisure time deliberately earmarked 'Alone' when we
seek to discover for ourselves that solitude can be creative; where we
seek the realization that the space inside us is in the dwelling place of
the most high God who converts our emptiness into his fullness.

If we take time to do this, we discover that in prayer we do not
simply cry, 'Help!', we know ourselves helped. We do not simply
ask: we will receive. We do not simply talk. We will know ourselves
heard, held and healed.

(Taken from Just Good Friends, pp 148, 149)

# The Friend who Betrays

*Jesus said to Judas 'Friend, why are you*
*here?'*
Matthew 26:50

W hen someone we love wounds us, we become like
frightened hedgehogs. We curl into a ball, withdraw
from others, push out the prickles to protect ourselves
and even stab those we love if they come too near too soon. This
ball-curling is not necessarily wrong as long as it is temporary.

Hedgehog prickles are God-made; designed for the hedgehog's
preservation. Similarly, the hurt and anger we experience when
hostility threatens the harmony of the home is a reflex action:
neither morally right nor morally wrong. Unless we recognize this,
we give Satan a foothold unnecessarily. He will whisper: 'What a
weak, pathetic Christian you are. Here you are, pretending to be so
Christ-like, yet you're hurt again. You hypocrite.'

Satan delights to condemn. Ignore him. It is not wrong to feel
hurt. The Bible records Jesus' expressed hurt when he stumbled on
his sleeping disciples in the Garden of Gethsemane; sleeping when
he had begged them for prayer support. This side of eternity we will
be angry and hurt. We must view these emotions, not as personal
failure, but as a choice to be made. What makes anger and hurt sinful
is not what we feel, but how we choose to express those feelings.

(Taken from Creative Conflict, p 86)

# Too Busy Caring for Others

## *If I just touch his clothes I shall be healed*
### Mark 5:28

I remember reading with a group the account of the healing of the woman who suffered from haemorrhaging for twelve years. We tried, at first, to visualise the scene: the pressing crowd, the poverty-stricken woman, and Jesus. We then tried to put ourselves into the scene to *become* the sick woman whose need to touch the hem of Jesus's garment was so urgent. As much as our imaginations allowed, each of us felt the hot, sweaty bodies of the crowd jostling Jesus and identified with the desperation that woman must have felt; in our own time and manner, each of us stretched out a hand and touched the bottom of Jesus's robe. And each of us saw Jesus turn, heard him ask that curious question, 'Who touched me?', basked in his acceptance and allowed ourselves to be drawn to him. But one member of the group, described rather tearfully how she had spent the entire meditation carrying a sick friend to Jesus. When she heard other members of the group relate how Jesus had touched and spoken to them, she felt envious. 'That's typical of my life at the moment,' she admitted. 'I'm so busy caring for others that I don't give Jesus a chance to care for me.'

(Taken from Listening to God, pp 199–200)

# Loving Ourselves

*Come to me, all of you who are tired from carrying heavy loads, and I will give you rest. Take my yoke . . . and learn from me, because I am gentle and humble in spirit; and you will find rest. For the yoke I will give you is easy, and the load I will put on you is light*
**Matthew 11:28–30 (GNB)**

To love the self means . . . to pay attention to the real situation: the battered baby within each one of us who does need our care and our patience. It means refusing to condemn or punish ourselves, to find ourselves contemptible or disgusting, but on the contrary gentling ourselves along through all the ups and downs of existence with real charity of heart, finding ourselves touching, funny, interesting, attractive, as we would a real child.[69]

Dependency, petulance and fear are often cries for help. They are soothed by tenderness, understanding and patience. Just as it is both folly and cruelty to smack a hurt child, so we need to avoid blaming or punishing the weeping child within our partner or ourselves. Just as you would cuddle a real child you must find ways of expressing love to the suffering child who lives within each adult. I am not suggesting that we 'spoil' the child by giving in to unrealistic demands, whining or manipulation but we need to learn to cherish one another.

To bottle up emotion and play the part of the tough, unyielding 'example to everyone' is storing up trouble for the future and probably stems from pride rather than real nobility. Jesus did not say, 'When things are hard, put a brave face on it, stick it out.'

Bringing our loads to Jesus often helps us to share them with someone else as well.

(Taken from *Two into One*, pp 115, 116)

# Come Apart and Rest

### *Let us go somewhere else!*
### Mark 1:38

I n Mark 1 we read of a certain Sabbath when Jesus had taught in the synagogue in Capernaum, delivered a man of an evil spirit, healed Peter's mother-in-law, and at sundown had ministered to crowds of needy people. Before sunrise he retreated to a solitary place to be with his Father, but on returning to Capernaum the disciples alerted him to a new set of demands: 'Everyone is looking for you!' Whereupon Jesus replied: 'Let us go somewhere else' (Mark 1:37,38). And although we are told that the 'somewhere else' was nearby villages where he would preach again, we also know that the walk to those villages would have given Jesus the space and exercise he needed to replenish his own resources.

I take great comfort from Jesus' example, from his command to the seventy-two after their exhausting mission, 'Come apart and rest'.

When I am trying to help people whose pain is clearly not going to evaporate overnight, I need to retreat to a quiet place to be alone with God. And I also need to spend time creating lovely things which bring quick returns. Without these, my life lacks balance and I become a dreary, depressed and depressing person.

(Taken from Listening to Others, pp 121, 122)

# Walking With Us

*Do you believe that I can heal you?*
Matthew 9:28

We all need someone who will recognize the pain of our personal vulnerability; someone who will, in turn, expose their vulnerability. We all need someone who will seek to understand our quota of defeats and tell us about theirs. We all need someone who will pierce the layer of superficiality, understand it for what it is: the pseudo-confidence which is a cover-up for insecurity; someone who will admit, 'I identify with your pain because I'm a wounded healer too.' We all need someone to stay alongside us while we discover what maturity is all about; someone who will permit us to stay alongside them while they make similar discoveries.

We long for someone with whom we can feel safe, to whom we can belong, to whom we can give ourselves to the fullest extent of our being and who will similarly give of themselves in return; someone who does not mind admitting that they love with the 'L' plates on, that they have not yet learned all there is to learn about this mystery called loving relationships.

(Taken from Just Good Friends, p 46)

# Welcome to my World

## *God so loved us*
### 1 John 4:11

We all have a basic need to be accepted just as we are.
To accept someone involves making a place for them within yourself, carving out time for them, meeting their unexpressed but deeply felt needs *at cost to yourself*. Acceptance is not condoning all they do or agreeing with all they say. It means receiving a person to yourself, offering the security which creates the free and fearless space in which he/she may develop.

Accepting love is unconditional love. Unconditional love, *agapē*, 'forgives a guilty spouse, affirms an unlovely spouse, bears with bad taste, insensitive neglect, stupid decisions and cruel aggressiveness'.[70] And as John Powell rightly says, unconditional love is the only kind of love which enables persons to change and grow.

Love in marriage receives the other unconditionally, it forgives unfailingly and finds ways of expressing approval. Love gives to the other a sense of worth. It rescues the other from despair and loneliness and heals the wounds of a life-time.

(Taken from Two into One, p 124, 125, 126)

# Becoming Real

*That you may know how extraordinarily great
is his power in us who believe*
Ephesians 1 18:19

'What is REAL?' asked the Rabbit one day when he and
his close friend the Skin Horse were lying side by side
near the nursery fender. 'Does it mean having things
that buzz inside you and a stick-out handle?'

'Real isn't how you are made,' said the Skin Horse. 'It's a thing
that happens to you. When a child loves you for a long, long time,
not just to play with, but REALLY loves you, then you become
Real.' ...

'Does it happen all at once, like being wound up ... or
bit by bit?'

'It doesn't happen all at once,' said the Skin Horse. 'You become.
It takes a long time ... Generally, by the time you are Real, most
of your hair has been loved off, and your eyes drop out and you get
loose in the joints and very shabby. But these things don't matter
at all, because once you are Real you can't be ugly, except to people
who don't understand.'[71]

The Skin Horse was very wise and extremely accurate. 'Real' is
not how we were first made. It implies growth and maturing. We
become 'real' through the patience of those who love us.

Most people admit that they want to be understood and cared for
by someone else. This gives them permission to be 'real' with a least
one other person in this brash, uncertain world.

(Taken from Just Good Friends, p 73, 74)

# Everyday Help

*Keep doing everything you learnt from me
and were told by me*
**Philippians 4:9**

Most people in need still turn, not to a professional, but to a friend for help. Gary Collins claims that 'if these peer counselors . . . can recognise their limitations, they can with very little training make a significant impact on the mental health of people around them. This is real people helping.'[72]

Michael Jacobs, suggests that: 'We have as a society effectively deskilled the ordinary man or woman in those tasks which are part of common life.' He goes on to point out that there are many occasions when the ordinary skills at the fingertips of most men and women are quite sufficient to help a person in need. 'What is frequently missing is the confidence to apply them.'[73]

# Love with Your Sleeves Rolled Up

*Put on love which binds everything together*
**Colossians 3:14**

L ove is caring enough for others to offer practical help when needed: hoovering, cooking, gardening – being prepared to love with your sleeves rolled up. It has been a sadness to me to discover that fewer people volunteer for this hidden ministry of caring than for the more 'glamorous', up-front tasks of counselling and prayer ministry. Love-in-action, can be the cinderella of today's ministries.

(Taken from Listening to Others, p 231)

# Bearing Burdens

*Day in day out, there is the pressures on me*
*of my anxiety for all the churches*
2 Corinthians 11:28

Sharing someone else's burden can be like carrying a heavy rucksack: a strain. I sometimes come to God over-burdened, exhausted and identifying with a complaint made by Michel Quoist:

Lord, why did you tell me to love all men, my
brothers? . . .
They are bending under heavy loads; loads of injustice,
of resentment and hate, of suffering and sin . . .
They drag the world behind them, with everything
rusted, twisted, or badly adjusted.
Lord, they hurt me! . . .
They are consuming me! . . .
What about my job?
    my family?
    my peace?
    my liberty?
    and me?[74]

(Taken from Listening to Others, p 124)

# Two in One Flesh

*The Lord God said 'It is not good for the man to be alone. I will make a helper suitable for him'*
Genesis 2:18

In the first book of the Bible we read how God conceived the concept of the marriage relationship.

Sin had not yet polluted the world, Adam's surroundings were absolutely perfect, yet he was weighed down by loneliness until God created a companion for him. God had made Adam in his own likeness; that is, ready for relationships. In the absence of relationship Adam's health was under threat, so God made him 'a helper' in the form of a wife.

The Hebrew word for 'helper', carries a variety of meanings. It means, among other things, a person who assists another to reach complete fulfilment; a person who comes to the rescue of another; a person qualified to complete or correspond to another in the sense that they provide the missing pieces from the puzzle of the other's life. This word 'helper' is never used of an inferior. Indeed, very often, the word 'helper' is used of God himself. So we read the psalmist's joyful testimony: 'God is my helper . . .' (Ps 54:4, RSV).

(Taken from Marriage Matters, p 78)

# The Heavenly Bridegroom

*The mountains may depart, the hills may*
*be shaken but my love for you will never*
*leave you*
Isaiah 54:10

In the Old Testament God is described as the bridegroom of Israel. As bridegroom God becomes thoroughly involved with his wayward bride. He pours out tenderness, care and material provision upon her. Ezekiel describes the Lord's child bride whom he discovers and cherishes through each phase of her life (Ezk. 16:6–10). God expresses unending love for his bride: 'With everlasting love I have taken pity on you . . . (Is. 54:8 JB). He makes physical and emotional provision for her despite her disloyalty, coolness and adultery. His ready acceptance and approval of Israel draws forth all her potential beauty, here seen as masculine, 'I will love them with all my heart . . . I will fall like dew on Israel. He shall bloom like the lily . . . he will have the beauty of the olive and the fragrance of Lebanon' (Ho. 14:5–6 JB).

This symbolism is developed in the New Testament which describes the church as the bride of Christ. The incarnation is about intimate involvement. The crucifixion is about painful identification. The message of the ascending Christ is that he departs in order to prepare a place where his bride might join him, where she might be involved with him for ever.

(Taken from Two into One, pp 27, 28)

# Leaving: a New Number One

*A man shall leave his father and mother and be joined to his wife, and the two shall become one flesh*
Mark 10:7–8

Popular opinion may mock and the sick marriages of society may appear to substantiate the claims that marriage is outmoded, but that does not alter this admonition of Jesus. He does not start with man, nor with anthropology, but with God: 'from the beginning of creation, "God made them male and female"' (Mk. 10:6). I am not suggesting that we disregard all the opinions of sociologists. I believe they have valuable insights to share. I am saying that, as Christians, we take our authority from God and we need to re-examine the instructions of our Lord, to leave, cleave (be joined) and become one flesh. Our Creator always wants what is best for us and His instructions for marriage are exactly fitted to men and women as they really are . . .

And God instructs married couples 'to leave': 'to recognise that when we marry, life must now revolve around a new number one – our partner. To leave means to put the partner before oneself, to wake up each morning and ask: "How can I make my partner happy today?"'

(Taken from Two into One, p 34, and Marriage Matters, p 42)

# Cleaving: A New Order of Priorities

> *'A man leaves his father and mother and cleaves to his wife and they become one flesh'*
> Genesis 2:24 (RV)

The literal sense of the Hebrew word for 'to cleave' is 'to adhere to' or 'to be glued to' a person. Partners in marriage were to be welded together so that the two became one. But the Bible's use of this word nowhere implies a relationship which is needy, greedy or claustrophobic, wooden or restrictive . . . Ruth 'clave' to Naomi when they were both widowed. Her request that Naomi should not ask her to leave her suggests a warm, loving, supportive relationship, a togetherness and healthy interdependence which applied equally to times of joy and times of pain, to times of stability and security and to times of change.

We also read that David's attendants 'clave' to him through thick and thin, implying that 'cleaving' includes faithfulness: the desire to make the well-being of the partner in marriage a top priority . . .

When two married people donate quality time to one another, they convey several non-verbal messages: you matter to me; our relationship matters to me, and I want our love to deepen with the years, not to fade or die. And when a couple donate quality time to one another, both partners receive certain assurances: I am of sufficient worth to my partner for him or her to want to spend time with me; I am loved, and I am lovable. These are the most healing messages anyone in the world can hope to receive. They bring in their wake a sense of well-being. Couples who transmit and receive these messages regularly to one another and receive them from one another find that life is well worth living. The architect of marriage knew this when he commanded couples to leave and to cleave.

(Taken from Marriage Matters, pp 55–56)

# Oneness includes Sharing

*A man leaves his father and mother and*
*cleaves to his wife and* they become one
Genesis 2:24, emphasis added

I n *A Severe Mercy* Sheldon Vanauken pinpoints the importance
of sharing and oneness.
'If one of us likes *anything*, there must be something to like
in it – and the other one must find it. Every single thing that either
of us likes. That way we shall create a thousand strands, great and
small, that will link us together. Then we shall be so close that it
would be impossible – unthinkable – for either of us to suppose that
we could ever recreate such closeness with anyone else. And our trust
in each other will not only be based on love and loyalty but on the *fact*
of a thousand sharings – a thousand strands twisted into something
unbreakable.

Our enthusiasm grew as we talked. Total sharing, we felt, was the
ultimate secret of a love that would last for ever. And of course we
*could* learn to like anything if we wanted to. Through sharing we
would not only make a bond of incredible friendship, but through
sharing we would keep the magic of inloveness. And with every
year, more and more depth. We would become as close as two
human beings *could* become – closer perhaps than any two people
had ever been. Whatever storms might come, whatever changes the
years might bring, there would be the bedrock closeness of all our
sharing.'75

# Creating Oneness

*Adam had intercourse with his wife, and she became pregnant. She bore a son and said, 'By the Lord's help I have acquired a son'*
Genesis 4:1

When two people fall in love, life revolves around the loved one. All that seems to matter is the well-being of the loved one. Nothing seems to be too much trouble: no chore, no sacrifice, no offering of time or attention, no donation of money or possessions. Humbled by love, they each promote the other. And when that in-love-ness matures, mellows and turns to genuine, authentic love, the couple cannot contain it. It overflows to create a home which bears the hallmark of both, it gives birth to babies or ministries, projects or dreams. It embraces others.

(Taken from The Smile of Love, p 24)

# Oneness Reaches Out

*Abraham looked up and saw three men*
*standing near him . . . He said 'Let me*
*fetch you a little bread and you can refresh*
*yourselves before going further'*
**Genesis 18:2,5**

One purpose of marriage is to reach out to others. This reaching out is always costly.

I think of one young couple who opened their home every Sunday to students and 'homeless' single people. They would always cook for more than their family in case a newcomer attended church. There would always be a house full of people on a Sunday afternoon. As their family grew and the fifth child was born they could ill afford the money, the inroads on their privacy or the battering to their furniture which such demanding hospitality involved but they viewed these as love-offerings for Christ. I remember the wife speaking to me of the joy they experienced as they watched lonely people gradually find their feet in a strange town. She spoke of the thrill of seeing young people searching for Christ and finding him in their home.

A circle of loving was formed which seemed to have no beginning and no end. The couple poured out love at great cost, but God replenished their resources with his own blessing. And, of course, they were never short of babysitters. The home was a place of laughter and joy.

(Taken from Two into One, pp 63, 64)

# Spiritual Oneness

*Where two or three come together in my name, there am I with them*
Matthew 18:20

Most Christians pay lip-service to the desirability, even the necessity of spending time alone each day with God, but, as Stephen Doyle observes, 'If people were asked, "Do you have a relationship with Jesus?" most Christians would answer "yes". If they were asked, "When did you last talk with Him?" most would have difficulty in answering.'[76] If this is true of individuals, it is even more true of married couples. I recently asked a dozen couples, 'How important is prayer to your marriage?' They replied, 'It's very important.' But when I asked, 'How often do you pray together?' with the exception of one couple, they all replied, 'Hardly ever'. This inconsistency between our belief and our way of life leads to impoverishment. Prayer enriches relationships.

Alice Gavoty, the wife of a French diplomat, records in her diary how shared prayer with her husband Joseph enhanced their joy in one another and in God. 'From the start we used to say our prayers together . . . We found the Lord more and more in each other and we regarded this as the blessing on our union which He had willed. Near Joseph, I almost always had an actual sense of God's presence.'[77] As Bishop Theophan writes: 'Prayer is the test of everything. If prayer is right, everything is right.'

(Taken from Two into One, pp 53, 54)

# Praying Together

*'Wherever two or three people come together in my name, I am there, right among them!'*
Matthew 18:20 (JB Phillips)

There was an Archbishop who lived in the nineteenth century called Archpbishop Theophan. He once said: 'When prayer is right, everything is right.' Or as the old maxim puts it: 'Those who pray together stay together.'

I want Jesus right in the middle of our relationship. The open sesame to having him there is prayer. We pray with each other just for the joy of acknowledging the presence of Jesus in our relationship.

One of the reasons why some couples find it difficult to pray together is that the emphasis has always been on using words in prayer. The extrovert finds it very easy to use words when they pray. The introvert, on the other hand, finds this very difficult. We miss out on a whole dimension of prayer if we cannot be silent together. My husband and I enjoy a few moments of silence together before lunch most days. These are our most powerful times of prayer because here we can 'just be' before the God whose love enriches our relationship.

# Practical Oneness

*There is more happiness in giving than in receiving*
Acts 20:35

The Bible insists that Christians are accountable to the Divine Treasurer for what he entrusts to us. This alone should push us into establishing an organized, systematic, responsible attitude to financial matters. The Chief Executive is God. The earthly treasurer might be the wife or the husband. What matters is that they agree a policy, and allow the one more adept at figures to deal with the practicalities.

In order to agree on the way to spend money, each one needs to know the full extent of the joint income, the assets and the probable expenditure. To ensure that expenditure does not exceed income, it is helpful to draw up a budget placing known items (tax, insurance, mortgage payments, gas bills, electricity bills, *etc.*) alongside income. Then balance the books. For the Christian, budgeting will not be determined by wants but by needs. Decisions will be governed by the recognition of what can be done without. It will not be governed by what we must have to be like neighbours, Personal needs have to be placed within a global perspective, taking into account neighbourhood needs and church needs.

Christ makes demands on those who are rich, and that includes all who live in the west. But God is no one's debtor. The same God from the abundance of His resources, gives blessings and has promised that this will continue (See 2 Ch. 31:3–10; Pr. 3:9–10.)

(Taken from Two into One, pp 109, 110)

# Sensitive Oneness

*A man must leave his father and mother*
*and be joined to his wife, and the two will*
*become one body. This mystery has many*
*implications. But I am saying it applies to*
*Christ and the church*
**Ephesians 5:31–32**

'Let there be spaces in your togetherness.'[78] Space is the breath which is vital to the growth of individuality which in turn strengthens intimacy.

Allowing the other 'space' demonstrates a high degree of trust. Without trust, there is no love.

If love is to grow, you each must possess the ability to receive. When you drink in the love which you read in another's eyes for you, it fills you with an intoxicating sense of well-being and worth. It brings security and peace and the deep assurance that, 'I am loved for who I am.'

As each one becomes open to the love God pours out each becomes capable of love which is 'other-centred' rather than self-centred. Each one becomes capable of love in action; the love which by-passes feelings and provides for the needs of the loved one even when feelings are not warm or particularly loving. God equips us to love with the will as well as with the feelings and this kind of loving is required of every husband and wife whose desire is to mirror the love between Christ and His bride, the Church. Such love is not easy to practise or to understand. But couples dare not embark on Christian marriage without it.

> Love so amazing, so divine,
> Demands my soul, my life, my all.

(Taken from *Growing into Love*, pp 104, 105, 106)

# Caring Confrontation

*Martha, Martha . . . you are worried and upset about many things, but only one thing is needed. Mary has chosen what is better, and it will not be taken away from her*
Luke 10:42

Space is as essential to relationships as the gap between rungs of the ladder. Shared lives within fixed boundaries spell security. Shared lives stripped of such separateness spell, at best an exposure from which one party will eventually run, at worst, an unhealthy bondage where two or more people are held together by the confidentiality of secrets shared. As Henri Nouwen puts it, 'Space can only be a welcoming space when there are clear boundaries.'[79]

If each person's privacy is to be thus preserved, and if the individual's pressing needs are to be met realistically, the art of sensitive confrontation must be learned by each member of the family. Some Christians fear the very word confrontation. It conjures up ugly images: a head-on collision, a ding-dong battle, cruel clashing of personalities and views, angry outbursts, wounding experiences.

This fear of confrontation is regrettable. It results in resentment and the hard-heartedness that divides. And it is not Christlike. Jesus was confrontational as a person without stooping to becoming argumentative. In this, as in everything, he is our model.

(Taken from Creative Conflict, p 78)

# Modern Marriage

*Love each other as I have loved you*
John 15:12

Fifty years ago marriage offered a definitive way of life. The husband went out to work, controlled the finances and made major decisions. His wife cleaned the house, cooked the meals and looked after the children. Modern marriage acknowledges no such conclusive boundaries. This is both liberating and perplexing. It is liberating because it gives scope for creativity, experimentation and exchange of roles.

It is perplexing because there are few rules to this new game. Couples must make up their own and that is not as easy as it sounds.

Love is not always 'doing what comes naturally'. Love has to be learnt in the hard school of experience. We all know the theory of love, but it takes hours of patient practice to translate theory into a life-style.

Modern marriage may well be more rewarding, and perhaps more biblical than the marriages of yesteryear. But past patterns still haunt us.

'I still feel guilty when I leave Mike to cook his own supper.' 'I feel *I* ought to organize our finances, although I know Sheila would be more efficient.' These persistent voices from the past prohibit harmonious sharing unless couples discuss the rules of their game. Discussion has to continue until you are sure that your proposed life-style coincides with what your partner wants. If it doesn't the marriage will be in trouble.

(Taken from Growing into Love, pp 49, 50)

# Space and Togetherness

*After six days Jesus took with him Peter*
*and James and John and led them up a high*
*mountain apart by themselves*
Mark 9:2

I t is essential for each partner to recognize that their spouse's needs may differ from their own. While one may relish company for most of the day, the other can only cope with people if it is possible to escape from them from time to time. One may value shared prayer, while the other appreciates praying with others so long as private devotions can be safeguarded. Each partner should place their own needs alongside the needs of their spouse so that both sets of needs can be met. Sensitive oneness only occurs in couples who trust one another sufficiently to experiment with varying degrees of togetherness and varying degrees of time spent separately.

(Taken from Marriage Matters, p 80)

# The Meaning of Headship

*The husband is the head of the wife as Christ is the head of the church, his body of which he is the Saviour*
**Ephesians 5:23**

The Bible's teaching on equality and authority is rooted in paradox. On the one hand it underlines the sexual and spiritual equality of married people in acknowledging that they become 'one flesh' and that they are 'heirs together' of the Kingdom of God. On the other, it places before them the fact that the husband is the divinely appointed 'head' of the relationship (Eph. 5:23). Headship in a partnership of equality can only be understood when its nature has been examined. And Paul leaves Christians in no doubt concerning the style of headship which he is recommending. 'The husband is the head of the wife as Christ is the head of the church, his body, of which he is the Saviour' (5:23).

Paul's emphasis here is not on the authority and power of Christ but on his self-giving: Christ's own words to his disciples help us to understand his attitude: 'Whoever wants to become great among you must be your servant, and whoever wants to be first must be slave of all. For even the Son of Man did not come to be served, but to serve, and to give his life a ransom for many' (Mk. 10:43–45). The husband's headship, far from containing rights to be claimed, presents a superlative standard of self-sacrifice which leaves many Christian men asking, 'Who is equal to this task?'

(Taken from Two into One, p 44)

# For Husbands

*Husbands, love your wives, just as Christ
loved the church and gave himself up for her*
Ephesians 5:25

When Paul instructs Christian husbands in the art of loving their wives, he makes it clear that the familiar picture of the tyrannical husband finds no place within a Christian framework. Harshness is forbidden (Col. 3:19). Paul's entire emphasis is on the duty a Christian husband has, because of his 'headship', to become his wife's self-forgetting companion. The husband's prototype is to be found in Jesus. The husband's main aim should be to emulate the love Christ demonstrates for his bride, the church. This kind of loving is not just an emotion; it is an orientation, a chain of choices, a series of actions which are planned to bring about the wife's well-being, happiness and ultimate wholeness.

When a husband loves his wife in this way he draws out her full potential and Paul implies that this is another of the husband's duties (v. 26). Fulfilment of this duty is one of the greatest gifts a husband can give to his wife. It is liberating. It enables her to recognize her unique beauty and to acknowledge her own worth. A husband whose aim is to promote his wife will avoid 'putting her down', he will not try to 'score points' off her or make derisive comments about her. Rather he will find opportunities to affirm her and to sing her praise (Pr. 31:10).

(Taken from Two into One, pp 45, 46)

# A Forgiving Love

*Father, forgive them for they do not know*
*what they are doing*
Luke 23:34

J ust as the bride of Christ is continuously on the receiving end of the undeserved goodness of the God who freely forgives her, so a Christian husband or wife has to learn to forgive, 'not seven times, but seventy times seven'. Forgiveness is the generosity which restores broken relationships. Forgiveness includes acceptance without acquiescence. It is the capacity to accept your husband or wife as a person even when you cannot condone their actions. Forgiveness, as Neville Ward puts it, is the ability a person has to bear 'injury without retaliation and without his love becoming even just a little frightened and therefore more cautious and reserved, so that there is now simply a richer love where that evil has been done.'[80]

Christ's love is an unbreakable love. John Powell describes unbreakable love in this way: 'I will always be there for you. If I say I am your man, I will always be your man.'[81] God says the same thing to Israel through the words of the prophet Jeremiah 'I have loved you with an everlasting love' (Je. 31:3), and Jesus repeats the message of unending love, 'As the Father has loved me, so have I loved you' (Jn. 15:9).

(Taken from Two into One, p 46)

# Unconditional Love

*Husbands should love their wives as their own bodies. He who loves his wife loves himself*
Ephesians 5:28

C hrist-like love is unconditional love (Eph. 5:28). Unconditional love is the only love which heals. This love is just
'there'. It declares, 'I am all for you, no matter what you are
like at the moment, no matter what you do.' This is the love Christ
offers to his bride, the church. It is not a blinkered love which fails to
recognize the loved one's blemishes. On the contrary, unconditional
love acknowledges faults, failures and defects and goes on loving.

Unconditional love conveys the message. 'I love you *with* your
deficiencies.'

The opposite of unconditional love is love as a reward for good
behaviour. It is approval granted only when certain conditions have
been met and is not really love at all

This so-called love gives rise to doubt. It leaves a bitter taste and
gives the impression, 'I am not loved for myself. I am loved only for
what I have to offer.' In the final analysis, this leaves the partner
feeling not so much loved as used. Do you love your partner, 'warts
and all'? Or are you hoping to change him/her?

(Taken from Growing into Love, p 100)

# Yonggi Cho's Challenge

*Husbands, treat your wives with consideration . . . since you are joint heirs of the grace of life and so your prayers will not be hindered*
1 Peter 3:7

Paul Yonggi Cho, was pastor of the Full Gospel Central Church in Seoul, Korea. Yonggi Cho's church was both the biggest and the fastest growing church in the world. But this success story has a shadow side.

Early on in his ministry, tensions arose in the pastor's marriage: Yonggi Cho found it all too easy to dismiss his wife's emotional needs, protesting that through his wife the devil was scheming to divert him from his first calling: to win the people of Korea for Christ.

One day, in desperation, he prayed, 'Lord, change her or otherwise we must separate!'

God heard that prayer and answered it by revealing to Yonggi Cho how God required *him* to change. He began by showing him how vital it was that he met his wife's needs. What kind of testimony could he give if his wife were to leave him and he ended up divorced? His primary role in life was not to win Korea for Christ but to love his wife in the same way as Christ loved the church.

When God speaks, Yonggi Cho obeys. He cancelled certain evangelistic campaigns and began an entirely new lifestyle which included his wife.

Today they are both used by God to win Korea for Christ but, under the lordship of Christ, their marriage sits on the top rung of their ladder of priorities. Everything else, including their pastoral responsibilities which escalate with the years, find their pecking order after that.

(Taken from Marriage Matters, pp 50, 51, 52)

# Woman's Work

*Make it your aim to be at one in the Spirit,
and you will inevitably be at peace with one
another*
Ephesians 4:3 (J B Phillips)

Many Christians go into marriage nursing the secret ambition to transform their partner's habits, beliefs or lifestyle. I remember one bride who paused at the door of the church immediately after her wedding to whisper to me, 'Let's pray now that he will start coming to church with me.' In some respects that is an unfair prayer. She married a non-church-goer. She may long and pray that he will turn to Christ, but she has no right to demand that he changes his Sunday time-table just because they are husband and wife. Unconditional love requires her to accept her husband with his habitual absence from church. If she cannot accept this, she should not have married him. Of course, it is not wrong that she should want him to turn to Christ. But if compliance to her every whim becomes a condition of her love, it is not true love. Change in marriage must not be in response to the nagging of the spouse. Rather it must be the inner compulsion of love to love. You change your habits because your love for your partner is greater than your obsession with a particular way of life.

(Taken from Growing into Love, pp 100, 101)

# The Meaning of Submission

*Wives submit to your husbands as to the Lord*
**Ephesians 5:22**

Submission within marriage is the inner compulsion of love to love. It is not playing 'Let's pretend'; let's pretend women are brainless, skill-less, weak. Rather, submission is having the courage to acknowledge one's strengths and to place them first at the feet of one's spouse for their welfare, growth and wholeness. Herein lies the crunch, of course. The world persuades us to seek self first. Self-fulfilment, self-indulgence, self-seeking are preferred to sacrifice. But, as Christians, we are called to run counter to worldly suggestions. And this submission results in the kind of exhilarating, adventurous, successful partnership which the writer of Proverbs implies.

Deliberate self-renunciation is hard. But doesn't love want to make sacrifices? John Powell suggests that it does:

Love implies that I am ready and willing to forgo my own convenience, to invest my own time, and even risk my own security to promote your satisfaction, security and development.[82]

(Taken from Growing into Love, p 116)

# More About Submission

*A perfect wife — who can find her? She is far beyond the price of pearls. Her husband's heart has confidence in her; from her he will derive no little profit.*
Proverbs 31:1,2

The Bible portrays marriage as an egalitarian relationship where husband and wife enjoy a social partnership, sexual oneness, spiritual togetherness and a procreative responsibility. Moreover, Galatians 3:28 makes it clear that in Christian circles there must be no talk of precedence and inferiority. We 'are all one in Christ Jesus'.

Women who allow themselves to be used, who fail to contribute to the decision-making of the marriage, who think of themselves as inferior to their husbands, have misunderstood what Paul is saying in Ephesians 5.

Proverbs 31 speaks of a wife who was a powerful woman. This strong woman voluntarily gave her administrative skills, her counselling insights, her quick brain, her practical capabilities first to her husband, then to her children and thirdly to the needy. Her submission was a positive yielding of all that she had and all that she was to others.

(Taken from Growing into Love, pp 115, 116)

# The Perfect Wife

*She is clothed in strength and dignity, she can laugh at the days to come. When she opens her mouth, she does so wisely; on her tongue is kindly instruction*
Proverbs 31:25,26

The book of Proverbs presents us with a picture of a gifted married woman who seems to have enjoyed submitting herself to her husband. This 'perfect wife' (Pr. 31:10 ff.) certainly did not pretend that she had no strengths. She appears to have been, among other things, an accomplished needle-woman, a shrewd administrator and a successful business woman. She seems to have possessed boundless energy, a compassionate nature and a discerning mind. The narrative implies that she voluntarily invested all of these strengths in her husband's welfare. She did not lose her personal identity or become overwhelmed by him. They interacted as two autonomous people. She provided him with mental stimulus, and clearly he admired and respected her.

This submissive wife did not restrict her activities to her home and family. Her abilities spilled over into the circles in which she moved. This fulfilled, creative, strong woman whose talents were channelled to promote her husband, her children and the needy made a significant contribution to the society in which she lived.

Women today who recognize their worth may reject the injunction to submit as a reaction against those Christian women who become insipid non-persons out of false humility. Jesus' revolutionary attitude towards women should allay some of the fears women can harbour.

(Taken from Two into One, pp 49, 50, 48)

# Superman or Wonder Woman?

### *Submit to one another . . .*
#### Ephesians 5:21

The average person is equipped to give support and advice to others on occasions but not qualified to be dependable, rock-like and strong all of the time. There are situations in life which expose the weakness of the strong, which uncover the vulnerability of the well-integrated person and which cause the rock-like to crumble. On such occasions they are the ones who stretch out a desperate hand and need to be rescued. You may think you have married one of the world's helpers, someone who is always prepared to mount a rescue operation. But, at best, your partner is no more than a wounded healer who will sometimes prop you up and who will, on occasions require support from you.

Couples need to be generous enough and mature enough to see the need for giving as well as receiving. They recognize that they married a real person, not Superman, or Wonder Woman.

Christian couples know that there is a resource in Jesus to which they can always turn. He is our safe place, our refuge, the supplier for our deepest needs. With this recognition, we can release our partner from unrealistic demands. We are free to explode the myth that marriage meets our every need. We are at liberty to see the marital relationship and our partner for what they are, one of the vehicles, but only one, which God chooses to use to meet our need for love.

(Taken from Two into One, pp 99, 100)

# Tension

*Each of you should look not only to your own interests, but also to the interests of others*
**Philippians 2:4**

T ension is to marriage what birth pangs are to childbirth. They are the unmistakable warning that new life is coming. They provide the motivation to strain every muscle and nerve to bring forth the life which is part of both of you. Healthy attitudes to conflict:- the ability to understand its causes, willingness to modify behaviour patterns, and respect for the 'otherness' of ones partner, are antiseptics, preserving the new life. Loyalty, communiction and accurate listening, are anti-toxins preventing disease destroying what you create.

Two highly motivated people, harnessed to their Creator-God, possess all the resources required to arrest the malaise of marital disharmony. The sustained centrality of the lordship of Christ, over all aspects of marriage and the availability of the miracle-power of prayer provide unlimited resources in times of conflict.

C.S. Lewis wrote of the tension which existed in his own marriage: 'The most precious gift that marriage gave me was this constant impact of something very close and intimate yet all the time unmistakably other, resistant — in a word, real.'[83]

(Taken from Two into One, pp 102, 103)

# Hold Your Ground

*Your enemy the devil prowls around like a*
*roaring lion looking for someone to devour*
1 Peter 5:8

Satanists are fasting and praying for the breakdown of Christian marriages and, in particular, the marriages of those in Christian leadership. But we need not be daunted. Satan, unlike God, is not present everywhere at the same time. And although he seems to have an efficient, well-tried network of evil with which he oppresses us, we must never forget that he is the defeated foe. As Christians we hold the trump-card: prayer in the name of Jesus. The thrilling thing is that couples who obey the biblical injunctions and combat Satan and his minions by resisting him, fighting him, and holding their ground are among those who are finding that, mysteriously and miraculously, their marriages are being sustained or mended by God; and that prayer and spiritual solidarity against the powers of darkness work. 'For our struggle is not against flesh and blood, but against the rulers, against the authorities, against the powers of this dark world and against the spiritual forces of evil in the heavenly realms. That is why you must rely on God's armour, or you will not be able to put up any resistance when the worst happens, or have enough resources to hold your ground' (Eph. 6:12,13).

(Taken from Marriage Matters, p 103)

# Striving for Unity

*Jesus saw that they were making headway*
*painfully for the wind was against them*
Mark 6:48

The Chinese symbol for crisis is made up of two characters. One means 'danger', the other means 'opportunity'. Christians who are committed to one another are those who are committed to treat conflict as homework to be done, who resolve to benefit from it and learn from it. They are wise enough, in the face of conflict, to ask certain questions: 'Are we *for* each other or against each other?' 'Do we want this relationship to work to glorify Christ, or is the price we may have to pay too high?' 'Lord, is there something in *me* that is disrupting this relationship?'

These are the questions we must ask when we are locked in conflict with another. Isn't this what the apostle Paul meant when he exhorted the Philippians to 'strive together' or when he admonished the Ephesians to 'make every effort to keep the unity of the Spirit'? The picture is of Christians straining every nerve and muscle, pulling together like the members of a boat crew, striving to reach the goal: unity. Anything that falls short of this commitment is to be confessed and I am not allowed to pin the blame for crab-catching on my brother or sister, husband or wife.

(Taken from Two into One)

# Hatred is Love Hurt

*Euodia and Syntyche, please, I beg you, try*
*to agree*
Philippians 4:2

The dividing line between love and hate is gossamer thin as I rediscovered recently. My husband and I had enjoyed a day out together: browsing in the market of a country town near our home, tramping in the hills under a steel-blue autumn sky, going out together for the evening on our own, a rare treat.

When we arrived home, I went to the kitchen to make the bedtime drinks. David wandered off to watch the news on television. And something inside me snapped. I felt irritated, annoyed, abandoned. It may be irrational, but I wanted him to be with me. It had been such a good day, why stay apart now? When he went off like that, I felt rejected. Of course I hadn't actually *said*, 'Let's make the drinks together.' Neither had he said, 'Do you mind if I watch the news?' But the hurt inflicted resulted in me rediscovering the horrifying truth that hatred can displace love as quickly as you can snap open an automatic umbrella.

(Taken from Creative Conflict p 105)

# Mr Right

*May the Lord increase and enrich your love
for each other*
1 Thessalonians 3:12

Val used to dream of the handsome curate she would marry one day. He would be her spiritual leader and she would help him in his work. They would serve God side by side. Then Val fell in love with Paul. But Paul was not a curate, and he was not particularly handsome. What is more, this civil servant had been a Christian only a few months when they met. But they were in love and they got married. Val still secretly 'blames' Paul for not being the strong Christian of her dreams. Her fantasies prevent Paul from becoming the husband God meant him to be. Until she lets go of the fantasy, she traps Paul in an unrealistic mould. She stifles his growth.

Men, I find, also conceal a mental short-list. Peter's list described the glamorous, sylph-like figure of the girl he would marry. When he married Sue, he kept the secret list. Unfortunately, the list did not tally with Sue's measurements. At times he uses his fantasy to taunt his wife, inflicting deep hurt.

Do you have a short-list? Does it contain the 'essential characteristics' of your future partner? Burn it. Erase the memory. This is an act of the will which requires humour and prayer. It frees you to offer unconditional love to your partner, thus setting him/her free to be the person God made him/her to be.

(Taken from Growing into Love, p 43)

# Gradual Change

*The Holy Spirit of the Lord will come upon*
*you in power . . . and you will be changed*
*into a different person*
1 Samuel 10:6

Sometimes the changes God wants to bring about take years. At one time, pages of my prayer journal were devoted to the anger and frustration which poisoned my life and which stemmed from the growing tensions in my marriage to David.

In prayer I would whine to God about my husband: 'It really feels as though he doesn't care about me at all . . . How little is his understanding and how very limited his compassion.' In prayer I would throw down the gauntlet and challenge God to change my husband so that the quality of our marriage could improve. In prayer I would pour out the self-pity that filled me to the brim: 'There's a big part of me, Lord, which is tired of trying, weary of forgiving, exhausted with the agony of gingerly putting my nose out of my hedgehog prickles only to have it stepped on again.'

And in prayer, God would come to me, hear me out, absorb my bitterness, touch my bruised and battered heart, and gently but persistently show me, not where David needed to change, but where *I must* change.

By God's grace we both changed so that the sharing of our lives today is more mutually fulfilling and fun-filled than it has ever been. Painful though it was at the time, I look back with gratitude at the patient surgical skills with which the Holy Spirit operated on me to break me, recreate me and to rid me of spiritual diseases in the hospital of prayer.

(Taken from Listening to God, pp 210, 211)

# The Best is Yet to Be

*Jacob worked for seven years for Rachel and they seemed to him like a few days because he loved her so much*
Genesis 29:20

On our silver wedding anniversary, my husband and I were strolling, hand in hand, along a beach on a Greek island, and I put to him the question: 'Are you glad you married me?' When he replied in the affirmative, I asked: 'Why? Why are you glad?' And he answered: 'Because, even after all these years, you are my best friend.'

In the silence which followed, I thanked God for our growing relationship. If I had asked those questions a few years earlier, I might have received some rather evasive answers. I looked up to the mountains which framed the beach where we were walking, felt the warmth of the sun tanning my body and heard the whistle of the wind which was playing on the waves. As I gave thanks for these signs of the love of God, I gave thanks, for an even greater sign of his love. This Creator God stoops down to touch us in our need, to draw married people together when life threatens to drive them apart and to perform the miracle of mending their marriages.

(Taken from Marriage Matters, p 57)

# Listening Love

*I hear my love.*
*See how he comes*
Song of Songs 2:8

The first duty of love is to listen.

These lines from George Eliot never fail to move me.

'Oh the comfort, the inexpressible comfort of feeling safe with a person; having neither to weigh thoughts nor measure words but to pour them all out, just as it is, chaff and grain together, knowing that a faithful hand will take and sift them, keep what is worth keeping, and then, with the breath of kindness blow the rest away.'

(Taken from Listening to Others, p 101)

# Transfiguration

*This is my son, the Beloved, he enjoys my*
*favour.*
*Listen to him*
Matthew 17:5

There is a moving scene in the Gospels which shows us how to receive guidance, how to establish to whom to go and when. Jesus has taken his disciples with him to the top of a mountain. There he turns his eyes away from earth towards his Father and his whole form is transfigured in a way which fills the disciples with awe. As his hand-picked companions Peter, James and John watch him, they notice that he is not alone. He is in consultation with two glorified companions: Moses the lawgiver, and Elijah the prophet. They also detect the presence of the Father, whose voice they clearly hear (Matt. 17:1–5).

We are not told in detail what Jesus was asking, saying or doing. What we are told is that he was deep in conversation with these three, that they were discussing his imminent death. He was to emerge from this prayer time with a clear vision of what he was to do next. The Father would tell him what to do. As Jesus himself admitted, he was utterly depending on his Father for such instructions. What we are also told is that we, similarly, need to consult with Jesus before we take any kind of action. 'Listen to him,' the Father reminds us.

(Taken from Open to God, p 176)

# Transforming Power of Love

*Naomi, taking the child, held him to her breast; and it was she who looked after him*
Ruth 4:16

When a mother welcomes her new baby, and pours acceptance into this helpless little life, the baby begins to enjoy what psychiatrists call 'a sense of being'. Security. The assurance that 'it is all right to be me'.

When that child is on the receiving end of generous and gracious relationships with father, grandparents, uncles, aunts, friends of the family and neighbours, it enjoys a sense of 'well-being' – good spirits, courage, personal vitality.

In time, as the child grows and matures, its existence will be positive and joyful. It will enjoy a free flow of energy and it will be highly motivated to invest its personality, energies and interest in persons and concerns outside itself. Such children will care for others because they, themselves, have been cared for. Compassion, generosity, kindness, warmth, reliability and patience flow from them because loving relatives and friends have poured these resources into them in the first place. A sense of 'being' and 'well-being' generate a longing to expend our resources in caring for others. This is the transforming power of love.

(Taken from The Smile of Love, pp 22, 23)

# Your Will be Done

*Joseph arose and took the child and his*
*mother by night, and departed to Egypt*
Matthew 2:14

The father of a new-born baby once expressed to me his feelings for his wife and child:

'I've never loved anyone like this before. I can think of no one but them. I just want to be with them doing whatever I can for them. When they are distressed, I am distressed. When they are happy, I am happy. Nothing else matters to me at the moment — only them.'

The biblical notion of the will of God is like that. It means that God's longing and desire, love and joy are focused on his people. He delights in them. He safeguards them. He yearns over them. That is why the Christian can say with confidence, in the words of Julian of Norwich: 'I saw that he is to us everything that is good.'

*'Lord, you know what I desire, but I desire it only if it is your*
*will that I should have it. If it is not your will, good Lord, do not*
*be displeased, for my will is to do your will.'*

Julian of Norwich

(Taken from Reflections for Lent, p 38)

# I Can't Cope

### *Jesus learned obedience through what he suffered*
**Hebrews 5:8**

I recall visiting a young mother and her new-born child in hospital. The baby was born with a ventricular hole in the heart. She had an oesophageal reflex which would necessitate keeping her upright day and night. It seemed unlikely that she would keep her food down for long. As the husband walked from the ward to the hospital entrance with me, he confessed that he could not cope with a responsible lecturing post, a wife who must be totally absorbed in her sick baby, three other children *and* all the normal household chores. We recognized that his feelings were realistic. We acknowledged that this was where the support of the 'body of Christ' could find expression, and he began to think of people in the church who might be asked to help regularly. I admired that husband. He refused to pretend that all was well when it was not. He recognized where help was needed and was unafraid to ask for it. He carefully worked out his own scale of priorities in a stressful situation. It was a good example of the creativity of pain.

(Taken from Two into One, p 114)

# Transforming Love

*God chose what is weak in the world*
1 Corinthians 1:27

L ove transcends worthlessness and communicates acceptance, affirmation and commitment.

This dimension of love was brought home to me recently while watching television. The cameras zoomed in on a mother sitting by the bedside of one of her children, the twelfth. The child sat in the hospital bed whimpering like a frightened animal: helpless. From the waist up, the infant's emaciated body was covered with weeping sores and scorch marks. Her thin face was also discoloured and scarred: the effects of a bomb blast. Yet the mother leant over this scrap of suffering humanity and contemplated her with love. It was as though this child was the only one who had ever been born.

(Taken from Living Free, pp 55, 56)

# Faithful Fathers

## *The eyes of the Lord are towards the righteous and his ears towards their cry*
### Psalm 34:15

The love of faithful fathers for their children was once communicated most movingly in a television documentary. Five fathers appeared on the programme. All of them were separated from their wives and had been granted little or no access to their children. One of the men had not been visited by his children for nine years. Choking back his tears, he admitted, 'I sometimes walk the streets of the town just to catch a glimpse of them to make sure they're all right.' Another man broke down in front of the camera as he tried to describe how the enforced separation feels. A third explained how he lives for the weekends when he can take his four-year-old daughter to a hotel for a night. 'She's a part of me,' he said. 'It feels so good being her father.'

This is the kind of love one of the Psalmists attributes to God. 'God loves me so much, he can't take his eyes off me.'

(Taken from The Smile of God, p 97)

# God's Children

*Fathers, do not irritate your children or they will lose heart*
Colossians 3:21

Children are God-made personalities in their own right. Though they are offshoots of parental love, God created a unique mould for each one. That is why you often hear parents exclaim, 'They're all *our* children but they are all so different.'

The challenge of parenthood, from the toddler stage onwards, is the challenge to succour and yet to let go. The toddler must be given the warmth and security of the parents' love but must also be given free and fearless space away from parents where he can try life without them. Unless the toddler takes the initiative at this stage and gains autonomy there will be trouble later in leaving home and travelling on alone. As parents, we must hold these two child-needs in tension: keep a healthy balance between providing the home-soil where our children can put down roots and where their uniqueness may flourish and at the same time grant them appropriate freedom, the separateness from us where they learn to take initiative. Much of the friction that erupts in the family happens because as parents we wear huge L plates. We are learners, not experts. Friction teaches us where we need to adjust our parenting so that it more accurately meets the needs of our children.

(Taken from Creative Conflict, p 94)

# Love Your Children

*The infant will play over the den of the adder;*
*the baby will put its hand into the vipers lair.*
*No hurt nor harm will be done*
Isaiah 11:8,9

Children need warmth and acceptance, appreciation and autonomy, time and attention, yet some parents treat their children harshly, magnify their failures out of all proportion and absent themselves in pursuit of pleasure or success.

In later years, such children will build on these foundations if they are subjected to the kind of teaching which presents God as an authoritarian father-figure who demands perfection in all things: 'Be perfect . . . as your heavenly Father is perfect' (Matt. 5:48). And such teaching, alas, is prevalent in our churches today. The implication is that unless we conform to a rigid set of rules, we are unacceptable to God. If we fail to conform and are punished and ostracised, the conviction deepens that 'I am a hopeless case'. Belief in a god, who shows no understanding of human frailty, does not induce confidence to look in trust into the face of the loving Creator who beckons us.

(Taken from The Smile of Love, p 142)

# Too Busy

*From the Father of all, his whole family in*
*heaven and on earth takes its name*
Ephesians 3:14,15

As parents, we do not model ourselves sufficiently on the Fatherhood of God. We make ourselves available to our children when it suits us: when the commercials are on, when the news has finished, 'When I've finished the ironing'. Children are quick to detect this reluctant, limited availability. They resent it and rebel.

God offers us unlimited availability. With the heavenly Father we neither need to choose our time carefully nor have an access card to come into his presence. The invitation is unambiguous and clear. 'You may come into my presence with boldness at any time.' This is the availability we should offer to our children.

Of course, I do not mean that we should waive aside the need for discipline, that we should encourage our children to clamour endlessly. What I am suggesting is that we should share the *attitude* that clearly characterizes God: total availability. There is a paradox here. When a child knows that he or she is welcome at any time and can have our undivided attention when it is needed the child clamours less and not more. Such a child is secure in the availability of love.

(Taken from Creative Conflict, pp 96, 97)

# He/She Did It

*'Have you eaten from the tree I commanded you not to eat from?' The man said, 'The woman you put here with me — she gave me some fruit from the tree, and I ate it.' Then the Lord God said to the woman, 'What is this you have done?' The woman said, 'The serpent deceived me, and I ate'*
**Genesis 3:11,13**

Don't blame the other person. Most of us fall into this trap. Indeed, we fell into it years ago when we were children. When an adult rebuked us for intolerable behaviour we would find someone on whom to pin the blame: 'It wasn't my fault. He made me do it.' This practice is as old as creation. Adam and Eve used it when God came to them in the garden after they had disobeyed him defiantly and deliberately.

When confronted by God, Adam tries to apportion the blame between God and his wife while Eve pins the blame onto the serpent. Neither is prepared to accept personal responsibility

(Taken from Marriage Matters, p 69)

# They're Getting at Me

*All have sinned and fall short of the glory of God*
**Romans 3:23**

'I'm tired of being woken up every morning by a baby that isn't my own and I'm really fed up with forever tripping over toddler's toys when that toddler isn't mine.'

'Life at home's become unbearable since my gran moved in. She fusses over me as though I'm a little girl. She thinks I should be in by ten every night. She can't bear it if even faint strains of my radio reach her ears but she turns *her* television set up full volume. And she's so demanding of my time; always expecting me to sit in her room and talk to her.'

Notice the common thread running through these complaints. Blaming. When hostility hangs over the home like a thunder-cloud, most of us look for someone to blame; someone, anyone, other than ourselves, at whom to point the finger. Most of us refuse to acknowledge that *we* are blameworthy or that we must shoulder at least a portion of the blame.

Why not give God an opportunity to put his finger on *your* habits or your attitudes. Allow him to change them for the wellbeing of others.

(Taken from Creative Conflict, pp 72, 73, 74)

# Using Friction

*Whatever someone sows, that is what they will reap*
Galatians 6:7

W hen friction threatens to disrupt, five questions must be faced: First, 'What new insights can I glean from this situation: about myself, my family, life, God?' Second, I must take full responsibility for my share in the blame and ask, 'What mistakes have *I* made?' Third, 'What is going on underneath the surface, causing this conflict to erupt?' Fourth, 'Is the underlying cause pain and sadness in the person with whom I am cross. Do they need compassion rather than my annoyance?' Fifth, 'What is God trying to teach me through this frightening situation?'

When friction flies round family life like a bluebottle in summer, ask yourself some forthright questions. Is friction highlighting slip-shod parenting? Am I modelling myself on the Fatherhood of God or has worldliness crept into our family philosophy? What is God trying to say to me through this situation? How is he trying to bring me into alignment with his will? Is he asking me to grow in certain areas: the ability to trust, the selflessness that places parenthood above profession or pride, the guts to give guidance?

No family will ever be fully free of friction. But by God's grace, many families can discover that friction propels people into ever increasing freedom.

(Taken from Creative Conflict, pp 103, 104)

# Johnny the Snail

*Love does not insist on its own way*
1 Corinthians 13:5

Ll parents know how easy it is to allow friction to flame into a consuming fire. You take little Johnny to the shops. You are in a hurry. Johnny chooses today to contemplate every daisy and rose bud *en route*. Your irritation level rises until you snap. Johnny gets a spanking.

You feel a failure because you smacked little Johnny because he dawdled. Little Johnny was fractious in the supermarket because you were cross with him on the way there. You scold him for whining. And so on . . . By the end of the day the feelings of failure are overwhelming and you are tempted to ask. 'Lord, why on earth did you entrust me with children?'

The surface reason for friction was Johnny's snail-like progress to the shopping precinct; but the underlying reason is the challenge of parenthood. Faced with the demands of the newborn baby, we are confronted with the need for supreme self-sacrifice. For a few days or weeks, we give of ourselves gladly and generously. But the novelty soon wears off. We are confronted with the truth about ourselves: we were born with a bias to sin and self-centredness. We want our own way just as badly as the baby. The years spread out before us not as a joyous, romantic adventure but as a dark tunnel through which we must crawl, denying self. In the face of the need for such selflessness, we squeal.

(Taken from Creative Conflict, pp 92, 93, 96)

# All My Fault

*If you go snapping at one another and tearing
one another to pieces, take care. You will be
eaten up by one another*
Galatians 5:15

God sees me just as I am, 'warts and all', and loves me just as
I am. The lack of this accepting love in families fans friction
into flames. An eleven-year-old sums up the situation well
in a poem called *Me'*:

If anyone's in trouble,
it's Me!
If a knife drops, or a door bangs,
it's Me!
Me! Me! Me!
it's always Me! . . .
If the baby starts screaming,
it's Me!
If the fuse is broken,
it's Me!
Me! Me! Me!
It's always (guess who!)
ME!
Susan Stowe (age eleven), *Fresh Voices*, NCER, 1979 p 59

When a child is bombarded with continuous criticism, when parents
fall into the trap of viewing their children as flesh-and-blood
Pinocchios, puppets to be controlled rather than children to be
loved, when parents offer love in exchange for good behaviour, the
scene is set, not just for friction, but for something far more serious:
the smouldering resentment that becomes the seed-bed for doubts
about personal self-worth and lovability. God never measures out this
cruel treatment. Instead he offers us acceptance in such large doses
that we, ourselves, desire to change as a response of love to Love.

(Taken from Creative Conflict, p 100)

# Anything For a Quiet Life

*Whoever is free with correction loves their child*
Proverbs 13:24

Our heavenly Father makes absolute demands on his children and expects unwavering obedience; even when he requires his first-born to stagger under Calvary's cross. Many parents do not operate within this biblical framework. They are afraid to discipline, afraid to set clear goals for their children, afraid to demand absolute obedience. Where there is little obedience there is little trust. Where there is little trust there is little love. Where there is little love there is much friction. Friction arises because of the insecurity lack of discipline brings. Love for children expresses itself in nurturing them with self-sacrificing availability but also provides plenty of information and clear instructions about the 'how to' of negotiating the uphill struggle of life. Children may resist these demands. They may call parents 'square', 'fuddy-duddy', 'mean'. But eventually they will understand, love them and maybe even thank their parents.

This happened to a friend of mine unexpectedly. She had set limits of the amount her daughter could spend on shoes. 'Am I being stingy?' she had asked herself at the time. But her daughter after admitted: 'I'm glad you didn't allow me to spend as much as I liked. I was really pushing you to see how far you'd let me go. I need your guidance, your wisdom and your help.'

(Taken from Creative Conflict, pp 97, 98)

# Remember to Praise

## *I have not found such faith in Israel*
### Matthew 8:10

Donate your leisure time to your children. Explore life together so that they are exposed to stimulating experiences. Broaden their horizons, but do it with them. Swim with them. Walk with them. Watch television with them. Much of the whining that triggers off quarrels will stop when our children are assured that we love them enough to give them our time.

Children need affirmation from their parents. They are growing up in an increasingly competitive world.

A certain amount of competition is healthy; adds zest to life. But all competition and no affirmation results in inner loneliness and insecurity. God, our heavenly parent-figure, frequently affirms his children. 'You are my friends.' 'I have told you everything.' 'Well done, good and faithful servant.' 'I haven't met such faith in Israel.' Similarly, we must affirm our children. When the toddler walks, uses new words, learns to use the potty for himself, praise him. Build up his self-esteem. This will not turn him into the dreaded spoilt child. It will give him the certainty that he is lovable, capable of worth. It will spur him on to greater achievements.

(Taken from Creative Conflict, pp 98, 99)

# Nobody Wants Me

*Can a woman forget her baby at the
breast . . .
feel no pity for the child she has borne?
Even if she were to forget
I shall not forget you'*
Isaiah 49:15

Hurts caused during the first seven years of life may leave a permanent scar.

Alice felt the draught of her love-less childhood well into adulthood: 'When I was a tiny little girl, I was put in an orphanage. I was not pretty, and no-one wanted me. But I can recall longing to be adopted and loved by a family as far back as I can remember. I thought about it day and night. But everything I did seemed to go wrong. I tried too hard to please everybody who came to look me over, and all I did was drive people away. Then one day the head of the orphanage told me a family was going to come and take me home with them. I was so excited, I jumped up and down and cried. The matron reminded me that I was on trial and that it might not be a permanent arrangement. But I just knew it would be. So I went with this family and started school in their town – a very happy little girl. And life began to open up for me, just a little.

'But one day, a few months later, I skipped home from school and ran in the front door of the big old house we lived in. No-one was at home, but there in the middle of the front hall was my battered old suitcase with my little coat thrown over it. As I stood there and looked at that suitcase, it slowly dawned on me what it meant . . . they didn't want me. And I hadn't even suspected . . . That happened to me seven times before I was thirteen years old.'[84]

(Taken from *Living Free*, pp 90, 91)

# How Far Can They Go?

## *There is no fear in love*
### 1 John 4:18

Decisions, decisions, decisions. Fear, fear, fear. This is the world of the teenager's parent. You have never travelled this way before. How are you supposed to know the answers to these questions that crowd in on you every day? Where does trust end and parental irresponsibility begin? This underlying uncertainty and parental panic is one of the chief causes of conflict at the teenage stage. To love appropriately sometimes demands difficult decisions. It sometimes requires unpopular restrictions. Unless you are secure in yourself and in the Lord, you will find yourself torn in shreds emotionally, an insecurity that will express itself in the nagging syndrome teenagers so dread.

Teenagers can behave in a brash, insensitive way which is often a mask camouflaging insecurities and uncertainties. It is easy to believe that we have a duty to point out weaknesses. But in doing so, we often magnify the failure that already plagues the teenager. Your son or daughter longs for affirmation and affection instead of criticism so try to reflect back all that is of worth in them. This will encourage them to press on towards personal growth and it will also increase their respect for you. Life will not be friction-free because a certain amount of friction is inevitable in family life. But where the pervading atmosphere is affirmative and affectionate love, friction can be liberating.

(Taken from Creative Conflict pp 95, 99)

# Friends Across the Generations

*Wherever you go I shall go,*
*wherever you live I shall live.*
*Your people will be my people*
*and your God will be my God*
Ruth 1:16

Young people can be impetuous and unrealistic in their expectations. The fortunate ones are prepared to hear the opinions of others, and ready to weigh the advice of parents and concede that it might contain a glimmer of the truth. I am not suggesting that young people have to accept all the advice they are given. But relationships are strengthened when they are generous enough to ventilate plans and choices with those who have watched development for a good number of years. One young wife told me that she sometimes asks her husband's mother for advice even when she doesn't need it. It gives her mother-in-law a feeling of being wanted and deepens their friendship.

Most parents enjoy and secretly hope for friendship with their adult children. Friendship includes letting another in on some of your plans about the present and the future, and love produces more love.

(Taken from Two into One, p 107)

# Mother and Son

*Jesus said to his mother 'Woman, this is your son.' Then to the disciple he said 'This is your mother'*
John 19:26

The concern and love of Jesus for his mother knew no limits. We see this truth supremely illustrated at Calvary. While he hangs on the cross, dying a criminal's death, his heart goes out to his watching mother. Laying aside his own anguish and need, he recognizes her need for support and companionship as she faces the sting of bereavement and he supplies this need by giving her his closest friend, John. It is John who records how, with great tenderness, Jesus demonstrates to Mary that he understands the bitter pain which fills her heart and mind and shows her that he wants to alleviate her loneliness by making available to her someone who would stand by her in her darkest hour.

We honour our parents and we show them that we love them. And we do this most effectively by recognizing what their needs really are and by being prepared to meet those needs lovingly, generously and at cost to ourselves.

(Taken from Marriage Matters, pp 27, 28)

# Love One Another

*Father, if I become angry, do not let my anger
lead me into sin; do not let me use harmful
words, but words that build up and do good
to those who hear me; and do not let me make
your Holy Spirit sad. Help me to get rid of all
bitterness and hate; help me to be kind and
tender-hearted; and help me to forgive, as
you have forgiven me through Christ.*
Based on *Ephesians* 4:26, 29–32

An elderly, hard-bitten man once described his tangled
relationship with his daughter-in-law. He spoke of her
with venom and the hatred of years. Some months later,
his tone of voice had changed when he mentioned her. He seemed
softer, almost loving. When I asked what had brought about his
change of heart, he invited me to inspect the rose-bed she had
weeded for him while he was bed-ridden. He waved his hand in
the direction of the windows she had cleaned and showed me the
tray, tastefully prepared for his afternoon tea. It was true that
their views about almost everything clashed. But now there was
an understanding between them. They no longer fought each other.
They were 'for' each other.

Like the legendary mouse who gnawed away at the ropes which
bound a man until the frayed edges snapped, this woman learned
that persistent love really works. Love is patience personified. It is
kindness incarnated in the middle of strife. It is shown by a person
who never gives up working towards reconciliation. As Christians,
we are to love each other like that.

(Taken from Two into One, p 104)

# Blaming God

*The Almighty has made my life very bitter.
I went away full, but the Lord has brought
me back empty . . . The Lord has afflicted
me; the Almighty has brought misfortune*
**upon me**
Ruth 1:20,21

Naomi was a woman who had lost everything: her home, her
possessions, her husband and her sons. She blamed God
for marring her life.

The Bible gives no hint that God rebuked Naomi for blaming
him in this way. On the contrary, he gives Naomi a treasure in the
form of her daughter-in-law, Ruth. Ruth refused to abandon her
embittered, bereaved, needy mother-in-law. Instead, she brought to
Naomi the steadfastness of God's persistent love: 'Don't urge me to
leave you or to turn back from you. Where you go I will go, and
where you stay I will stay. Your people will be my people and your
God my God. Where you die I will die, and there I will be buried.
May the Lord deal with me, be it ever so severely, if anything but
death separates you and me' (Ruth 1:16–17).

As the story unfolds it becomes clear that God's love for Naomi is
constant. Creative. He loves her through Ruth and gradually melts
her hardness. And by the end of the book, there are smiles all
round as the women of Bethlehem celebrate the arrival of Naomi's
grand-child, the son of Ruth and her new husband, Boaz. As the
curtain falls, we catch a glimpse of the most touching scene of all:
'And Naomi took the child to her own bosom and she became his
nurse' (4:16, JB).

(Taken from The Smile of Love, pp 31, 32)

# Sensitive Giving

### *Let me give you*
Ruth 2:8

Boaz said to Ruth, 'Let me give you some advice. Don't pick up corn anywhere except in this field. Work with the women here; watch them to see where they are reaping and stay with them. I have ordered my men not to molest you. And whenever you are thirsty, go and drink from the water jars that they have filled' . . . At meal-time Boaz said to Ruth, 'Come and have a piece of bread, and dip it in the sauce.' So she . . . ate until she was satisfied, and she still had some food left over.

To his workers, Boaz said: 'Let her pick (the corn) up even where the bundles are lying, and don't say anything to stop her. Besides that, pull out some corn from the bundles and leave it for her to pick up.' (Ruth 2:8,9,14,15)

Boaz, shows us how to enjoy life while supporting those God brings across our path.

Ruth and her mother-in-law Naomi were not homeless but they were living below the poverty line. They never knew where their next meal was coming from. Naomi therefore encouraged her widowed daughter-in-law to go to the fields at harvest-time and to glean whatever she could. And Boaz, the wealthy landowner, spotted and supported her. The result of this sensitive giving was that both Ruth and Naomi had more than enough to eat and they overflowed with thanksgiving that their needs had been met.

At the same time, we see how Boaz enjoyed the harvest feast. He knew how to celebrate and to sacrifice, how to throw a party and how to stay sensitively alongside those in need.

(Taken from New Daylight, Sept–Dec 1990, p 42)

# Rejoice With Those Who Rejoice

*Your hearts will rejoice and no-one will take your joy from you*
John 16:22

Louis Evely tells us that the inability to receive joy is a universal problem; though Jesus made us depositaries of his joy and though Christianity is a religion of joy and though God has filled his world with joy, Christian people have not yet learned to cherish this priceless gift. We are much more inclined to mourn with Christ than to rejoice with him. We are better disposed to be sorrowful with Christ and to share his sufferings than his joy.[85]

After the crucifixion, a few faithful friends lingered at the foot of Christ's cross. But on the morning of the resurrection, no one was present to witness him bursting the bonds of death or to watch while the angels rolled the stone away. Consequently part of Jesus' post-resurrection task was to convert each of his friends so that they could receive the reality of his joy. But he had to take them by the hand, one by one, and teach them how to receive his joy.

(Taken from Listening to Others, p 242)

# Rejoice With Those Who Rejoice

*Rejoice in the Lord always, again I say rejoice*
Philippians 4:4

Before I can hope to receive joy from another, I must be stripped of my preoccupation with self, be prepared to let go of those things on which my security seems to depend and abandon myself afresh to God. I'll never be able to receive joy with genuineness while another's good news seems to threaten my security![86]

I remember the occasion when a close friend of mine announced her engagement. She had talked to me at length about her relationship with the young man she was in love with. And through these conversations our closeness with each other had deepened. But when, eventually, she made her commitment to her husband-to-be, I realised that the dynamics of our relationship would need to change. I would have to step back. In time, after she married, I would lose her because she would move away from our area. And because her joy threatened my security, though I made all the right happy noises about being glad for her and though I congratulated him, I had not received their joy with the care I would have received their pain if they had announced that they were separating.

(Taken from Listening to Others, p 243)

# A High-Risk Proposition

*An unmarried man can devote himself to*
*the Lord's affairs, all he need worry about*
*is pleasing the Lord . . . In the same way*
*an unmarried woman, like a young girl, can*
*devote herself to the Lord's affairs; all she*
*need worry about is being holy in body and*
*spirit*
1 Corinthians 7:32,34

'I really want to marry. But if it's better for the kingdom of God, I will stay single.' The young man who said this is an eligible bachelor already much used by God. It sums up the conflict felt by many Christians. Should I marry? Or can I be of greater service to God if I remain single? Is celibacy a higher calling than marriage?

St Paul certainly accentuates the advantages of singleness. He reminds us that the unmarried person enjoys freedoms which are denied to married people.

However, celibacy is not a higher calling than marriage. Rather, it is different. Single people are not necessarily more useful to God than married people. They bear fruit in different ways, achieve wholeness in different ways and learn the art of selflessness in different ways. For self-actualization is not to be realized in marriage or in singleness. Its source rests in God.

In order to discern our own call and act upon it, we have to discard all that is not of God. And if we truly seek His will, we find it. But the discovery of His chosen path calls for obedience. It demands sacrifice. Only God knows what we leave behind and what we choose to sacrifice. And only God replenishes the inner joy which makes the choice of a high-risk proposition possible.

(Taken from Growing into Love, pp 18, 25)

# For the Sake
# of the Kingdom

*Although he was the Son, he learnt to obey
through suffering*
Hebrews 5:8

J esus was unafraid to swim against the tide: the cultural norm at the time was for men to marry and he remained single.

But he developed warm and tender relationships with men and women alike. The Gospels lead us to believe that John and Peter, Lazarus, Martha, and others of his friends were really important to Jesus. Jesus shows that a man can be alone, yet emotionally fulfilled; in his state of singleness he can enjoy maturity and wholeness.

It is easy to dismiss this and bleat, 'it was all right for Jesus. He was perfect.' He was. But he learned the obedience of perfection through the things which he suffered (Heb. 5:8). Did this suffering include the mental torment of knowing that some women were drawn to him by the magnetism of erotic love? Did it mean that he suffered the anguish of finding some women attractive, while being denied the opportunity to express these strong feelings? The Gospels do not tell us. I believe that Jesus' life, was as much a potential collision course as our own, that he confronted such temptations head-on. But he never sinned.

(Taken from Just Good Friends, pp 38, 39)

# Single Blessedness?

*About remaining celibate, I have no directions*
*from the Lord, but give my own opinion as*
*one who, by the Lord's mercy has stayed*
*faithful*
1 Corinthians 7:25

Some single people long for marriage, not just for the companionship – though that is an important consideration – but for status. Despite the clamour of feminists in recent years, there is still a supposed stigma attached to the single state. Marriage appears to provide a higher status. But for the Christian, status is something to be relinquished. Our goal in all things should be to obey God, whom our souls love, and to follow the path which he unfolds for us. If this path leads to marriage, that is our highest vocation. If it is singleness, this is the calling which will lead us most directly to himself, the source of joy.

When parental pressure is exerted, this obedience to God needs to be recalled. Parents, friends and relatives perpetuate the myth that the only road to fulfilment leads through marriage. This is not the truth. Many fulfilled, joyous and fruitful Christian people demonstrate the falsity of this claim. It is possible to love deeply and to be loved in return without being married.

Marriage is not the best way of life for everyone – but the way of self-giving love is.

(Taken from Growing into Love pp 53, 26)

# Who Walk Alone

## *We are poor but make many rich*
### 2 Corinthians 6:10

The unattached person enjoys complete freedom of movement, freedom of choice, freedom of friends. But, as Margaret Evening warns, 'there can be so much freedom in the single life . . . that one has to guard against selfishness.'[87] In her classic *Who Walk Alone* she enlarges on this. 'One extremely cold winter's afternoon, I lit a roaring fire, put my feet up and settled back for a cosy afternoon with a box of chocolates and a novel, *The Dean's Watch* by Elizabeth Goudge. I read of Mary Montague who was crippled by a fall as a child.

With no prospects of a career or marriage it seemed that she was doomed to life-long boredom, but then in a moment of awakening, it dawned upon her that *loving* could be a vocation in itself, a life work. It could be a career, like marriage or nursing, or going on stage. Loving could be an adventure. Firstly, she accepted the vocation and took a vow to love.

God spoke to me through Mary Montague that afternoon . . . I put the novel on one side . . . and went to fetch a young colleague who lived in a dingy bed-sit. I found her huddled over the one bar of a totally inadequate electric fire, still wearing the anorak that she had put on that morning whilst the room 'warmed up'. She came home with me and together we toasted our toes in front of the fire and talked into the night. For both of us there was far more warmth in that weekend than came from the fire blazing in the hearth.'[88]

(Taken from Growing into Love, p 19 and Just Good Friends pp 136, 137)

# Trust in God

*Jesus took the loaves, and when he had given*
*thanks he distributed them*
John 6:11

George Müller's concern for destitute children in the West of England prompted him to found orphanages there in the early years of the nineteenth century.

The homes were run on a shoe-string budget but George Müller had resolved never to purchase anything unless cash was available. One day to his horror he realised that no money meant no bread for his three hundred orphans. That night, instead of going to bed, he stayed awake to pray. He reminded God that these were *his* orphans; that he had declared himself the Father of the fatherless; that this work was *his* work and that the honour of his name was at stake. He begged God to prove afresh his faithfulness.

Next morning he came down to the refectory to find that the tables were laid as usual but the bread-plates were empty. Nevertheless, watched by three hundred hungry-eyed children, he said grace thanking God for the food they were about to receive. The children were about to sit down to face a row of empty plates when the sound of cart-wheels on the gravel drive drew every eye to the window. This noise heralded the arrival of the local baker who had felt compelled that night to bake an extra batch of loaves and to bring them as a gift to 'Mr Müller's children' before he began his morning rounds. The cart was unloaded, the hungry children were fed, and trust soared in George Müller's never-failing God.

(Taken from Listening to Others, p 76)

# Use Me, Lord

*The peace of God which passes all understanding will keep your hearts and your minds in Christ Jesus*
Philippians 4:7

P ray the prayer of St Francis, aware that God is attentive to you and indwelling you.

Lord, make me an instrument of your peace.
Where there is hatred, let me sow love,
Where there is injury, pardon,
Where there is doubt, faith,
Where there is despair, hope,
Where there is darkness, light,
Where there is sadness, joy.

O Divine Master, grant that I may not so much seek
to be consoled as to console,
not so much to be understood as to understand,
not so much to be loved, as to love;
for it is in giving that we receive,
it is in pardoning that we are pardoned,
it is in dying that we awake to eternal life.

(Taken from The Smile of Love, p 60)

# God's Tender Love

## *I will lead her into the desert and speak to her heart*
### Hosea 2:16

G od's love, is not so much a feeling as a never-ending series of positive, constructive, creative actions whose purpose is to promote our long-term well-being. That is not to say that God never feels warm towards us. He does. His love, as portrayed in the Bible, is as tender as the love of a good mother, as persistent as the love of a faithful father, as passionate as the love of a bridegroom for his bride, as committed as the love of one who has taken solemn vows and meant them. His love is patient and kind, long-suffering and forgiving and, though undeserved, God's love never gives up.

(Taken from The Smile of Love, p 27)

# Grace and Love

*He did not spare his own Son, but gave him*
*up for us all*
Romans 8:32

God could quite easily just have abandoned us to our fate. He could have left us alone to reap the fruit of our wrongdoing and to perish in our sins. It is what we deserved. But he did not. Because he loved us, he came after us in Christ. He pursued us even to the desolate anguish of the cross, where he bore our sin, guilt, judgement and death. It takes a hard and stony heart to remain unmoved by love like that. It is more than love. Its proper name is 'grace', which is love to the undeserving.[89]

(Taken from The Smile of Love, p 119)

# Infinite Love

*God shows his love for us in that while we were yet sinners Christ died for us*
**Romans 5:8**

I find that, while watching parents with their children, I often catch glimpses of the kind of love God offers us.

I think of an occasion when I was attending a conference under canvas. One evening, as the sun was setting behind the pine trees and a breeze blew into the tent where we were meeting, we all began to shiver. The small group of which I was a part was being led by a young couple whose little girl had tired of the creche and come to join us. She shivered too. But she knew where to go — to her mother. I watched her climb onto her mother's knee, snuggle into her mother's arms and smile as she felt herself wrapped round in the big, blue cardigan which her mother was wearing.

A few minutes later, tell-tale sounds and facial expressions betrayed the fact that she was dirtying her nappy. What would her mother do? Scold her? Remove her from the tent? Tell her she was 'a dirty girl'?

The mother did none of these things. She continued to hold her daughter tight as though she smelt of the most fragrant baby powder. So the little face peeping from the big, blue cardigan quickly regained its contented smile.

God's love is like that — only more so.

# God's Glorious Love

*Yes, you are my rock and my fortress*
Psalm 31:3

Find in me your true and lasting peace . . .
I am a secure anchor for you, a safe harbour.
I am an overhanging rock beneath which you can shelter.

I am the one who runs to pick you up when you fall.
My arms embrace you to give you comfort and hope.
Trust yourself to me.

Let me kiss your hand as a mother kisses her wounded child.
Let me speak words of endearment to soothe you and words of encouragement
to set you on your feet.

I will do this for you because my love is purer than any mother's love. Were you afraid to tell your mother of your secret woes? Don't be afraid of me. I know the depths of your heart already. Is there anything in you that I don't know? My word is the truth: I love you.

Therefore be joyful in my love whatever befalls you. My glorious love is the foundation of the earth.[90]

(Taken from The Smile of Love, pp 114, 115)

# Endless Love

*The steadfast love of the Lord is forever
and ever*
Psalm 103:17

When we fall he holds us lovingly, and graciously and swiftly raises us.[91]

Though we sin continually he loves us endlessly, and so gently does he show us our sin that we repent of it quietly, turning our mind to the contemplation of his mercy, clinging to his love and goodness, knowing that he is our cure, understanding that we do nothing but sin.

If there be anywhere on earth a lover of God who is always kept safe from falling, I know nothing of it – for it was not shown me. But this was shown: that in falling and rising again we are always held close in our love.[92]

(Taken from The Smile of Love, p 126)

# Completely Yours

*For the son of God, Jesus Christ . . . was not*
*yes and no. But in him it is always yes*
2 Corinthians 1:19

Since he is wise he loves you with wisdom.
Since he is good he loves you with goodness.
Since he is holy he loves you with holiness.
Since he is just he loves you with justice.
Since he is merciful he loves you with mercy.
Since he is compassionate and understanding
  he loves you with gentleness and sweetness.

He loves you with the greatest humility and the deepest respect . . .
He joyfully reveals his face to you, saying to you, 'I am yours,
completely yours. And my happiness is to be who I am so that I
may give myself to you and be all yours.'

(Taken from The Smile of Love, p 124)

# Devoted Love

*Nothing in all creation can separate us from the love of God in Christ Jesus our Lord*
**Romans 8:39**

Be absolutely certain that our Lord loves you, devotedly and individually; loves you just as you are. How often is this conviction lacking even in those souls most devoted to God. How little they realise that God loves them incomparably more than they will ever know how to love him. Think only of this and say to yourself, 'I am loved by God more than I can either conceive or understand'. Let this fill your soul and prayer and never leave you. It contains the whole of St John's teaching. 'As for us, we have believed in the love which God has for us.' Give yourself up with joy to a loving confidence in God and have courage to believe firmly that God's action towards you is a masterpiece of partiality and love . . .

Remember that it is our souls which are his joy, not on account of what we do for him, but on account of what he does for us. All he asks of us is to accept his kindness, generosity, tolerance and fatherly love.[93]

# Enfolded in Love

*The Lord set his heart on you and chose you*
**Deuteronomy 7:7**

God is everything that is good.
He is our clothing. In his love he wraps and holds us.
He enfolds us for love, and he will never let us go.[94]

As the body is clad in clothes, and the flesh in skin, and the bones in flesh, and the heart in the whole, so are we clothed, body and soul, in the goodness of God and enfolded in it.[95]

From him we come, in him we are enfolded, to him we return.

And he showed me more, a little thing, the size of a hazel-nut, on the palm of my hand, round like a ball. I looked at it thoughtfully and wondered, 'What is this?' And the answer came, 'It is all that is made.' I marvelled that it continued to exist and did not suddenly disintegrate; it was so small. And again my mind supplied the answer, 'It exists, both now and for ever, because God loves it.' In short, everything owes its existence to the love of God.[96]

# From Love to Love

*God saw all he had made and indeed it was*
*very good*
Genesis 1:31

Lord my God,
    when your love spilled over into creation
    You thought of me.
I am from love
  of love
    for love.
Let my heart, O God, always recognise, cherish and enjoy
Your goodness in all of creation . . .
Direct all that is in me toward your praise . . .
Energise me in your service.
Lord God, may nothing ever distract me from your love . . .
Neither health nor sickness, wealth or poverty,
    honour nor dishonour, long life or short.
May I never seek nor choose to be other than you intend
    or wish.[97]

# Does He Love Me?

*The Lord your God will be true to the*
*covenant . . . he will love you and bless you*
**Deuteronomy 7:12,13**

We have invented a religion of sadness and fear. Invariably we create a God in our image. Because we do not love him very much, we are led to think that he does not love us much. Because we do not worry much about him, we imagine that he does not worry very much about us. Because we are not very happy with him, we conclude that he is not very happy with us.

But the whole of revelation protests. Revelation teaches us that God is not like us, that we should not consult how we feel towards him in order to know how he feels towards us, that God is good even if we are bad, that God loves us even if we do not love him, that God loved us first.[98]

# Identikit God

### *If God is for us, who is against us?*
### Romans 8:31

When we pray we have in our minds and imagination, however faintly, 'an identikit image of God'99 which we have formed from infancy onwards. The biggest piece of this jigsaw was handed to us by our father – not through the words he said but through the person he was. Our mother's personality contributed another major piece of the picture. Sunday School teachers (if we had them), teachers, youth group leaders, the mass media and preachers have all contributed other parts of the picture. And for some people that is bad news because it has given them the impression that God, like a punitive policeman, drives behind them on the motorway of life, captures on video every mistake they make and pulls them off the road to punish them for the most minor offence.

The origins of this picture can sometimes be traced back to seemingly godly parents who teach their children about God, take them to church and Sunday School and pray with them, but fail to embody Christ's love to them: the forgiving, unconditional, compassionate love which Paul describes in Ephesians 5:22 ff: the love which is patient and kind, protective and trusting, positive and persevering; the love which shuns rudeness, the keeping of scores, selfishness and envy (1 Cor. 13:4–7).

(Taken from The Smile of Love, pp 141, 142)

# Disappointed in God

## *We had hoped that he was the one to redeem Israel*
Luke 24:21

A person who perceives God as a policeman is unlikely to fall at his feet in 'wonder, love and praise'. And the person who believes that God has let him down may well scoff at the concept of God as love.

J.B. Phillips, the translator of the New Testament, describes their problem powerfully:

'Here,' such people say, resentfully and usually with more than a trace of self-pity, 'is One whom I trusted, but He *let me down*.' The rest of their lives is consequently shadowed by this let-down . . . Some . . . rather enjoy this never-failing well of grievance. The years by no means dim the tragic details of the Prayer that was Unanswered or the Disaster that was Undeserved. To recall God's unfaithfulness appears to give them the same ghoulish pleasure that others find in recounting the grisly details of their 'operation'.[100]

I understand why some people believe God to be a very disappointing God – But is he?

We need not be trapped for ever in the web of our distorted view. One way out is to welcome the realisation that we may be wrong. This is a moment of grace.

(Taken from The Smile of Love, pp 145, 146, 147, 148)

# Sugar Daddy God

*You must love the Lord your God with all
your heart and with all your soul*
**Deuteronomy 6:5**

The 'Me Generation' have produced a Sugar Daddy God. As Jim Packer points out, those who worship him reduce

. . . 'religion to magic, treating the God who made us as if he were Jeeves to our Bertie Wooster, or the genie of the lamp to our Aladdin . . . It involves the idea that God's promises are like magicians' spells: use them correctly and you can extract from God any legitimate pleasant thing you wish . . . Petitionary prayer is perceived as a technique for making God dance to your tune and do your bidding . . . Prayer as our way of managing and directing God's energies is never far from its heart. Bad!'[101]

One reason why this is 'bad' is that while the person who worships this Sugar Daddy god is succeeding in bending their god's will to meet their own needs, their hearts are full of love for him and their mouths full of praise. When, on the other hand, he appears not to have heard their request, or worse, refuses to give them their heart's desire, then their life falls apart and their faith in a good God dies.

(Taken from The Smile of Love, p 149)

# Spoil-Sport God

*How can I give you up . . . ?*
*How can I hand you over . . . ?*
*All my compassion is aroused . . .*
*For I am God, and not man —*
*the Holy One among you.*
*I will not come in wrath.*
Hosea 11:8–9

The spoil-sport god is not the God of the Bible. He is the figment of the imagination of our own conscience and the product of certain preachers who preach from their own over-active, misguided conscience rather than from the Word of God.

But this god lives on in the hearts and the imaginations of many people both in and out of our churches. It is very unlikely that such people will be moved to look into the face of God lest they see, not a smile, but a scowl of disapproval.

God is in love with his people. He commits himself to them in love. Nothing can quench this love, even though, as Charles Elliott puts it, his loved ones play fast and loose: 'Like an accomplished flirt, they play at a relationship they don't mean, and never give a thought to the damage they do to the victim of their flirtation.'[102]

If God had been a punitive policeman, he would have annihilated his people. Instead we hear his anguished cry through Hosea

(Taken from The Smile of Love, pp 140, 141)

# Other-Worldly God

### *Eat your bread with joy drink your wine with a glad heart*
Ecclesiastes 9:7

Countless Christians equate God with their conscience and, in doing so, consider him to be a kill-joy. Delia Smith describes this so-called god well:

He is the other-worldly one, bent on stifling human life, dead against pleasure or achievement: sensual pleasure is taboo, sexual pleasure not to be thought of. Eating is all right, so long as you don't enjoy the food too much; alcohol forbidden under any circumstances. He is not at all happy with success or creativity . . . The life-stifling god is at odds with human intellectual powers: he would suppress all science, philosophy, theology . . . 'Keep 'em down' is his motto: if they get a chance to enjoy and achieve too much they will get out of hand.[103]

That god is the antithesis of the God of the Old Testament, the image of the incarnate God we see in Christ, and the teaching of the apostles. *This* God gives us all things richly to *enjoy* as well as to share (1 Timothy 6:17). *This* God is scorned for enjoying himself too much – even accused of being a 'glutton and a drunkard'! (Matthew 11:19). *This* God delights in giving good gifts: 'Everything that lives and moves will be food for you.' (Genesis 9:3). *This* God created men and women for the unique joy of sexual oneness in marriage (Genesis 2:24)

(Taken from The Smile of Love, p 140)

# The Smile of Jesus

## *Let the little children come to me*
### Matthew 19:13,14

If we are ever tempted to believe that God does not smile, we need only look at Jesus. He came, among other things, to show us what his Father is like. And, although the word 'smile' is not used specifically of Jesus' interaction with people, there are many times when his smile is self-evident.

Is it conceivable, for example, that there was no smile on Jesus' face when the mothers brought their little children to him, requesting that he would lay hands on them and bless them? I think not. Surely, his face would have been wreathed in smiles as he held out his arms, inviting the children to cluster round him with his welcoming words, 'Let the little children come to me' (Matt. 19:13,14).

Or is it remotely possible that he would have ministered to Simon's mother-in-law without a smile? Surely, as he visited her bedside, took her hand, felt the fever leave her and helped her up from bed, there would have been smiles and laughter on his face and hers? That house must have been full of joy as she prepared lunch for them (Mark 1:29–31).

And I sometimes wonder whether it was the warmth which danced in his eyes and shone through his smile when 'the woman of ill repute' anointed him and kissed him in the house of Simon the Pharisee, which gave rise to Simon's silent scorn: 'If this man were a prophet, he would know who this woman is that is touching him and what a bad name she has' (Luke 7:39, JB).

(Taken from The Smile of Love, pp 40, 41)

# Preparing for Harvest

*Cain brought some of his harvest and gave it as an offering to the Lord. Then Abel brought the first lamb born to one of his sheep, killed it, and gave the best parts of it as an offering. The Lord was pleased with Abel and his offering, but he rejected Cain and his offering*
**Genesis 4:3,4**

'Harvest Thanksgiving? What's that?' Some Christians in Singapore once asked me those questions when I mentioned to them our custom of celebrating God's goodness at harvest-time. Why *do* we have Harvest suppers and Harvest services? Where does the practice spring from? Are such celebrations still relevant in today's world? If so, what gifts please God?

In Genesis 4 we can learn what kind of attitude and gift brings God pleasure and what kind of gift brings him only pain.

'Cain brought *some* of his harvest' – imagine him finding a few left-overs – and deciding to take these to the service of thanksgiving. Then picture Abel holding and cherishing his new-born lamb.

Abel's gift brought God great joy while Cain's gift brought only disappointment and sorrow. Abel's gift was a love-gift; a sign that Abel's life revolved around God not himself, while Cain's gift was brought out of duty and not gratitude – it showed that Cain's life revolved, not around God but around Cain.

(Taken from Bible Reading Fellowship notes, Sept-Dec 90, pp 39, 40)

# The Smile of Love

*How often would I have gathered your*
*children together as a hen gathers her*
*chickens under her wings*
Luke 13:34

God wants us to be re-energised by his love – particularly in those times when we feel most defeated and most discouraged.

Mike Mitton, the Director of Anglican Renewal Ministries, tells of an occasion when God seemed to underline this for him. He was on retreat at the time and, just before lunch one day, he went for a brief walk. As he approached a stile he heard God say, 'Don't go on. Turn back to the gate behind you. I have something to show you.'

Protesting, because he did not want to be late for lunch, Mike obeyed.

Near the gate he saw a rabbit nibbling the grass contentedly – until it picked up the scent of a human. Whereupon it kicked up its back legs in fright and scampered into the woods.

'Why did it scamper off like that?' God asked Mike.

'I don't know, Lord . . . I suppose it thought I was going to harm it,' Mike replied.

'Were you?' God asked.

'Of course not, Lord.' Mike was indignant. 'How could I harm such an innocent creature?'

'Mike, do you realise you're sometimes like that rabbit? You scamper away from me as though I would harm you if you came close. But I love you. I bear you no malice. I will never hurt you.'

(Taken from The Smile of Love, pp 144, 145)

# Hound of Heaven

*If I take the wings of the morning and dwell in the utter most parts of the sea, even there thy hand shall lead me and thy right hand shall hold me*
Psalm 139:9,10

God has his own way of breaking through. Francis Thompson's poem, *The Hound of Heaven*, reminds us of this glad fact:

I fled Him, down the nights and down the days;
I fled Him, down the arches of the years;
I fled Him, down the labyrinthine ways
of my own mind, and in the mist of tears
I hid from Him . . .
From those strong Feet that followed, followed after.[104]

The hound of heaven pursues gently, sensitively, persistently, and he conquers.

# Know, Love and Serve God

*May the Lord bless you and keep you;*
*May he let his face shine on you and be*
*gracious to you;*
*May he show you his face and bring you*
*peace*
**Numbers 6:24–26**

God created us so that we might know, love, serve and
worship him in this life and enjoy oneness with him for
ever. God's purpose in creating us was to draw from us a
response of love to his love outpoured. Every man, woman and child
was therefore created capable of worshipping God. As the Scottish
Catechism puts it: 'I was created in order to worship God and to
enjoy him for ever.'

*O Lord, lift up the light of your countenance upon us*
*that in thy light we may see light;*
*the light of self-knowledge*
*whereby we may repent;*
*the light of faith*
*whereby to choose your will;*
*the light of guidance*
*whereby we may advance;*
*the light of grace*
*whereby we may attain;*
*the light of glory*
*which shines more and more pointing toward the perfect day*
*and towards you, the very Light of Light;*
*who lives and reigns in the brightness of*
*the holy and undivided Trinity*
*blessed for ever and ever.* 105

# On the Road to Perfection

*You must be perfect as your heavenly father is perfect*
Matthew 5:48

The God of the Gospels wants us to be perfect and he has given us a framework for living: 'Love the Lord your God with all your heart and with all your soul and with all your mind . . . Love your neighbour as yourself' (Matt. 22:37–38). But perfection, Christ-likeness, is the goal towards which we travel: it is not an existence any of us will enjoy this side of eternity. We need God's love to give us the strength and the courage to journey on as we 'fall and get up, fall and get up, fall and get up again.'[106]

God wants us to be re-energised by his love – particularly in those times when we feel most defeated and most discouraged.

(Taken from The Smile of Love, p 144)

# Enduring Love

*Give thanks to the Lord, for he is good.*
**Psalm 136:1**

*H*is *love endures for ever . . .*
    to him who alone does great wonders,
       *His love endures for ever.*
who by his understanding made the heavens,
    *His love endures for ever.*
who spread out the earth upon the waters,
    *His love endures for ever.*
who made the great lights –
    *His love endures for ever.*
the sun to govern the day,
    *His love endures for ever.*
the moon and stars to govern the night;
    *His love endures for ever . . .*
to the One who remembered us in our low estate
    *His love endures for ever.*
and freed us from our enemies,
    *His love endures for ever.*
and who gives food to every creature.
    *His love endures for ever.*
Give thanks to the God of heaven.
    *His love endures for ever.*
Psalm 136:4–9; 23–26

I am from love, of love, for love.
Lord God, may nothing distract me from that love.

# Love Without Beginning

*He [the Father] chose us in him [Christ]*
*before the creation of the world . . .*
*In love he predestined us to be adopted as his*
*sons through Jesus Christ . . .*
Ephesians 1:4,5

The love of God is eternal, having an absolute beginning in the Father, outside of time, which reaches back into the character of God as Trinity. It was in that beginning that God loved us — before we existed, before the universe was made. It was then that he predestined us and called us.

So our praise to God does not spring simply from what he has done for us in his Son. The work of Jesus restored and completed what God the Father had begun in creation — to make humans in his image and likeness.

Our worship of God focuses on what he determined to do before the world began.[107]

(Taken from the Smile of Love, p 115)

# No Abiding City

### *In this world you will have trouble*
John 16:33

The God of the Bible does not hand out to his followers insurance policies which guarantee them immunity from life's disasters. We see in Jesus how God copes with the traumas of life as we see him threatened in his own home-town of Nazareth (Luke 4:29); bereaved when his cousin, John the Baptist, was brutally murdered; despised for befriending prostitutes and tax-collectors; criticised for his teaching; sold by one of his disciples; and then murdered himself. In this world he encountered a great deal of trouble. What he never lost, except for that agonising moment on the Cross, was the sense of the Father's presence sustaining him through it all. And that is what he promises us: 'In me you may have peace' (John 16:33). Peace: that strange sense of well-being he can give which defies circumstances and keeps us sane in the middle of the storm.

(Taken from The Smile of Love, pp 148, 149)

# Channels of God

*Having this ministry by the mercy of God we do not lose heart*
2 Corinthians 4:1

Hurting people crave a touch of divine love, wisdom or healing through God's human agents.

Would-be helpers need to learn the art of listening to God because none of us has within ourselves the divine love which penetrates and communicates, which heals and consoles or challenges and confronts. But God will add these resources to us. And he will do it while we creep into him ourselves, make a deliberate attempt to lay on one side our preoccupation with our own needs and insecurities, fears and unresolved tensions and he will add to us sufficient resources to stay alongside broken people. Without this love much of the time we spend with hurting people may well be wasted.

It is in listening to God that we receive forgiveness and cleansing for the sin which would otherwise block us from being effective channels of God's power and holding, healing love.

(Taken from Listening to Others, pp 236, 237)

# Safe Forever

*He will feed his flock like a shepherd,*
*he will gather the lambs in his arms,*
*he will carry them in his bosom,*
*and gently lead those that are with young*
Isaiah 40:11

Father,
  You love me,
    not in some aloof, impersonal way,
but with the cherishing love a mother pours on her child;
with the adoring love a good father delights
to give his first-born.
with the disciplining love good parents give their children;
with the protecting love shepherds' shower on their lambs.
Your love for me now
is gift-love.
Faithful,
committed,
unchanging,
inextinguishable.
Grant me the grace to experience that love here on earth
even though on that glorious day when I see you face to face
I shall experience it in even richer measure;
and be eclipsed by it
for all eternity.

(Taken from The Smile of Love, p 108)

# The Good Shepherd

*The Lord is my shepherd, I shall not want.*
*He makes me lie down in green pastures,*
*he leads me beside quiet waters,*
*he restores my soul.*
*He guides me in paths of righteousness*
*for his name's sake.*
*Even though I walk*
*through the valley of the shadow of death,*
*I fear no evil, for you are with me;*
*your rod and your staff, they comfort me*
Psalm 23:1–4

The picture of the Good Shepherd is of a man who expresses his faithfulness through his availability: 'he leads me, restores me, is with me.' The Good Shepherd is one who involves himself in the life of his flock: he gathers the lambs together, carries them, leads the ewes with gentleness. The Good Shepherd is a dedicated person: he searches for the lost, heals the sick, bandages the wounded. Communication between sheep and shepherd seemed a two-way affair: the helpless sheep looked to the shepherd for guidance, wisdom and direction. These resources were given constantly. The relationship which grew between a sheep and his shepherd was one of intimacy.

Not only does Jesus *imply* that, as the Good Shepherd, he will communicate with his flock. He *promises* that the Holy Spirit will be a talking, teaching, acting agent of God whose mission will be to show us the truth by transmitting God's messages and to further lead us into the truth by revealing to us 'what is yet to come'.

(Taken from Listening to God, pp 80, 81)

# Knowing the Sheep

*[The Sovereign Lord] tends his flock like a*
*shepherd; he gathers the lambs in his arms*
*and carries them close to his heart; he gently*
*leads those that have young*
Isaiah 40:11

On a visit to Israel, my husband and I wandered out of Nazareth and met a youth carrying a new-born lamb, a shepherd boy.

He showed us his lamb with obvious pride. 'It's mine. It's not quite twenty-four hours old.' He also pointed to the other sheep grazing peacefully in the long grass. This boy was in charge of seventeen sheep including the baby lamb. Each sheep had a name. Each responded to that name. When the shepherd called, they followed. His relationship with these sheep, which belonged to his father, was intimate. He treated them not as possessions, but as persons. So he whisperd in the lamb's woolly ear in the same way as a mother would coo over her baby. He told his little flock his news as they walked from pasture to pasture. He chided them when they wandered away from him or when they strayed near a dangerous precipice. And as they walked home in the evening, he explained to them what was happening and told them of his plans for the next day

In the east you never see sheep without an accompanying shepherd. At home it's the exact opposite. You scarcely ever see a shepherd, just fields full of unaccompanied sheep.

(Taken from Listening to God, pp 79, 80)

# God in All

*Holy, holy, holy is the Lord God of hosts*
Isaiah 6:3

Father
Holy
Revered
Mysterious is your Name
May all my contacts and relationships
My struggles and temptations
My thoughts, dreams and desires
Be coloured by the loving reverence I have for you.
May your personality be reflected
In my work
In the words of my lips
And in the thoughts which lodge in my mind
So that all I am
And all I do
May become ever more worthy of your holy presence
Living in me.

God be in my head and in my understanding
God be in my eyes and in my looking
God be in my mouth and in my speaking
God be in my tongue and in my tasting
God be in my lips and in my greeting . . .
God be in my ears and in my hearing
God be in my neck and in my humbling . . .
God be in my hands and in my working . . .
God be at my end and at my reviving.

(Taken from Reflections for Lent, pp 37, 27, 28)

# Into the Eye of God

*Desire a better country that is a heavenly one*
Hebrews 11:16

Macrina Wiederkehr's poem reminds us that we are pilgrim people on a journey to God:

For your prayer
   your journey into God,
may you be given a small storm,
   a little hurricane named after you,
persistent enough to get your attention
violent enough to awaken you to new depths
strong enough to shake you to the roots
majestic enough to remind you of your origin:
   made of the earth
   yet steeped in eternity
   frail human dust
   yet soaked with infinity.

You begin your storm under the Eye of God.
A watchful, caring eye gazes in your direction
   as you wrestle with the life force within.

In the midst of these holy winds
In the midst of this divine wrestling
   your storm journey
   like all hurricanes
   leads you into the eye,
Into the Eye of God
   where all is calm and quiet.
A stillness beyond imagining!
Into the Eye of God after the storm
Into the silent, beautiful darkness
Into the Eye of God.[108]

# God of Surprises

*'I am the alpha and the omega' says the Lord God, 'who is, who was and who is to come'*
**Revelation 1:8**

I find prayer exciting because I never know in advance how God is going to meet with me. The Divine Lover sometimes comes as the Father, the one who is saving the best robe for the worst child, the Father who gave his own Son, such is the generosity of his loving. Sometimes my Lord comes as the loving, searching Shepherd, sometimes as life. Sometimes as energy.

My knowledge of God is becoming deeper. It is far less an intellectual knowing and progressing towards the intimate knowing experienced by a husband and wife: union. Sometimes he comes to me as the Bridegroom to his Bride and in that knowing there is such awesome love. As I write that now, it seems too wonderful that Almighty God – the generous one – should meet *me* in that way and yet that is part of his generosity that it is he who takes the initiative.

(Taken from Listening to God, p 69)

# To Pray Like Jesus

### *Say this when you pray: 'Father'*
Luke 11:2

No one had ever prayed like Jesus before because no one in the whole world had ever been conscious, as he was, that God was his Father, that God's love for him was total. When Jesus prayed, he frequently referred to God as 'Abba' – Father, Daddy. Jesus implores his disciples to do the same: to turn childlike, trusting eyes to God and simply to whisper: 'Daddy'.

A good father cherishes his child, provides security, stability, guidance and unconditional love. A good father makes sacrifices for his child. A good father delights in every stage of his child's growth. God is a good father. As Carlo Carretto puts it:

> If God is my father, I can be calm and live in peace;
> I am secure for life, for death, for time and for eternity . . .
> If God is my father, I count for something and in him find
> my own true dignity . . .
> God is God of the universe, even when the earth quakes and
> the rivers overflow, and he is my father, even if my hands get
> frost-bite and an accident makes me a cripple for life.'[109]

Because God is my Father, and because prayer is the place where, consciously, I call him Father, prayer is, supremely, the place where I know myself to be loved and held and met by God. In prayer I am conscious that God the Father comes to me, wipes away my tears, heals my hurts and enfolds me in his love.

(Taken from Reflections for Lent, p 34)

# Pen Pictures

## *No good tree bears bad fruit*
### Luke 6:43

Jesus seems to assume that we will exercise the gift of imagination when seeking to understand his teaching. This is the way we enter most fully and creatively into his pen pictures in Luke 6: figs growing on thorn bushes, grapes growing on briars and good fruit growing on rotten trees. It is possible, of course, to attempt to tease out the reasons why Jesus concocted these strange symbols but that would be a twentieth-century, Western approach to an Eastern style of teaching. Great Eastern teacher that he was, Jesus appealed to the eye gate and the ear gate more powerfully, in some instances, than to the intellect. He did so expecting his hearers to visualise the incongruities he was describing: clusters of grapes dangling from briars instead of adorning the vine; figs bursting from thornbushes rather than ripening on the fig tree. Similarly, he expected his hearers to enter into these parables with all their senses: to smell the yeast, to feel it crumbling in their hands, to see the bread rising (Matt. 13:33). In other words, Jesus recognised that, in the imagination, we have a source of knowledge which puts us in touch with hidden realities and offers us ways of relating to them.

(Taken from Open to God, p 56)

# Open to God

*Behold I stand at the door and knock; and
if anyone hears my voice and opens the door
. . . I will come in . . .*
**Revelation 3.20 RSV**

L et us use our imagination, and open the door of our lives
to Jesus.

Notice, in passing, whether, when we hear his knock, we
throw open the door in welcome or exasperation or gingerly from
reluctance, despair, fear or awe. When we feel we are ready, we invite
him inside. But instead of leaving him standing in the hall, we suggest
that we go on a tour of the house together. Take him into one room
at a time, noticing in passing which rooms we are happy for him to
inspect and which rooms we enter with reluctance or shame. Maybe
we even clutch in our hands the key of a room which we shall keep
firmly locked?

In the rooms we do enter with him, we notice his reaction as he
surveys the decor and the furnishings, the structure and the design.
We notice, too, whether he comments on the atmosphere which
permeates the place. And we remind ourselves that he is the love
which is patient and kind, gentle and anxious that the loved one
always enjoys the best. So at the end of the tour, we sit down with
him to listen carefully to his suggestions.

Then tell him that our home is his home and we invite him, not
only to make the necessary changes to the fabric and atmosphere,
but to invite into the home the guests of his choice. We listen while
he tells us who those people are.[110]

(Taken from Open to God, p 80)

# Listening Prayer

*In his longed for shade I am seated and his*
*fruit is sweet to my taste*
Song of Songs 2:3

On one occasion, while I was praying, a picture of a beautiful oasis rose before my eyes. The water in the pond was still and pure; the trees which surrounded it were stately and offered shade from the scorching sun. Beside the pond stood an animal: a deer which seemed to be looking for something. When a fawn appeared, the deer showed his delight. They nudged each other affectionately. The fawn snuggled into the deer's warm body. They drank together from the pool before resting in the warm grass. When I asked God what this delightful picture meant, he seemed to assure me that this was a representation of my listening prayer. The time I set aside to develop my relationship with him becomes an oasis. In this still place he waits, more eager for an encounter with me than I am to encounter him. He seemed to show me that on the occasions when I come to this place of refreshment, I must be unashamed to delight in him; that he, similarly, will show me that he delights in me; that I am the focus of his love, the object of his affection and care. During these times he would nourish me. Like the bride in the Song of Songs I would sit under his shade and taste the fruit of his love.

(Taken from Listening to God, pp 99, 100)

# Breaking Free

*By faith Abraham obeyed . . . and he went
out not knowing where he was to go*
Hebrews 11:8

While teaching, lecturing, and writing about the importance of solitude, inner freedom, and peace of mind, I kept stumbling over my own compulsions and illusions . . . What was turning my vocation to be a witness to God's love into a tiring job? . . . Maybe I spoke more about God than with him. Maybe my writing about prayer kept me from a prayerful life. Maybe I was more concerned about the praise of men and women than the love of God.[111]

Henri Nouwen plucked up the courage to clear his desk and his diary and become a Trappist monk for seven months to reassess his priorities and change his lifestyle.

(Taken from Listening to Others, p 165)

# Discipline is the Key

### *Pray constantly, give thanks*
### *in all circumstances*
1 Thessalonians 5:17–18

The pressing problem is busyness and John Eudes' advice to Henri Nouwen reinforces the need to deal with it:

* Establish a new rhythm of prayer, make it known and make it a priority.
* Make a daily discipline of listening prayer a must by plotting periods of the day when you determine that you will 'waste time' with God.
* Recurring days of retreat will be really fruitful only when this daily discipline is firmly established.
* Integrate prayer and work: 'Lecturing, preaching, writing, studying and counselling ... would be nurtured and deepened by a regular prayer life.'[112]

(Taken from Listening to God, pp 165, 166)

# Anchored in God

*When you pray, go into your room and shut the door and pray to your father who is in secret*
Matthew 6:6

If I am to receive God's message into myself so that it strikes root, germinates and bears fruit, I need silence. This silence – 'Be still and know that I am God' (Ps 46:10) – is difficult to achieve. But it is the prerequisite of listening and it involves telling myself, firmly and authoritatively, to stop chattering, to shut up!

When I resist the temptation to go straight from breakfast to my desk and start writing but, instead, move to my desk via my prayer corner, the quality of my work improves because, deliberately, I take time to drop anchor into God. I know this to be true. I have proved it over and over again.

(Taken from Listening to God, p 166)

# Looking Back

*The Pharisee stood and said this prayer to himself 'I thank you that I am not like every one else' . . . the tax collector standing far off did not dare even to raise his eyes to heaven*
Luke 18:11–13

I t is quite possible to go through the motions of prayer and remain unaware of the activity of the Holy Spirit in us.

There is value in spending five minutes each day watching an action re-play of the past twenty four hours and asking God to slow down the film when he wants to remind us of the good gifts he has given us.

Sometimes God shows us where love, joy, peace, patience, kindness and self-control have been offered to us by others . . . Or where we have been enabled to do things which in our own strength, we would be incapable of achieving. He does this by bringing to the surface of our memory occasions when we have been uncharacteristically kind or patient or moments when what we have said or done has clearly been inspired by him, or times when he has prompted us to pray for someone just when they most needed it. Such memories are humbling and draw from us gratitude that the Spirit of Jesus continues to transform us.

# Making the Best of the Day

*Do not worry about tomorrow. Each day has enough trouble of its own*
Matthew 6:34

On dark days when the future seems bleak and we feel battered and bruised it is easy to be beguiled into believing that there is nothing for which to praise God. But that assumption is usually far from the truth . . .

On one such day I struggled to recall tiny signs of God's love and beauty. When I paused to look back I recalled 'the dawn chorus', time to pour out my pain to the God who cares . . . a wonderful sunny summer's morning . . . a cloudless slate blue sky. And I was forced to admit that my seemingly dismal day had been punctuated with good gifts which were in danger of being overlaid by gloom.

(Taken from the Prayer Journal)

# The Jesus Prayer

## *God be merciful to me a sinner*
### Luke 18:13

I once visited a Greek Orthodox monastery where, for three days, I joined in the rhythm of prayer practised by the monks and nuns who live there. The special feature of this monastery, for me, was the use these people made of what is known as 'The Jesus prayer', a prayer which consists of the words, 'Lord Jesus Christ, Son of God, have mercy on us.'

For two hours every morning and two hours every evening, the community meet in the chapel to pray. They use these words and these only: 'Lord Jesus Christ, Son of God, have mercy on us.' As I prepared to visit this monastery, I feared that to recite this prayer would be nothing more than vain repetition. What I found as I joined in the prayer with these men and women was that, for four hours each day, I was listening to God on a profound level. I cannot speak for the others who participated in this prayer cycle, but, for me, I became acutely aware of two realities: the holiness of God and my own innate sinfulness. In one sense, this was not new. In another sense, it *was* new because of the manner in which I 'saw' the mystery and the 'otherness' and the glory of God and because of the manner in which I became equally conscious of my own nothingness before him. The fact that I am nothing, he is everything, and yet he loves me.

(Taken from Listening to God, pp 203, 204)

# Everywhere

*If I ascend to heaven, you are there; if I make my bed in the underworld, you are there*
Psalm 139:8

Short ejaculatory prayers can help to keep alive a loving awareness of Christ. I often use a prayer of Amy Carmichael 'Holy Spirit, think through me till your ideas become my ideas.' And John Wesley's words express my desire to stay in tune all day: 'Jesus, strengthen my desire to work and speak and think for you.'

In this way prayer need not be divorced from everyday routine, but can become an integral part of it. As Guy Brinkworth puts it: 'a background yearning for God can be sustained in the middle of any activity as a kind of "celestial music while you work".'[113] 'The internal burning sign of love need not, with practice and adaptation, interfere with the efficiency of the "secular" side of the contemplative's activity.'[114] In-tuneness with God's will and mind need not cease when we take up a pen or a newspaper or a gardening fork.

(Taken from Listening to Others, pp 173, 174)

# Pondering the Word

*Mary kept all these things, pondering them in her heart*
Luke 2:19

Richard Foster says of *lectio divina*: 'It is a kind of meditative spiritual reading in which the mind and the heart are drawn into the love and goodness of God . . . We are doing more than reading words . . . we are pondering all things in our heart as Mary did. We are entering into the reality of which the words speak.'[115]

The Carmelite mystic Teresa of Avila often went to prayer with a book in her hand: 'often the mere fact that I had it with me was enough.'[116]

# Word of Knowledge

*You have had five husbands and the man you now have is not your husband*
John 4:18

A word of knowledge is an insight implanted by God about a particular person or situation for a specific purpose. Alex Buchanan, summarised the gift helpfully:

The word of knowledge may be the revelation of the whereabouts or the doings of a man, the nature of his thought, or the condition of his heart. It is a gift of revelation. It becomes vocal when shared with others. It is a fragment of divine knowledge which cannot be attained by study or consecration. It is a divinely granted flash of revelation concerning things which were hopelessly hidden from the senses, the mind, or the faculties of men.

I was to discover that Jesus exercised this gift. His use of it astounded the Samaritan woman who talked with him at the well. Although Jesus had never encountered her before, so far as we know, he seemed well informed about her sex life. This word of knowledge not only astonished the woman, it resulted in a complete change of life-style.

(Taken from Listening to God, pp 130, 131)

# Living Words

*The water that I shall give will become a*
*spring welling up to eternal life*
John 4:14

Teachers of prayer have struggled to describe meditation. St John Cassian called it 'the rocking of the heart' which rises and falls like a ship dipping in the swell of the spirit. Sister Margaret Magdalen likens it to a tumble drier. The heart 'tumbles and turns the word of God until it has made it its own.'[117] People in the Middle Ages used another evocative metaphor: *ruminari* – the *chewing* of the Word. Commenting on the aptness of this metaphor, André Louf suggests that it conjures up a tranquil picture of sleepy cows chewing the cud patiently and incessantly. Like those cows, he recommends that Christians digest and chew God's Word. Then rest before regurgitating and chewing the same phrase all over again. As we discipline ourselves to do this, we find that our aim is being achieved. This living Word will so penetrate and permeate and nourish and become a part of us that, when we pray, it will spring into our minds and flow from our lips with the same sort of spontaneity as it did with Jesus.

(Taken from the Introduction to Praying with the New Testament, p xii)

# Prayer is an Adventure

## *Whatever you ask in my name I will do*
### John 14:13

When Christians pray together miracles happen. Behind Peter's release from prison (Acts 12:1–17) was a group of Christians in prayer. Shared prayer preceded Pentecost. The Welsh revival of 1905 was anticipated by Christians praying together. Couples praying in partnership have unwittingly influenced the world. André Louf, for example, dedicates his book *Teach us to Pray*, to 'mother and father whom I frequently saw at prayer and from whom I learned to pray.' As Ralph Martin expresses it, 'prayer is not a pious addition to things . . . it is a force allowing things to happen which could not have occurred without it.'

Prayer is an adventure because prayer is the work of God's Spirit within us (Rom. 8) and as Peter Hocken puts it, 'The Spirit makes fresh what has become stale, puts new flesh on old bones, and causes new life to pulse through the old body.'[118]

The paradox about prayer is that it is both a gift from God through the Holy Spirit (Rom 8:26) and at the same time it is an art to be learned.

(Taken from Two into One, pp 55, 57)

# God Believes in Me

*When we cry Abba Father it is the Spirit
bearing witness that we are children of God*
**Romans 8:15–16**

To know oneself loved, believed in, understood, accepted, trusted and constantly renewed by God is a humbling experience.

This is the nature of the encounter, not that I am stumbling towards the Abba Father, but that the Abba Father is running towards me. It is not that I love God but that God believes in me. The discovery at the heart of contemplation is not that I am contemplating the divine love, but that the divine love is contemplating me. He sees me and understands and accepts me, he has compassion on me, he creates me afresh from moment to moment, and he protects me and is with me through death and into life beyond.[119]

(Taken from Listening to God, p 70)

# Come Apart

## *Come away to a desert place*
### Mark 6:31

Brother Ramon claims that 'whenever a new chapter opens in God's dealing with people in Scripture, whenever God reveals himself in a new and deeper way, whenever there are moments of revelation, redemption, sanctification – then the person who is the spearhead of such events is called into the mountain, or deep into the desert for confrontation with himself and God.'[120]

When the Holy Spirit draws us deeper and deeper into spiritual mysteries, we find within ourselves the desire to carve out whole chunks of time to be quiet so that we may become more open to God. Whenever we do this, whether we realise it or not, we are following in the tradition of the prophets, the patriarchs and of Jesus himself. 'Abraham walked in the desert under the star-filled night. Jacob dreamed in his wilderness solitude at Bethel . . . And Moses received the revelation and call at the burning bush in the wilderness beneath Horeb'.[121]

The New Testament paints a similar picture. There we see John the Baptist spending his entire childhood and adolescence 'on retreat' in the desert and Jesus himself spending whole nights under the velvet, star-studded sky in solitary prayer and adoration of his Father.

(Taken from Open to God, pp 67, 68)

# Hold It!

## *They came up and worshipped him*
### Matthew 28:9

'Hold it!' Perhaps that is the simplest and most accurate definition of contemplative prayer: the deepest, most mysterious method of listening to God.

The phases of prayer are rather like pieces of a jig-saw puzzle. When you fit them together you realise that God has been preparing you for the moment when you 'hold it'; when your heart and mind and will are relaxed, focused on him, surrendered to him, cleansed and renewed so that you are ready to gaze on him in adoring love and to know yourself the object of his undivided affection and attention.

Archbishop Anthony Bloom captures the nuances of this dimension of listening prayer with a simple story of a peasant who had formed the habit of slipping into a certain church at a certain time of day with clockwork regularity. There, day by day, he would sit and, apparently, do nothing. The parish priest observed this regular, silent visitor. One day, unable to contain his curiosity any longer, he asked the old man why he came to the church, alone, day in, day out. Why waste his time in this way?

The old man looked at the priest and with a loving twinkle in his eye gave this explanation: 'I look at him. He looks at me. And we tell each other that we love each other.'

(Taken from Listening to God, pp 63, 64)

# Resting in God

## *The face of Moses was radiant because he had been talking to God*
### Exodus 34:29

C ontemplation gives rise to deep, heart-felt wonderment and worship. To contemplate means to pay rapt and loving attention to a person or object. So to contemplate God means to pay rapt and loving attention to him and to allow him to do the same to us. Contemplative prayer involves being totally absorbed – abandoned to God. 'Contemplative prayer is like taking a sun-bath; like soaking up the radiant heat of the living Christ . . . it is just being naked before God, totally exposed to him and to his penetrating Word.'[122]

When we contemplate, our task is simply 'to be silent and to let the Word of love speak to the middle of *our* being, so that it becomes heart knowledge as well as head knowledge.'[123]

If we are to do this, we may find that we need 'ways in' to contemplation such as music, phrases of Scripture, pictures and quotations from books.

(Taken from Open to God)

# Into the Hands of God

### *When I saw him I fell at his feet*
### Revelation 1:17

Contemplation is about putting ourselves in the hands of the God who loves us, experiencing that love, basking in its radiance and warmth; being overwhelmed by its power, responding to it; being transformed by its tenderness, strengthened by the giver's compassion; being met in our emptiness by the fullness of God, being found in our lostness by the Shepherd who cares; being refreshed by his never-failing well-springs, being refilled by his life-giving Spirit; discovering by experience the truth of his promises: 'I will come to you', 'My strength is made perfect in your weakness.'

In the silence and solitude of my prayer room I sometimes lie prostrate at the foot of the cross which hangs on my wall and admit to God: 'All I have to offer you is my emptiness. Please fill me.' And very often the tenderness of his presence and love creep over me and the words of this hymn take on new meaning:

O the deep, deep love of Jesus!
vast, unmeasured, boundless, free;
Rolling as a mighty ocean
In its fullness over me.
Underneath me, all around me,
Is the current of Thy love;
Leading onward, leading homeward,
To Thy glorious rest above.
    (Samuel Trevor Francis 1834—1925)

(Taken from Listening to Others, pp 125, 126)

# Soul Friend

*To each is given the manifestation of the*
*Spirit for the common good*
1 Corinthians 12:7

Contemplative prayer and listening to God are disciplines which lay the Christian wide open to eccentricities, extremes and errors. To protect them from sallying forth on some mystical ego-trip most people find that a mentor and guide to set them on course from time to time is essential. Thus St Basil (330–379) urges his readers to find a man 'who may serve you as a very sure guide in the work of leading a holy life', one who knows 'the straight road to God'. He warns that 'to believe that one does not need counsel is great pride.'[124] St Jerome (340–420) pleads with his friend Rusticus not to set out on an uncharted way without a guide. And St Augustine (354–430) is emphatic: 'No one can walk without a guide.'[125]

Not everyone would agree that spiritual direction should be given by a friend. Nevertheless, I was grateful for the friendship I enjoyed with those to whom I turned for help along the way. To me, they were 'soul friends', to borrow Kenneth Leech's memorable phrase.

(Taken from Listening to God pp 179, 178)

# The Intimate Stranger

*How can I understand unless someone guides me?*
Acts 8:31

A soul friend is the intimate stranger who, as a person experienced in the life of prayer, will be committed to you in an adult/adult relationship in an attempt to set you on the path of prayer, assist you in discerning the breathings of the Spirit, bring you to a place of greater self-knowledge and self-acceptance and help you find the will of God. The soul friend will avoid encouraging excessive dependence, but will accept you as you are as well as confront and challenge when occasion demands. A soul friend might draw alongside the person of prayer in their confession of failures to God. The soul friend might be God's instrument of healing using prayer counselling, the laying-on of hands or anointing with oil. To those of us who have been privileged to receive the help of a soul friend, a certain Celtic saying elicits a loud 'Amen': 'Anyone without a soul friend is a body without a head.'

My 'soul friend' listened to my confusion on more than one occasion. With him the jumble of conflicting thoughts and emotions would tumble out. With him I could express my uncertainties and fears. He would listen, attune his ear to the Holy Spirit of God, disentangle the threads, present them with order and clarity and explore with me what God was asking of me. He would make suggestions but never demand that I obey him implicitly.

(Taken from Listening to God, pp 179, 180)

# Facing Oneself

*O, the depths of the riches and wisdom and*
*knowledge of God*
**Romans 11:33**

My soul friend instilled in me the courage to face myself as I really am: not the successful, coping person I like to project to the world, but the mixture of success and failure, honesty and deception, saint and sinner which I really am. It was he who confronted me with the need to change. His own pilgrimage of prayer proved to me that listening to God is a journey where joys are found as much in the travelling as in the arriving. His child-likeness in prayer drew from me a child-like eagerness to reach my destination even when the destination, I knew, lay at least in part on the other side of eternity.

> Saint Catherine of Siena, Lord,
> said you are like the sea.
> The more we know of you,
>    the more we find;
> And the more we find of you,
> the more we want.
> Yet we never really understand you.[126]

(Taken from Listening to God, pp 181, 182)

# Closer to God

*God has given revelation through the Spirit*
*and the Spirit searches everything*
1 Corinthians 2:10

I t is the task of the Holy Spirit to pinpoint inconsistencies. His one desire is to draw us nearer and nearer to God. If he highlights areas which need cleansing or attention it is only because he wants the garden of our life to bring pleasure to God, to others and to ourselves. We need therefore to accept such revelations as moments of grace and give thanks for them.

Search me, dear Lord, and show me myself
Show me if there is anything hurtful in me
Show me, too, where I am growing in grace

(Taken from the Prayer Journal)

# Deeper Into God

*We do not know what we ought to pray for,*
*but the Spirit himself intercedes for us with*
*groans that words cannot express*
**Romans 8:26**

As the Holy Spirit takes us deeper and deeper into God he may entrust us with a burden for particular people in trouble or distress. As we pray for these people we may find ourselves weeping or groaning before God. Paul warns us to expect this and explains in Romans 8 why it happens.

He shows us that the Spirit is prompting us to pray 'in accordance with the will of God'.

(Taken from the Prayer Journal)

# Dark Night of the Soul

## *Without having seen him you love him*
### 1 Peter 1:8

One of the methods God uses to bring about inner harmony in some people is sometimes called 'the dark night of the soul'. This describes the phases of the spiritual journey when the senses no longer pick up the felt presence of Christ but seem to be conscious only of nothingness. During this winter of the senses God seems to be, not present and attentive and loving, but completely absent. Thomas Merton refers to this experience often and describes it variously: 'spiritual inertia, inner confusion, coldness, lack of confidence'. 'What at first seemed rosy and rewarding suddenly comes to be utterly impossible. The mind will not work. One cannot concentrate on anything. The imagination and the emotions wander away.'[127]

Thomas Merton makes the claim that these night times of the senses increase in frequency as time goes on, that there is a sense in which they can be taken as signs of progress provided the pray-er does not give up but determines to respond to the challenge, refuses to view this hollowness as spiritual doom or punishment for sin, but sees it, rather, for what it really is: the opportunity for growth.

I still shudder when prayer dries up on me, when I listen and hear nothing, when I yearn for God and find emptiness, but I am learning, slowly, that the darkness is but the shadow of his hand, silence but the herald of his call, and nothingness the space prepared for the return of never-ending love.

(Taken from Listening to God, pp 212, 215)

# Coming Soon

*Though you do not now see him you believe
in him*
1 Peter 1:8

I remember clearly one of those horrifying patches when God seemed to have absented himself never to return, when a complete revulsion for prayer swamped me. Engulfed by this darkness, and in panic, I telephoned my soul friend and asked if I could see him. Sensing the depths of my despair he fixed an appointment for the following day. As I described the darkness, the fear, the nothingness, the pain, I also voiced my self-doubts. Had I sinned? Was that why God had disappeared? Was I deluding myself about this pilgrimage of prayer? Was I expecting too much, expecting to encounter God in the way I had enjoyed? Or were the doors to contemplation and listening to God closing?

When my tale of woe had been told, this wise man of God closed his eyes, held his head in his hands, and went quite silent. I knew him well enough to know that he would be praying. A hush stole over the room and I waited.

After several minutes he looked up and I noticed that his eyes twinkled and an excited smile spread across his face. 'Joyce!' he said, 'I feel so excited by this darkness of yours. You see, when you stand in the howling desert like this, you never know how God will next come to you. What you do know is that he will come. I believe God is encouraging you to look for him round every corner because he *is* coming – and he's coming soon.'

(Taken from Listening to God, p 180)

# Grieving in Prayer

*While we live we are always being given up to*
*death for Jesus' sake*
2 Corinthians 4:11

J ust as listening to God can elicit paeans of praise so it can plunge
the person at prayer into a deep and terrible pain. When this first
happened to me and prayer triggered off uncontrollable weeping,
I wondered what was happening. Now, I think I understand.

When we stand before God and tune into him, we pick up some
of the heart-break he feels for a needy world. In this way God gives
us the privilege of 'knowing him' and entering into the 'fellowship
of his sufferings', to use the language of St Paul.

A little while ago a friend called to see me. He is a teacher, a
person God is drawing into listening prayer. He spelt out the horror
he felt as he watched certain pupils in his school fight one another
physically, just like little tigers. 'It hurts even to think about it,'
he admitted. 'I don't understand why they want to be so cruel to
each other.' I suggested that his inner turmoil and pain might have
found a mooring in his heart for a purpose: because God wants him
to weep and groan in prayer, not just for the situation at school,
but because peace in the world has been pillaged, because in the
world at large strife sets man against man on a bigger scale than
this school scene.

(Taken from Listening to God pp 208, 209)

# The Absence of God

*You have wrapped yourself in a cloud too thick for prayer to pierce*
**Lamentations 3:43**

Gerard Hughes claims that the experience of desolation is a good sign; an invitation to grow:

Desolation will only be experienced by those whose lives are essentially directed to the praise, reverence and service of God. If a person is turned away from God in the core of their being, they may experience the occasional sting of remorse, but in general the felt absence of God will not cause them any pain . . . If we imagine ourselves to be in the hands of God as clay in the hands of the potter . . . we can see desolation as a turning of the clay so that it becomes a vessel which can contain life-giving water which as unformed clay it could not hold. Desolation, as it were, gouges us out, so that we can receive more. At the time, the process simply feels painful: when it is over we become aware of new areas of feeling and perception within us.[128]

# Self-Centredness

*When I was a child, I spoke like a child, I*
*thought like a child*
1 Corinthians 13:11

Thelma Hall tells us why conversion may be difficult.

From our emergence from our mother's womb into this world, our almost immediate experiences of conscious reality proceed to confirm the illusion that we are the centre of the universe: the crying infant is comforted; hungry, it is fed. Its every need is attended to for its very survival and growth; everything is given, nothing demanded of it . . . 'Watch out for No. 1!' becomes an implicit and instinctive motto . . .

This basic egocentricity is opposed to God-and-other-centredness . . . This is why conversion may be described as a 'shifting of one's centre', away from narcissistic self-love and self-serving, to the self-giving love and serving of God and others.[129]

# Spring Thaw

*Come then my beloved,*
*my lovely one come.*
*For see winter is past,*
*the rains are over and gone*
Song of Songs 2:10,11

As John Powell testifies he had known about the love of God for many years before the moment of revelation came.

From the early morning till the darkened moments while waiting for sleep, I kept inviting Jesus into my house of many rooms. I kept reassuring Him that I was ready to admit my own [spiritual] bankruptcy, my own helplessness to direct my life, to find peace and joy . . . I begged the Spirit to free me from the ingrained habit of competition, from the insatiable hunger for success . . . and adulation.

What began to happen to me almost immediately can be compared only to springtime. It seemed as though I had been through a long, hard-frozen wintertime. My heart and soul had suffered all the barrenness, the nakedness of nature in winter. Now in this springtime of the Spirit, it seemed as though the veins of my soul were thawing, as though blood was beginning to course through my soul again. New foliage and new beauty began to appear in me and around me.

Once more I had the sensation of putting on a new pair of badly needed glasses and seeing all kinds of things that had been obscured.[130]

It is the work of God's Spirit to bring such joy.

# The Real World

*Let both wheat and weeds grows together
until the harvest*
Matthew 13:30

Over the centuries, the cumulative and escalating effect of millions of individuals choosing to please themselves rather than to serve Christ and their neighbour has ensured that tragedies will occur. It often seems that we do not live on a planet where good is rewarded and evil is punished. We live in a curious place where God, for his own good reasons, allows the wheat and the weeds to co-exist. Justice will only be fully vindicated when the final harvest is reaped, when the heavenly Gardener reappears and we are brought into the 'Real World'[131] – that place where the sun and moon cease to shine because 'The glory of God gives it light, and the Lamb is its lamp'.

(Taken from The Smile of Love, p 148)

# You did it for me

## *I was in prison and you visited me*
### Matthew 25:36

When Brian Greenaway was a prisoner in Dartmoor prison, he received an unexpected visit from a stranger. In *Inside* he describes how the thought of a visitor helped him to feel like 'a teenager on his first date' — really stirred up inside. And he tells how this 'chance' visit changed the direction of his life.

'Anything I can get you?' the stranger asked Brian. 'What about a book?'

Brian had seen an advertisement for *The Living Bible* a few days before so he asked: 'Would you know a thing called *The Living Bible*? It's sort of new and has a yellow cover and I've seen it in this ad . . .

I stopped, held by the look of amazement in his eyes. Without a word he bent down and opened his case . . . His hand came out with two books. One was a yellow book. On the cover were the words LIVING BIBLE. It was my twenty-seventh birthday . . .

I picked up the Yellow Bible, my fingers fumbling and searching for a page, any page. I let it all open where it wanted to and began to read. It was a chapter from John's Gospel:

'I have loved you even as the Father has loved me. Live within my love.'

Suddenly, in the stillness I felt a Great Presence surrounding me and pouring into me. I felt a surge of love ripping into me, tearing away all the layers of filth and dirt, boring down to my heart, dissolving the hate and the bitterness, swallowing up my tortured self-centredness. A blast of joy rushed through me, clearing me out like a vacuum cleaner . . . It was the rushing Spirit of Christ . . .

There was a turning of the key in the lock and the flat of a hand on the door. It was time for association. I got up and walked unsteadily out of my cell. Shaker, the pimp, was on the landing . . . 'Shaker, something's happened. Something very strange. I don't know how but . . . I've just become a Christian.'[132]

# God of the Gospels

*They said to Jesus, 'by what authority are*
*you doing these things?'*
Mark 11:28

There is nothing insipid about the Jesus of the Gospels. He is a revolutionary. But how many Christians see this? Their 'meek and mild' god persuades them to collude with social injustice by keeping quiet where the Jesus of the Gospels, the real God, would speak and act.

How many people who are involved, day by day, in the cut and thrust of the business world have failed to recognise the love of God, because the god who has been presented to them through the language of hymns and prayers is not the God of the Gospels, but an old man in the sky? But the God of the Gospels continues to call us; continues to love.

(Taken from the Smile of Love, p 155)

# Whatever You Do . . .

## *When you did it to one of the least of my brethren, you did it to me*
### Matthew 25:40

If we sense the agony of God's loved ones, we sense the agony of God himself.

Mother Teresa of Calcutta believes that, when she scoops up the dying from the streets of Calcutta she holds in her arms, the body of Christ.

Teresa of Avila wrote 'Though we do not have our Lord with us in bodily presence, we have our neighbour, who, for the ends of love and loving service, is as good as our Lord himself.'

And Henri Nouwen tells us that, 'The hunger of the poor, the torture of prisoners, the threat of war in many countries, and the immense human suffering we hear about from all directions can call us to a deeply human response . . . if we are willing to see in the brokenness of our fellow human beings the brokeness of God.'[133]

(Taken from The Smile of Love, p 187)

# Carry Each Other's Burdens

### *As the body without spirit is dead, so faith without deeds is dead*
James 2:26

What good is it, my brothers, if a man claims to have faith but has no deeds? Can such faith save him? Suppose a brother or sister is without clothes and daily food. If one of you says to him, 'Go, I wish you well; keep warm and well fed,' but does nothing about his physical needs, what good is it? In the same way, faith by itself, if it is not accompanied by action, is dead . . . You see that a person is justified by what he does and not by faith alone . . . As the body without the spirit is dead, so faith without deeds is dead. (Jas 2:14–17, 24, 26)

Share with God's people who are in need. Practise hospitality . . . Rejoice with those who rejoice; mourn with those who mourn. (Rom. 12:13, 15)

Carry each other's burdens, and in this way you will fulfil the law of Christ . . . Therefore, as we have opportunity, let us do good to all people. (Gal. 6:2, 10)

It is possible to read God's word, to understand it with our intellect but to fail to pick up with our spiritual antennae the message it is trying to convey. And it is equally possible for Christians to know a great deal about God without really knowing him just as it is easier to be familiar with Christ's commands than to obey them.

(Taken from Listening to Others, pp 73, 74)

# Who is My Neighbour?

*I was hungry and you fed me, thirsty and you*
*gave me drink*
Matthew 25:36

Lying in the ditch of convalescence after a major operation I contemplated the parable of the Good Samaritan from the vantage point of the vulnerable one, the victim, rather than through the eyes of the lawyer who asked: 'Who is my neighbour?' Like the lawyer, before I was admitted to hospital, from a position of strength and vitality, I was wanting to set goals and define boundaries. Now I viewed the question differently. The poor, cannot be classified. We are everywhere. I say 'we' because I now recognise that I am one of them. When people touch us in the pit of our need, we are assured that we come constantly under the caring eye of God. When people stay away, for whatever reason, we lie in danger of reading into this absence, not simply the neglect of humankind but the absence of God.

Caring for the poor is Kingdom activity, even if it simply means drawing alongside one person and sharing nothing more than vulnerability. It was one reason Christ came to earth; it was his way of demonstrating to the world what God is like.

'The poor and the weak have revealed to me the great secret of Jesus.

If you wish to follow him
you must not try to climb the ladder of
success and power,
becoming more and more important.
Instead you must walk *down* the ladder,
to meet and walk with people
who are broken and in pain . . .'[134]

(Taken from Under the Caring Eye of God, pp 214, 215)

# Do You Love Me?

*O God, you are the true God keep us safe*
*from false gods*
1 John 5:20–21

The call of the King inevitably involves some kind of identification with the powerless – the people among whom Jesus was born and lived and died. This conviction deepened during my stay in hospital. It gave birth to a disturbing dissatisfaction with the middle-class interpretation of the Gospels which I had imbibed for most of my life: teaching which insists that Christians must feed their minds through study of the Scriptures yet remains strangely silent about the Bible's insistence that Christ's followers should, at the same time, be feeding the poor; teaching which emphasises the need Christians have to soak up the love of God yet says nothing about the parallel importance of expressing that love to those for whom the name of God means nothing – particularly those who have nothing to eat, nothing to wear; teaching which presents Jesus as the Saviour who will bless us abundantly, even guarantee that we get rich quickly, but fails to present him as the One who requires us to turn from our selfishness; to become like him – especially in his attitude to the poor and those who suffer unjustly. 'What are the implications for me?'

(Taken from Under the Caring Eye of God, p 218)

# Jesus Disguised

*Lord, when did we see you hungry and feed*
*you, or thirsty and give you something to*
*drink? When did we see you a stranger and*
*invite you in, or needing clothes and clothe*
*you? When did we see you sick or in prison*
*and go to visit you?*
Matthew 25:37–39

A dream helped me to understand this parable. In my dream I saw a tramp stagger through my garden gate. He was dressed in dirty, tattered clothes and was clearly unwell. I watched him bend over my herb garden. I heard him vomit. My heart went out to him. I felt great warmth for him. I wanted to help him. But before I could move, I woke up.

The dream remained vivid. So I talked to God about it. 'Lord, you know that I'm not normally like that. The real me would have been angry if that had happened. Why was I so different in my dream?'

'In your dream, you reached the heart of the matter,' came the reply. 'I was the tramp. You sensed this. That is why you saw, not the tattered clothing, but me; that is why you were concerned, not with the smell and the mess, but with the person. When you felt warmth for that tramp and wanted to go to him, you were feeling warmth for me. Learn to live as you reacted in your dream.'

(Taken from The Smile of Love, pp 186, 187)

# Christ Still Cares

*He took the loaves and the fish, and after
giving thanks he broke them and began
handing them to the disciples, who gave them
to the crowds*
Matthew 15:36 (JB)

Thousands in our world are still hungry: hungry for bread, hungry for love, hungry for God. People in pain are still powerless. Helpless. Cast on the mercy of others, they cry out for compassion, relief, release, gentleness, generosity.

The risen, ascended Christ has not ceased to care. His compassion for the destitute and the dying, the sick and sorrowing, the bereaved and the depressed is as intense and passionate now as it was when he walked this earth. He comes to them now as he came when he was enfleshed with our humanity. He comes with that mysterious, hidden, felt presence which has supported so many sick and grief-stricken people down the ages. He comes, too, through the love expressed by others. Indeed, the chief channel through which his healing, consoling compassion now flows to the needy is through the eyes and the touch, the embrace and the kindness of other people. For this reason he still pleads, 'You feed them. You love them.' He still begs his followers to place the little they have to offer into his hands so that they can help him in alleviating a fraction of the sorrow afflicting our world.

(Taken from The Smile of Love, p 170)

# The Bread of Life

*. . . For my flesh is real food and my blood is real drink. Whoever eats my flesh and drinks my blood remains in me, and I in him*

The service of Holy Communion celebrates this self-gift of Jesus. 'Eucharist' means 'thanksgiving'. Every time we attend such a service it provides us with an opportunity to return to God humble thanks that he gave his Son so that we might live.

The service of Holy Communion also provides the setting where we may regularly receive the life-restoring food Jesus describes: his body and his blood. Christians down the ages have been divided about how the bread or wafer and the wine sustain us. But most would agree that in some sense the bread is Christ's body just as the wine is his blood and that this food nourishes and builds us up.

But the service does not end there. It moves us from thanksgiving, to feeding, to adoration and finally to making our personal response of love. And so it invites us to pray: 'Send us out in the power of your Spirit to live and work to your praise and glory.' In other words, having feasted at the banqueting table of God we go out to become harvest people – those who give to others the love God gives to them.

(Taken from Bible Reading Fellowship notes, Sept-Dec 90, p 45)

# What Might Have Been

*I will not leave you desolate*
John 14:18

We need this assurance because we are vulnerable. Most people react to loss by clinging to the past, demanding their 'rights', clasping their fingers around that which remains lest someone should prise the little they have left from their reluctant hands. But in the face of suffering we must learn to say goodbye to what might have been, the closeness, the friendship and fulfilment, so that we are free to receive the present and the future. We have to unclench our fists so that the past falls away, so that, with open palms, we may receive what God offers of peace, consolation and joy, in the present.

When we keep glancing over our shoulders to the past, regretting the loss of what might have been, the question which rises from deep within is 'Lord, why?' 'Why did he have to die now?' 'Why couldn't you have warned me?' 'Why . . . ? Why . . . ? Why . . . ?' And the Christian must learn that there is no answer to the question 'Why?' But if you allow the past to remain in the past, if you learn to live in the present, then a new question is prompted, 'Lord, what do you want me to learn from this situation?' The comfort is that the second question has an answer and though the reply may be painful because the lessons to be learned are costly, there is that awareness deep down that we are moving forward, into the present with God.

(Taken from Two into One, pp 118, 119, 120)

# Terminal Cancer

## *If I walk through the valley of the shadow of death I fear no evil*
### Psalm 23:4

In *Fear No Evil*, David Watson shares his sense of powerlessness in the face of terminal illness.

'When I first heard . . . that I had cancer, the news hit me like a thunderbolt. All human hopes and securities were suddenly shattered. "it *can't* be true," I said to myself foolishly and anxiously. "That sort of thing doesn't happen to me!" But it did, and my deepest fears were realised . . . The worst times for me were at two or three o'clock in the morning. I had preached the gospel all over the world with ringing conviction. I had told countless thousands of people that I was not afraid of death since through Christ I had already received God's gift of eternal life. For years I had not doubted these truths at all. But now the most fundamental questions were nagging away insistently, especially in those long hours of the night. If I was soon on my way to heaven, how real was heaven? Was it anything more than a beautiful idea? What honestly would happen when I died? Did God himself really exist after all? How could I be sure? Indeed, how could I be certain of anything apart from cancer and death? I literally sweated over these questions, and on many occasions woke up with my pyjamas bathed in cold sweat! Never before had my faith been so ferociously attacked.'[135]

# Life's 'Little Deaths'

*Distress and anguish held me in their grip,*
*I called on the name of the Lord . . .*
*The Lord looks after the simple.*
*When I was brought low he gave me strength*
Psalm 116:3,6

L ife challenges us to undergo loss — the loss of a limb through accident or amputation, the loss of a child through miscarriage, the loss of a job through redundancy, the loss of hope through the inability to conceive a child, the loss of parts of our body through disfigurement or surgery: the closing of a chapter when we retire. Looked at in this way, we are surrounded in life by people who are suffering the trauma of mini-deaths and we experience many of them ourselves.

Very often it is the Psalms which bring to us the comfort of God when our emotions are in turmoil.

It is not clear from the text of Psalm 116 whether the Psalmist is thanking God for deliverance from the jaws of death or whether he has been strengthened in one of life's mini-deaths. But it is clear that, he has found in God a sensitive listener, a rescuer and protector and one whose love is constant and tender.

After the death of her husband, Ingrid Trobisch wrote: 'Prayer for me . . . means . . . to crawl up on my heavenly Father's lap and let myself be loved.'[136]

(Taken from SU notes on death)

# Where is She Now?

*We are always full of confidence, realising*
*that as long as we are at home in the body we*
*are exiled from the Lord, guided by faith and*
*not yet by sight; we . . . long instead to be*
*exiled from the body and to be at home with*
*the Lord*
2 Corinthians 5:6–8 (JB)

'I wonder where she is now?' That's a question my father and I used to ask after my mother died. And we found that Paul gave us various clues. My mother was a believer so we knew that, wherever she was she was 'with Christ' and that that was far better for her than her life on earth. We knew, too, that she had, as it were moved house; the tent of her earthly body had been dismantled and she had moved, instead, to a more permanent, more secure, luxury home – that perfect place Jesus had been preparing for her. Or, again to use the picture language of Paul, it was as though she had taken off a worn out set of clothes, her earthly body and was being groomed to receive a set of brand-new, tailor-made garments, the spiritual body in which she would be clothed at the Second Coming of Christ (see 1 Cor 15:51–53).

In an attempt to explain Paul's teaching, a bishop once likened watching a person die to watching a ship sail out to sea. Although the ship disappears from sight, and we say, 'She's gone', she has not, in fact, ceased to exist. She journeys on until, as she nears her destination, she hears the people on the other side of the ocean cheering her on; welcoming her.

(Taken from SU notes on death)

# Show Me You Care

*You had not the strength to keep awake with me one hour*
Matthew 26:40

A student nurse who knew she was dying wrote to her colleagues in an attempt to help them understand how they could best help her: 'Please believe me, if you care you can't go wrong. Just admit that you care. That is really what we are seeking. We may ask for why's and wherefore's, but we don't really expect answers. Don't run away – wait – all I want to know is that there will be someone to hold my hand when I need it. I am afraid. Death . . . is new to me. I've never died before.'

What Jesus was asking for when he begged his disciples to 'stay here and keep watch with me' was the same sort of alongside care and concern the student nurse struggled to describe. For Jesus, in these agonising hours in Gethsemane, experienced the same sort of feelings which are all too familiar to people who know that their time to pass from life to death has come: sorrow, depression, fear, bargaining with God, anger, acceptance and victory.

Jesus suffered intensely and because he suffered such anguish, he is well able to understand the emotional turmoil of people like the lonely, terminally sick student nurse.

(Taken from SU notes on death)

# The Shade of His Love

### *Hide me in the shadow of your wings*
### Psalm 17:8

Just as sheep seek the shelter of trees when the mid-day sun scorches the fields, so God offers us the shade of his love when pain of any kind comes to us or our loved ones. And the love he offers is the protective love of the One who created us; the love of the One who knows what makes us tick and what we most need. It is a love which is available in the lonely hours of the night as well as in the day And it reaches us wherever we are for those who have the bitter-sweet privilege of giving God's love to dear ones who are on the threshold of death. If you know anyone in this position, ask God to show you how best to support them. It may be through prayer or in practical ways – helping with the shopping, taking them a cooked meal or looking after the children for a few hours.

Jesus showed us what real love is. When others hurt, he hurt with them. When people were in need he was there – not offering empty words but affection expressed in practical ways – like cooking breakfast for his weary disciples.

(Taken from SU notes on death)

# United in Heaven

### *I will be with you always*
Matthew 28:20

When someone we love dies, we feel keenly their absence. The sense of loss and loneliness can hold us in its grip for many months. At such times, the thought of the grand reunion we shall enjoy when Jesus returns can bring untold comfort:

*Lord Jesus Christ,*
*Sometimes, I close my eyes and try to imagine*
*What it will be like*
*When you come in glory.*
*Will the sky blush, as with the sunrise?*
*Or will it glow as it does when the sun sets?*
*Or will your glory pierce through the clouds in*
*a sudden blaze of light?*
*Who can tell?*
*And who can tell how that grand reunion with*
*loved ones will happen?*
*Amid all these imponderables, thank you for*
*the certainty*
*That when you come to take us home*
*Our loved ones who loved you while they were*
*here on earth will be with you*
*And we shall be with you*
*In that place where death has lost its sting*
*Where goodbyes become a thing of the past*
*Where there is no more parting*
*Either from those we love*
*Or from you.*

(Taken from Approaching Christmas, pp 36, 37)

# Jesus Bereaved

*They went away in a boat to a lonely place by themselves*
Mark 6:32

After the beheading of John the Baptist, Jesus withdrew by boat to a solitary place.

But he was not allowed to enjoy the peace and solitude he sought. People spotted the boat in which he was travelling, anticipated his destination and made their way on foot to his designated place of prayer. By the time the boat sailed towards the shore, hundreds were flocking to meet him. Like an unruly crowd of football supporters, they invaded his space and intruded on his grief.

As the bereaved and still-stunned Jesus steps out of the boat, an unforgettable scene faces him: weeping women carrying their sick and starving children; lame people hobbling on crude crutches; the blind fumbling their way with the help of sticks; the deaf, the dying and the destitute, all contributing to this sea of human need. Whereupon Jesus reveals the depth of his care for the individual. Refusing to allow his own unresolved sorrow to obstruct the course of love, he enters into the pain and brokenness, the fear and confusion surrounding him.

When the sick and the starving, the emotionally crippled and spiritually deaf and blind come crowding into our lives; as their faces stare at us from our television screens, newspapers, magazines or books; as we meet them in the streets where we live or encounter them in our place of work or worship, the doctor's surgery or hospital, the dentist's waiting room, the bus or the train, we will find ourselves, like Jesus, hurting at gut level. The conviction will deepen that Jesus is imploring us to 'give them something . . .'

(Taken from The Smile of Love, pp 168, 171)

# The Art of Being Real

### *Weep with those who weep*
**Romans 12:15**

D r Gary Collins defines 'empathy' by tracing the word back to its German root *einfühlung*, which means 'feeling into', or 'feeling with'. Empathy asks: 'Why is this person so upset?' 'How does she view what is happening?' 'If I were in her shoes, how might I feel?' In other words, empathy seeks to view life through the troubled person's eyes, to experience another person's world as though it were our own while keeping the words *as though* in the forefront of our mind. It involves walking in the other person's moccasins until you feel where they rub. Empathy attempts to show the person in pain that their feelings are both understood and accepted.

Warmth, according to Gary Collins, is synonymous with caring. It is a non-smothering, non-possessive concern for someone which is communicated by a friendly facial expression, a gentle tone of voice, gestures and appropriate touch, posture and eye contact which communicate the genuine message: 'I care about you and your well-being.'

'Genuineness', Dr Collins describes as the art of being real. The genuine person is an authentic person who has no need to pretend or to project a false superiority. Genuineness is authenticity which refuses to contemplate the playing of a superior role. It is openness without phoniness. It is sincerity, consistency and it is full of respect for others.[137]

(Taken from Listening to Others, pp 38, 39)

# Sharing the Brokenness

*Blessed be the God and Father of our Lord*
*Jesus Christ who comforts us in all our*
*affliction so that we may be able to comfort*
*those who are in any affliction*
2 Corinthians 1:3,4

The word compassion comes from two Latin words *pati* and *cum* which put together mean 'to suffer with'. 'Compassion asks us to go where it hurts, to enter into places of pain, to share in brokenness, fear, confusion, and anguish.' 'Compassion challenges us to cry out with those in misery, to mourn with those who are lonely, to weep with those in tears . . . to be weak with the weak, vulnerable with the vulnerable, and powerless with the powerless.' 'Compassion means full immersion in the condition of being human.'[138]

Compassionate people continue to care even when such caring costs. In counting the cost and paying it, true joy is experienced. Henri Nouwen puts it well:

'Compassion is not a bending toward the underprivileged from a privileged position; it is not a reaching out from on high to those who are less fortunate below; it is not a gesture of sympathy or pity for those who fail to make it in the upward pull. On the contrary, compassion means going directly to those people and places where suffering is most acute and building a home there.'[139]

(Taken from Listening to Others, pp 20, 27, 28)

# Tuning in to Anguish

*God knows how much I miss you all, loving*
*you as Christ Jesus loves you*
**Philippians 1:8**

J esus was full of compassion for people. When they suffered, he
suffered with them. Jesus reacted to pain in this way because it
is the way that God reacts to human suffering. Jesus' solidarity
with our suffering reveals his Father's identification with the
depth of our need.

Jesus healed people for one reason only – not to impress them,
nor to prove his divinity, but because their pain created such an ache
within his own heart that he suffered with them. Hurting humanity
called from him this depth of concern for the sufferer so he stretched
out the helping hand which rescued, restored and, in many cases,
healed. He was the personification of compassion.

Jesus received this ability to tune in to human anguish and identify
with people's pain from his Father, and in turn passed it on to his
disciples. He passed it on to Paul who, we read, was filled with tender
compassion for the converts in Philippi (Phil. 1:8).

It is a quality all would-be carers and listeners need. For where
such Christ-like compassion is absent, stretching out to others
sometimes has a hollow ring about it. At best such help can come
across as dutiful, brash or insensitive. At worst it can even seem
unkind or cruel.

A desire to comfort and protect is a sign that the seeds of
compassion have been sown but not an indication that the mature
fruit has yet ripened.

(Taken from Listening to Others, pp 30, 31, 32)

# Love One Another

*Be compassionate as your Father is
compassionate*
Luke 6:36

The word 'God' will convey nothing to the majority of people. For some, God is synonymous with a spoil-sport, a tyrant, an ogre. Or it is simply a form of abuse. If we are to convey to them 'that God is not a distant God, a God to be feared and avoided, a God of revenge, but a God who is moved by our pain and participates in the fullness of the human struggle',[140] it is vital that we ourselves embody these characteristics. This may mean that we are given the costly role of staying alongside the broken and the powerless, supporting them with our presence as well as our presents for as long as it takes, trusting that through our support they will find Emmanuel, God with us. We shall be called to spend less time in the cosy corners of our Christian fellowships. Instead, compassion may ask us 'to go where it hurts, to enter into places of pain, to share in brokenness, fear, confusion, and anguish ... to cry out with those in misery, to mourn with those who are lonely, to weep with those in tears'. For 'compassion requires us to be weak with the weak, vulnerable with the vulnerable, and powerless with the powerless. Compassion means full immersion in the condition of being human.'[141]

(Taken from Under the Caring Eye of God, p 226)

# Concern for Others

*Daughters of Jerusalem, do not weep for me; weep rather for yourselves and for your children. For look, the days are surely coming when people will say. 'Blessed are those who are barren, the wombs that have never borne children, the breasts that have never suckled!' Then they will begin to say to the mountains, 'Fall on us!'; to the hills, 'Cover us!'*

Luke 23:28–30 (JB)

Too weak to carry his own cross, a cause of concern for the centurion in charge of the procession, Jesus' reaction to the 'women of Jerusalem' must surely have surprised everyone. In all probability, these women were part of an organized group who were called 'the charitable women of Jerusalem'. They were official mourners, people with permission to offer sedative drinks to condemned criminals. When they saw Jesus dragging one foot after the other along the rough road, they seem to have had genuine pity for him. Their tears seem to have been real tears of sorrow and Jesus summons the strength to speak to them.

Even the most selfless person, when suffering, finds it hard to think of anything but their own pain. Not so Jesus. Despite his physical frailty, he seems to have ignored his own pain and concerned himself with the anguish these women and their children would suffer when Jerusalem was razed to the ground and those who survived the atrocities were taken into exile.

(Taken from God's Springtime, p 100)

# He Yielded up His Spirit

*At the sixth hour darkness came over the
whole land until the ninth hour. And at the
ninth hour Jesus cried out in a loud voice,
'Eloi, Eloi, lama sabachthani?'
which means,
'My God, my God, why have you forsaken
me?'*
Mark 15:33,34.

Mark's account of the Crucifixion stuns in its solemnity.
When you see Jesus writhing on the cross before your very
eyes, you have to make a personal response of humble,
grateful surrender to such depths of loving.

(Taken from Listening to God, pp 151, 152, 153)

# Descent into Trust

*Do you believe that I can heal you?*
### Matthew 9:28

Just as, at his Baptism, Jesus descended into the green waters of the Jordan and was submerged by them, so in Gethsemane he descended into the depths of his own dread: the dread of being encrusted with the evil which pollutes the world; the deeper dread of being separated from his Father. As he makes his descent, a curious thing happens. Terror turns to trust. He drops, not into nothingness but into the arms of the indwelling Father who sustains him. From deep within himself he finds welling up the will to say 'Yes' to whatever his Father requires of him. His will becomes one with the Father's. In his weakness, he discovers the secret of strength: it lies within him in the person of his Father.

In the same way, as we listen to the language of our own pain, as we go further, and pluck up the courage to plumb its depths, we find that God's strength is, indeed, made perfect in our weakness. It brings us to the well-springs of life: that indwelling source of sustenance and renewal which always flows into us from the Father, the Son and the Holy Spirit and out of us to touch the world.

(Taken from Under the Caring Eye of God, p 221)

# Who are You Lord?

*I am Jesus, whom you are persecuting*
Acts 9:5

Saul was breathing out murderous threats against the Lord's disciples. He went to the high priest and asked him for letters to the synagogues in Damascus, so that if he found any there who belonged to the Way, whether men or women, he might take them as prisoners to Jerusalem. As he neared Damascus on his journey, suddenly a light from heaven flashed around him. He fell to the ground and heard a voice say to him, 'Saul, Saul, why do you persecute me?'

'Who are you, Lord?' Saul asked.

'I am Jesus, whom you are persecuting,' he replied. 'Now get up and go into the city, and you will be told what you must do.' (Acts 9:1–6)

Pray using the words of St Paul:

Convince me, Lord,
that neither death nor life,
neither messenger of heaven nor monarch of earth,
neither what happens today nor what may happen tomorrow,
neither a power from on high nor a power from below,
nor anything else in God's whole world
may possess any power to separate me from the love of God.

(An adaptation of Romans 8:38–9)

# Your Sight is Restored

*The Spirit told Philip, 'Go to that chariot and*
*stay near it.' Then Philip ran . . .*
Acts 8:29,30

The result of Philip's obedient listening is well known: the Ethiopian turned to Christ. Similarly, the punch-line of the Saul and Ananias story is familiar: Saul's sight was restored and the direction of his life changed.

The Lord told him [Ananias], 'Go to the house of Judas on Straight Street and ask for a man from Tarsus named Saul, for he is praying. In a vision he has seen a man named Ananias come and place his hands on him to restore his sight.'

. . . Then Ananias went to the house and entered it. Placing his hands on Saul, he said, 'Brother Saul, the Lord . . . has sent me so that you may see again and be filled with the Holy Spirit.' Immediately, something like scales fell from Saul's eyes, and he could see again (Acts 9:11–12, 17–18).

# Moved With Compassion

*He had compassion for them and healed their sick*
Matthew 14:14

Henri Nouwen describes Jesus' reaction to human suffering powerfully:

There is a beautiful expression in the Gospels that appears only twelve times and is used exclusively of Jesus or his Father. That expression is 'to be moved with compassion'. The Greek verb *splangchnizomai* reveals to us the deep and powerful meaning of this expression. The *splangchna* are the entrails of the body or as we might say today, the guts. They are the place where our most intimate and intense emotions are located . . . When Jesus was moved to compassion, the source of all life trembled, the ground of all love burst open, and the abyss of God's immense, inexhaustible, and unfathomable tenderness revealed itself . . .

When Jesus saw the crowd harassed and dejected like sheep without a shepherd, he felt with them in the center of his being (Matt. 9:36). When he saw the blind, the paralysed, and the deaf being brought to him from all directions, he trembled from within and experienced their pains in his own heart (Matt. 14:14). They moved him, they made him feel with all his intimate sensibilities the depth of their sorrow. He became lost with the lost, hungry with the hungry, and sick with the sick. In him, all suffering was sensed with a perfect sensitivity.[142]

# God's Radiance

### *The glory of God is the city's light and its lamp is the lamb*
**Revelation 21:23**

Symeon, a theologian of the eleventh century, tells how Christ revealed himself in a vision of light:

You shone upon me with brilliant radiance and, so it seemed, you appeared to me in your wholeness as with my whole self I gazed openly upon you. And when I said, 'Master, who are you?' then you were pleased to speak for the first time with me, the prodigal. With what gentleness did you talk to me, as I stood astonished and trembling, as I reflected a little within myself and said: 'What does this glory and this dazzling brightness mean? How is it that I am chosen to receive such great blessings?' 'I am God,' you replied, 'who became man for your sake; and because you have sought me with your whole heart, see from this time onwards you shall be my brother, my fellow-heir and my friend.'[143]

(Taken from Listening to God, pp 109, 110)

# Trusting Jesus

*Whether you turn to the right or the left, your ears will hear a voice behind you, saying, 'This is the way; walk in it'*
Isaiah 30:21

A woman told me of an experience which changed the direction of her life.

She was an unbeliever and was lying in her hospital bed knowing that she was suffering from cancer. In intense pain, she longed for the injection which would prepare her for the operation she was to undergo that afternoon. Since there was no sign of the nurse, she lay back on her pillow, closed her eyes and tried to relax. All of a sudden, standing by her bedside, she 'saw' a priest and another person whom she took to be Jesus. Jesus stretched out his hand and held hers. A calmness spread through her body. Jesus invited her to trust him for the future. She promised him that if she recovered from the anaesthetic, she would live life his way. She did survive. And she kept her promise.

She has turned her back on the past and faced towards the living God.

(Taken from Listening to God, pp 107, 108)

# Pray for a Miracle

*Hannah replied 'I am a woman in great trouble'*
**1 Samuel 1:15**

A young married couple once came for counselling. For several years they had tried to start a family. When the wife failed to conceive they both subjected themselves to the necessary tests. These tests revealed that the husband was infertile. Should they adopt a child? Should they follow the advice they had been given and conceive a child with A.I.D.?

While they talked about their disappointment and moral dilemma, the Holy Spirit of God seemed to whisper the words, 'Pray for a miracle' in my spiritual ears. I had never prayed for a miracle baby before and was not sure that my faith would stretch that far. But the voice persisted so eventually I asked, 'Has it ever occurred to you that God might want to perform a miracle and give you a baby by natural means?'

The wife's face lit up. She, too, had sensed that this might be God's answer to their problem. The husband was uncertain. 'Supposing we pray and nothing happens?'

By this time the conviction in me was so strong that I suggested the husband borrowed the combination of his wife's faith and the little I could muster and we prayed that God would give them the gift of a child.

Six months later, the phone rang. I know the husband well and recognised his voice: 'Joyce! I've got something to tell you. My wife's pregnant.'

(Taken from Listening to God, p 206)

# Miracle of Love

## *Be filled with the Spirit*
### Ephesians 5:18

To be filled with the Spirit means to be filled with God. To be filled with God means to be filled with love. This Spirit-filling is no optional extra for super-keen Christians. It is a requirement for us all. It is the way to reach our goal. It entails, allowing the fabric of your life to be held in the dye of Jesus' love until every fibre is tinged with that love. There must be no attempt at tie-dying, the process whereby some patches of cloth are deliberately protected from the dye-stain. Every particle must submit itself to the penetrating influence of divine love. Every particle must be transformed. Christians who expose themselves regularly to divine love, will find themselves displaying that Christ-like love: in word, touch, look, and will. It may take years. It often does. But the miracle of love will happen. And the person who truly loves is truly free.

(Taken from Living Free, p 105)

# Abounding Harvest

*The Lord has clothed me in garments of salvation he has wrapped me in a cloak of saving justice*
**Isaiah 62:10**

This prayer never ceases to move me:

Anoint the wounds of my spirit with the balm of forgiveness pour the oil of your calm on the waters of my heart take the squeal of frustration from the wheels of my passion that the power of your tenderness may smooth the way I love that the tedium of giving in the risk of surrender and the reaching out naked to a world that must wound may be kindled fresh daily to a blaze of compassion that the grain may fall gladly to burst in the ground — and the harvest abound.[144]

# Encountering God

*What we have heard, what we have seen with our eyes, what we have looked upon and touched with our hands is the word of life*
I John 1:1

A sk the Holy Spirit to open your spiritual eyes so as to encounter God in a new way:

Open my eyes, Lord,
I want to see Jesus,
To reach out and touch him,
To say that I love him,
Open my ears, Lord,
And help me to listen.
Open my eyes, Lord,
I want to see Jesus.

Reflect on these words written on the wall of a Nazi concentration camp.

I believe in the sun, even when it isn't shining,
I believe in love, even when I feel it not.
I believe in God, even when He is silent.

Recall some of the people and things and events which have helped to firm up your belief. Write down reasons why you may doubt that God loves you.

Tell God these doubts. Let him respond.

(Taken from the Smile of Love, p 163)

# Moulded by God

*We are the clay, you are the potter; we are all
the work of your hand*
Isaiah 64:8

One evening I was praying with my prayer group in my home. We had each been given a lump of clay which we worked while one of the group read verses of Scripture comparing our lives to clay in the heavenly potter's hands.

I was astonished to discover how quickly the crude, cold lump was warmed by the heat of my hands, how malleable it became and how I longed to make of it something beautiful. I pummelled it and rolled it, squeezed it and moulded it until, at last, I created a small dish with a scalloped edge. By that time it belonged to me even though it had an identity all its own. I held it in reverence. And when someone suggested that we might end the evening by placing the objects we had made back into the sack of raw clay, a wave of protest swept over me. 'I couldn't bear to do that, it's special.'

I placed it on a window sill and, for days, would finger it affectionately. I still have it in my prayer room and would be sad to part with it.

Others in the group confessed to similar feelings of attachment for the objects they had made. It underlined how precious each of us is to God; how precious, too, is each particle of his creation.

(Taken from the Smile of Love pp 36, 37)

# The Hands of the Potter

*'Go down to the potter's house, and there I will give you my message.' So I went down to the potter's house, and I saw him working at the wheel. But the pot he was shaping from the clay was marred in his hands; so the potter formed it into another pot, shaping it as seemed best to him.*
*Then the word of the Lord came to me: 'O house of Israel, can I not do with you as this potter does? . . . Like clay in the hand of the potter, so are you in my hand'*
Jeremiah 18:1–6

A lump of clay is full of potential. But clay, if it is to become sufficiently resilient in the potter's hands to become the beautiful vessel the potter always intended, must be malleable, free from all impurities, bubbles and grit.

When we meditate, whether we realise it or not, we are placing ourselves into the hands of the living God. And when we pray, God is at work, ridding us of the dirt which makes it impossible for him to re-shape us.

Feel the hands of the potter pushing and prodding, pressing and pummelling this clay of our life.

Is this painful or pleasant?

What do I want to say to the potter?

Notice whether the fingers of God are rough and chapped like some labourers' hands or long, gentle and skilful. Notice whether the touch of God calms or distresses you and why.

(Taken from Open to God, pp 109, 110)

# Heart of Flesh

*I shall give you a new heart and put a new
spirit within you. I shall remove the heart of
stone from your bodies and give you a heart
of flesh instead*
Ezekiel 36:26

B ecause of the death of Jesus, our sin-stained hearts and guilt
ridden consciences can be cleansed. Our stone-hard hearts
which are so slow to believe can be replaced with hearts of
flesh which are quick to discern and believe God's activity in the
world and the lives of his people. This purification and fertilisation
of the soil of our life happens most effectively when we are silent
before God and attentive to him. It is then that the seedlings of
God's Word can take root and begin to bear fruit.

(Taken from the Introduction to Praying with the New Testament,
pp x, xi)

# A Legion of Angels

*The angel of the Lord encamps around those*
*who fear him, and he delivers them*
Psalm 34:7

Billy Graham shares this with us:
'The Reverend John G Paton, a missionary in the New Hebrides Islands, tells a thrilling story involving the protective care of angels. Hostile natives surrounded his mission headquarters one night, intent on burning the Patons out and killing them. John Paton and his wife prayed all during that terror-filled night that God would deliver them. When daylight came they were amazed to see the attackers unaccountably leave. They thanked God for delivering them.

A year later, the chief of the tribe was converted to Jesus Christ, and Mr Paton, remembering what had happened, asked the chief what had kept him and his men from burning down the house and killing them. The chief replied in surprise, 'Who were all those men you had with you there?' The missionary answered, 'There were no men there; just my wife and I.' The chief argued that they had seen many men standing guard — hundreds of big men in shining garments with drawn swords in their hands. They seemed to circle the mission station so that the natives were afraid to attack. Only then did Mr Paton realise that God had sent his angels to protect them. The chief agreed that there was no other explanation. Could it be that God had sent a legion of angels to protect his servants, whose lives were being endangered?'[145]

# Ministering Spirits

*Angels are ministering spirits sent to serve
those who will inherit salvation*
Hebrews 1:14

Myriads of these exotic, glorious, non-material beings shuttle through the pages of the Bible fulfilling their ambassadorial vocation; they offer guidance and give specific instructions:

> An angel of the Lord appeared to Joseph in a dream. 'Get up,' he said, 'take the child and his mother and escape to Egypt' (Matt. 2:13).

They give advance warning of certain events:

> The angel of the Lord appeared to her and said, 'You are sterile and childless, but you are going to conceive and have a son' (Judg. 13:3).
> The angel said to her, 'Do not be afraid, Mary, you have found favour with God. You will be with child and give birth to a son, and you are to give him the name Jesus' (Luke 1:30).

These spokesmen sent from God stun me by their glory and silence my unbelief. In the days when the Bible was penned, angels existed, angels spoke and angels acted.

(Taken from Listening to God, pp 110, 111, 113)

# Heavenly Protection

*See I am sending an angel ahead of you to*
*guard you along the way*
Exodus 23:20

God still sends his agents to protect and direct us:

When I was visiting the American troops during the Korean war, I was told of a small group of American marines in the First Division who had been trapped up north. With the thermometer at 20° below zero, they were close to freezing to death. And they had had nothing to eat for six days. Surrender to the Chinese seemed their only hope of survival. But one of the men, a Christian, pointed out certain verses of scripture and taught his comrades to sing a song of praise to God. Following this they heard a crashing noise, and turned to see a wild boar rushing towards them. As they tried to jump out of his way, he suddenly stopped in his tracks. One of the soldiers raised his rifle to shoot, but before he could fire, the boar inexplicably toppled over. They rushed up to kill him only to find that he was already dead. That night they feasted on meat, and began to regain strength.

The next morning, just as the sun was rising, they heard another noise. Their fear that a Chinese patrol had discovered them suddenly vanished as they found themselves face to face with a South Korean who could speak English. He said, 'I will show you out.' He led them through the forest and mountains to safety behind their own lines. When they looked up to thank him, they found he had disappeared.'146

# Meeting Jesus

*Let us go to Bethlehem and see this event
which the Lord has made known to us*
Luke 2:15

'To know the reality of Jesus.' That for many people is precisely what happens when they begin to meditate on the Gospels using the gift of the imagination. I think of a priest who confessed, 'For years, God for me has been the great unknowable, the Other. But now, thanks to the gift of the imagination, I have encountered him in the depths of my being.' Or the woman who had been praying for years before she discovered the rich resource inside her – her imagination. When she first contemplated the new-born Christ-child in this way she wept. 'I actually saw the Christ-child. I saw his tiny fingers and his outstretched hands. What's more, Mary placed him in my arms. I couldn't believe her generosity. But I held him.' Others similarly have asked, 'Can Christmas ever be the same now that I have been present at his birth?' 'Present at Christ's birth?' In one sense of course they were not present. But in another sense, in their imagination, they have been there, assimilating the sights and sounds and smells; drinking in, too, that inexpressible wonder.

(Taken from Open to God, p 60)

# Presence

*Ours were the sufferings he was bearing,*
*ours the sorrow he was carrying*
Isaiah 53:4

Henri Nouwen writes movingly of the importance of presence:

'When do we receive real comfort and consolation? Is it when someone teaches us how to think or act? Is it when we receive advice about where to go or what to do? Is it when we hear words of reassurance and hope? Sometimes, perhaps. But what really counts is that in moments of pain and suffering someone stays with us. More important than any particular action or word or advice is the simple presence of someone who cares. When someone says to us in the midst of a crisis, 'I do not know what to say or what to do, but I want you to realize that I am with you, that I will not leave you alone,' we have a friend through whom we can find consolation and comfort . . . Simply being with someone is difficult because it asks of us that we share in the other's vulnerability, enter with him or her into the experience of weakness and powerlessness, become part of uncertainty, and give up control and self-determination. And still, whenever this happens, new strength and new hope is being born.'[147]

# Salvation

*'Zacchaeus, come down. Hurry, because
I must stay at your house today'* . . . *They
all complained when they saw what was
happening. 'He has gone to stay at a sinner's
house' they said*
Luke 19:5–7

Zacchaeus was a crook: greedy, fraudulent and ruthless like most Roman employees. And he was hated. But while Jesus was with him Zacchaeus vowed: I will give half my belongings to the poor, and if I have cheated anyone, I will pay him back four times as much' (Luke 19:8). Jesus' response to this vow was a triumphant one: 'Salvation has come to this house today' (Luke 19:9).

The word 'salvation' means deliverance from disease; so it implies health and wholeness. It also means rescue from the power and guilt of sin. 'Saviour', Jesus is the One who will save us from our sin. So quite literally 'salvation' had come to Zacchaeus' house that day. He had been set free from the greed which had held him in its grip for so long, delivered from the desire to live for self, released to serve others, and he had entertained in his own home the Saviour of the world.

Jesus went on to explain that the reason he had come to earth was to seek and to save the lost. Zacchaeus had been lost in the sense that he had lived like a traveller who had lost his way. He had been lost in the sense that he was like a man riddled with disease. He had not only been found, he had been made new. Jesus must therefore have gone on his way strengthened in his resolve to go on searching for the Zacchaeuses of this world, and to go on loving them, even though it would cost him his life.

(Taken from God's Springtime, pp 60, 61)

# Whole Again

*Forgive us our sins as we have forgiven those
who sin against us*
Matthew 6:12

W hen the healing balm of prayer is applied to inner hurts, we lose the desire to carry round with us pockets of poison: the bitterness we once clutched to our breast like a priceless treasure, the resentment we clenched in our tight fists like the last possession we would relinquish to anyone. Healed and restored by Jesus, we are ready to let go of these hindrances. So the next stage is to pour out to Jesus, possibly in the presence of a friend, pastor or counsellor, the full extent of the hostility. The abscess is thus lanced. The poison is drained away. And the blood of Jesus cleanses it from every vestige of sin. When we are thus released from the sin we have nursed, we let go of a burden. We are washed; made new. Whole.

'Forgive'. We must not evade this. Rather, unhesitatingly and generously we must forgive the person who inflicted the pain in the first place and also forgive the person, who, in the present relationship, has been pressing, albeit unwittingly, on past pain. What this means is that, in prayer, we must picture them wounding us. Look them in the eye. Say something like, 'It's really hurting. But just as the Lord has forgiven me, so I forgive you.'

(Taken from Creative Conflict, pp 50, 51)

# Christ Centred

### *What the Father has taught me is what I preach*
John 8:28

Jesus never demands, '*My* will be done,' but rather, 'Father, may *your* will be done'. Jesus never even prays without first pausing to lay the situation before his Father to ask what kind of request he should make (John 8:28). Moreover Jesus rejected outright the temptation to live for 'number one'. He resolved, instead, to respond to God's call to usher in the Kingdom; to keep his Father, not self, as the centre of his universe, no matter what it cost. In other words, he shows us that God exists, not that he might serve us but, rather, that we might serve him. Our need to understand and make this shift from self-centredness to Christ-centredness is more urgent in our day than it has ever been in the history of the Church.

(Taken from The Smile of Love, p 150)

# Kindle Your Love in Me

*'Martha, Martha, you are anxious and*
*troubled about many things'*
Luke 10:41

At last, dear Lord,
I come to you,
Weary from the busyness of a thousand things which
clamour for attention
But longing to feel your touch afresh
This Christmastime.
Kindle in me
A love for you
which finds time for you
which responds to you
which yearns for your return.
Cause my heart to leap for joy
As I anticipate that great fact of the future —
Your re-entry to earth.
Pour into me the certainty that believes
That all life is to be lived under the shadow
Of that miraculous return,
The courage to live life your way
And the resilience to hold on to that hope
When times are hard
Or my body tired.
Bring me to Christmas Day
Not irritated with the commercialization with which
it is surrounded
But rather, rejoicing in the message of the angels
To me, today,
Is born my Saviour
Hallelujah

(Taken from Approaching Christmas, p 7)

# The Joy of Christmas?

*Whatever you do, work at it with all your heart, as working for the Lord, not for men*
Colossians 3:23

The days leading up to Christmas are, for many of us, the most hectic of the year. So much has to be pushed into so few hours, it seems. For the Christian who longs to focus on the true meaning of Christmas – the fact that at this time of year we remember that God sent his Son into the world to be our Saviour – this busyness poses a problem. How can we enjoy to the full the special joys of Christmas-time: the fun, the festivities and the family togetherness, and yet remain God-centred?

Brother Lawrence, the cook in a busy thirteenth-century monastery, testifies that he was as conscious of God's presence when elbow-deep in potato peelings as he was when worshipping God in chapel. And it is said of St Teresa of Avila that she found God so easily among the pots and pans that she rejoiced in an acute awareness of the God who was her constant companion even in the middle of the chaos.

Just as Teresa and Brother Lawrence learned how to cast the occasional loving gaze at God, so we will find that even a kitchen can become a haven if we tune into the sound of God's silence no matter what is going on around us.

(Taken from Approaching Christmas, p 42)

# According to Your Word

*The angel went to Mary and said 'Greetings you who are highly favoured! The Lord is with you'*
Luke 1:28

We are not told what Mary was doing when the angel appeared to her. She was an ordinary peasant girl who was probably not more than fourteen years old. It is most likely that this ordinary girl was performing ordinary domestic duties when God sent his messenger to her. And in one sense what God asked of her was also very ordinary. He simply invited her to continue with the plans which had already been made for her – to marry Joseph. Outwardly her life would not change. But inwardly, in the secret places of her innermost being, as she surrendered to God the gift of her ordinary, everyday life and the gift of her humanity, mysterious and awesome changes would take place. He would infuse this ordinariness with his own divine energy and presence.

'She was not asked to do anything for herself, but to let something be done to her. She was not asked to renounce anything, but to receive an incredible gift.'[148]

Just as God needed all that Mary had and all that she was, to rescue our world from destruction, so he needs us: our souls and bodies, our talents and possessions, our humanity and our ordinariness. And just as he gave the incredible gift of his own life to Mary, so he longs to impregnate us with divine energy and power. But he needs our 'yes'.

(Taken from Open to God, pp 87, 88)

# The Birth of Jesus is Announced

*Be it done to me according to your word*
Luke 1:38

The little town of Nazareth nestled on the slopes of the mountains of Lower Galilee. Its busy, narrow streets rose above the market place in terraces and its houses were small with flat roofs.

The countryside was fragrant with the scent of orange and lemon blossom and aromatic plants. The fields were bright with wild flowers: scarlet anemones, golden crown daisies, and bright-eyed marguerites. Gnarled fig trees, silvery olive trees, dark green cypress trees and graceful palm trees formed a familiar landscape.

We know little about Mary except that she was probably still in her teens and engaged to a carpenter named Joseph when the same angel who had appeared to Zechariah visited her:

> The angel said to her, 'Do not be afraid, Mary; God loves you dearly. You are going to be the mother of a son, and you will call him Jesus. He will be great and will be known as the Son of the Most High. The Lord God will give him the throne of his forefather, David, and he will be king over the people of Jacob for ever. His reign shall never end.' (Luke 1:28–33)

And we see Mary's beautiful act of submission. In this way, Mary became the selfless space where God could become man.

(Taken from Approaching Christmas, pp 56, 57)

# Elizabeth's Son is Born

*Mary set out and went as quickly as she could to a town in the hill country of Judah. She went into Zechariah's house and greeted Elizabeth*
Luke 1:39,40

M ary stayed with Elizabeth for some three months before returning to Nazareth. Just imagine the feelings of excitement and anticipation in those three people: the old priest who had prayed for years that a miracle would happen; the elderly woman who now carried a child whom God clearly was blessing from the time of his conception, and the young girl who marvelled daily at the privilege God was giving her – of becoming the mother of his own Son. Luke describes the events surrounding the safe arrival of God's miracle and how Zechariah's speech is returned when they name the baby John.

The father of a newborn child once tried to capture for me the emotions he felt as he watched his first child being born. 'It was a miracle,' he said. 'Wonderful. This baby is God's baby.'

Zechariah and Elizabeth knew, too, that John the Baptist, as he was to be called, was God's baby. His mission was to prepare the way for Jesus.

(Taken from Approaching Christmas, p 62)

# Fear Not

*While Joseph was turning the matter over in his mind — an angel of the Lord appeared to him in a dream and said, 'Joseph, son of David, do not be afraid to take Mary as your wife! What she has conceived is conceived through the Holy Spirit, and she will give birth to a son, whom you will call Jesus ('the Saviour') for it is he who will save his people from their sins.'*
Matthew 1:20,21

For Joseph a dream would have seemed both a normal and powerful method through which God would communicate his plans. God's dream-vision set Joseph's mind at rest and he replaced thoughts of instant divorce with plans for an immediate marriage. In this way Joseph provided both Mary and the unborn Jesus with the most effective moral support and protection he could possibly give — even though this must have been at cost to himself and despite wagging, gossiping tongues.

*Did Mary lurch*
*From fear to faith*
*From despair to hope*
*From doubt to belief*
*Dear Lord?*
*Or did she remain*
*Calm and serene*
*While Joseph mistrusted her?*
*You do not tell us*
*But the assurance you do give*
*Is that you were there*
*In the pain*

*Caring*
*And sharing*
*Making your purposes plain.*
*When friends ill-treat me,*
*Keep me*
*Trusting in your faithfulness*
*And in your ability to speak,*
*To vindicate,*
*And to restore.*
*So that your perfect purposes*
*May be fulfilled in me*
*As much as in Mary.*

(Taken from Approaching Christmas, p 64, 65)

# Kingdom Moments

## *The kingdom of God is within you*
### Luke 17:21

One way of coming to God is to take advantage of life's 'little solitudes', to borrow Richard Foster's phrase – those early morning moments in bed before the family wakes up, that cup of coffee in the middle of the morning, sitting in bumper to bumper traffic during the rush hour, travelling by train or by car, queuing in the supermarket. Snippets of time I once heard dubbed 'Kingdom moments'. We can train ourselves to sense the presence of the indwelling Christ in such moments just as Mary did when God's Son was forming in her womb: She who began by enclosing God within her womb, herself needs no enclosure . . . Hers the busy day of cooking, washing, sweeping, shopping at the noisy bazaar, sewing, mending, nursing, but through it all, the awe-inspiring love-union with the Lord.[149]

Commuters and journalists, politicians and film-producers, pilots and firemen, office workers and social workers and others whose work day is notoriously stressful might envy Mary and question whether there are any kingdom moments in their day.

There are: the challenge comes to each of us to recognise them.

(Taken from Open to God, pp 27–28)

# The Birth of Jesus

*Mary gave birth to her firstborn son and laid
him in a manger*
Luke 2:7

The journey from Nazareth to Bethlehem was eighty miles –
not the kind of donkey ride most pregnant women would
relish. Travellers took their own food on such a journey and
were offered only the most primitive of accommodation. When Mary
and Joseph arrived in Bethlehem they found the tiny town already
overcrowded. That was why the Saviour of the world made his entry
into the world in a common cave. And that was why his crib was the
animals' feeding-trough.

There has never been a time when I have not accepted with my
head that Jesus, God's Son, was born in a humble cave in Bethlehem.
But it was not until I visited the Holy Land for myself that I grasped
fully this fact with my heart.

I remember the moment of revelation well. It happened in the crypt
of the Church of the Nativity in Bethlehem: the church which has
been built over the spot where it is believed that Jesus was born.

Gazing at the spot where the manger is supposed to have stood,
tears began to trickle down my face. These tears, I knew, were tears
of awe and wonder. Deep within me a certainty had taken root. God
really had sent his Son to earth. It had happened here in Bethlehem.
And he had come as a baby: dependent, wanting and needing to
be found and touched and held and loved by those among whom
he lived.

(Taken from Approaching Christmas, pp 67, 68)

# The Christ Child

## *To you is born a Saviour*
### Luke 2:11

Imagine that you are kneeling beside the new-born Son of God. Gaze, marvel, adore. Express any emotions which surface in any way which seems appropriate: with your body, your voice, through writing or drawing. And ask yourself:

Is there anything I want to say to him?

Is there anything I want to do for him?

What can I learn from him?

How do I want to answer his question: 'What do you want?'

Is there anything he wants to say to me?

Is there anything he wants me to do for him?

Is there anything he wanted me to do for him?

Do not hurry. Relish each moment and ponder the mystery of it all.

*Wisdom unsearchable*
*God the invisible*
*Love indestructible*
*in frailty appears.*
*Lord of infinity*
*Stooping so tenderly*
*Lifts our humanity*
*To the heights of His throne.*
*Oh, what a mystery,*
*Meekness and majesty,*
*Bow down and worship*
*For this is our God.*[150]

(Taken from Open to God, pp 118, 129)

# The Shepherds

*There were some shepherds living in the
same part of the country, keeping guard
throughout the night over their flock in the
open fields. Suddenly an angel of the Lord
stood by their side, the splendour of the Lord
blazed around them, and they were terror-
stricken. But the angel said to them, 'Do not
be afraid! Listen, I bring you glorious news
of great joy which is for all the people. This
very day, in David's town, a Saviour has been
born for you. He is Christ, the Lord. Let this
prove it to you: you will find a baby, wrapped
up and lying in a manger'*
Luke 2:8–12

The shepherds, still dazzled by the brilliance of the angelic
choir, somehow made their way up the terraced slopes of
Bethlehem to the cave where the newborn baby lay. The
sight of the baby – God in a manger – changed their lives. They
returned to their work of shepherding overflowing with wonder and
praise and awe.

*Loving Father, this Christmas, like the shepherds, I would bow
in awed wonder before the majesty of heaven revealed in the form of
a baby. Fill me afresh with love as I contemplate these mysteries.
Reveal yourself to me so that, like the shepherds and the angels,
my heart may be filled with joy. And transform me so that this
Christmas I may become more and more like this Christ-child I
worship: ready to do your will in everything, even at cost to myself.*

(Taken from Approaching Christmas, pp 70, 71)

# Guided by a Star

*We saw his star as it rose and have come to do*
*him homage*
Matthew 2:2

When Jesus came to earth as a baby, God made sure that all sorts of people knew he was coming. Matthew tells us how 'wise men' as far away as Persia discovered the secret of the Messiah's miraculous birth. They came to the capital, Jerusalem, looking for an infant king. Herod's advisers tell him that it is in Bethlehem that 'the Christ' will be born.

These wise men, or Magi, were professional astrologers who had been trained to read the language of the sky. We do not know quite what they saw in the heavens to tell them that a king had been born in Palestine. What we do know is that some heavenly brilliance assured them that a new 'king' had made his entrance into the world. So here again we see God speaking powerfully to people who are going about their normal everyday tasks — even when that task is to read the signs of the stars.

*All-powerful Father,*
*you have made known the birth of the Saviour*
*by the light of a star*
*May he continue to guide us with his light*
*Enlighten us with his radiance*
*And strengthen us with his care*
*Until, with joy,*
*He takes us to our eternal home.*[151]

(Taken from Approaching Christmas, pp 88, 89)

# Give Him Your Heart

## *Jesus looked at him and loved him*
Mark 10:21

What can I give him, poor as I am
If I were a shepherd, I would bring a lamb
If I were a wise man, I would do my part
Yet what I can I give him, give my heart.
(C. Rossetti)

'Give my heart.' When I sang that as a child, my heart would be strangely warmed. For years I used to think that that warmth was all that was needed because I was simply required to give my love, my adoration, my worship and my praise. But now I see that it means all of that and much more. For Christ calls us to give to him the compassionate heart that prompts us to serve him in others. He calls us, too, to give him our listening heart – the heart that listens to God and to others; that is sensitive to sorrow but is equally quick to tune into joy.

(Taken from Listening to Others, p 250)

# To be with You

*Though he was rich, yet for your sake he*
*became poor*
2 Corinthians 8:9

**W**hy, Lord, Why?
    Why did you exchange the spaciousness of heaven
    And the warmth of your Father's presence
For the squalor of a manger on earth
And the limitations of life as a man?
Why did you who made the heavens
The mountains
The stars
The sun
Strip yourself of your glory
To become a helpless, homeless baby?
Why did you come here
To this spot
To Bethlehem?

I came, my child, because I love you
I have always loved you
I will always love you
I came to rescue you from the clutches of the Evil One
To deliver you from sin
To be your Saviour.
And I came as the prophets foretold:
To Bethlehem
To a woman's womb
To indwell you as I indwelt her
To become
Emmanuel
God with you and God in you.

(Taken from Approaching Christmas, p 69)

# Beloved Author of my Faith

*Holy, Holy, Holy, is the Lord, the Almighty,*
*he was, he is and he is to come*
**Revelation 4:8**

George Appleton writes movingly of God's revelation:

*Open my eyes, O Lord,*
*that I may see the chariots of fire,*
*and the crowd of watching angels and saints,*
*the four living creatures of creation,*
*the hosts of the redeemed,*
*from every nation and every generation,*
*and thyself, standing in the place of power,*
*directing thy Kingdom*
*and strengthening every struggling follower.*
*So seeing thee,*
*may I be held quiet and unafraid,*
*ready and daring, to be and do and bear*
*all that thy loving wisdom allows or wills,*
*O beloved Author and Finisher of my faith.*[152]

# Bibliography

Approaching Christmas, Lion Publishing, Oxford, 1987
Approaching Easter, Lion Publishing, Oxford, 1987
Bible Reading Fellowship Notes, BRF, Oxford, 1990
Conflict, Friend or Foe, Kingsway, Eastbourne, 1984
God's Springtime (book), Bible Reading Fellowship, Oxford, 1992
God's Springtime (cassette), Eagle, Guildford, 1992
Growing into Love, InterVarsity Press, Leicester, 1982
Just Good Friends, InterVarsity Press, Leicester, 1986
Living Free, InterVarsity Press, Leicester, 1986
Listening to God, Hodder & Stoughton, London, 1986
Open to God, Hodder & Stoughton, London, 1989
Marriage Matters, Eagle, Guildford, 1991
Prayer Journal, Marshall Pickering, London, 1990
The Smile of Love, Hodder & Stoughton, London, 1990
Two into One, InterVarsity Press, Leicester, 1981
Under the Caring Eye of God, Eagle, Guildford, 1991

# Notes

1 Valeria Boldoni (ed) Paula Clifford (tr) *Praying with Saint Augustine* SPCK 1987 pp 29–30.
2 Rene Philombwo (Cameroon writer) quoted by J. Veltri SJ in *Orientations* Loyola Press 1979.
3 André Louf *Teach us to Pray* DLT 1974.
4 Jim Bigelow *Love Has Come Again* Lakeland 1979 p 48.
5 Catherine de Hueck Doherty *Poustinia* Collins Fount 1975 p 20.
6 Erich Fromm *The Art of Loving* Unwin Books 1975 p 26.
7 André Louf *Teach us to Pray* DLT 1974 p 38.
8 Corrie ten Boom *The Hiding Place*, Hodder & Stoughton.
9 John Tauler, quoted in Tony Castle *The Perfection of Love* Fount 1986 pp 45–46.
10 John Powell *He Touched Me* Argus 1974 p 79.
11 Catherine de Hueck Doherty. *Poustinia* Collins Fount 1975 p 20.
12 F.B. Meyer *The Shepherd Psalm* Marshall, Mogan & Scott 1953 pp 28, 30.
13 Abraham Schmitt, *Listening with Love* Abingdon Press 1977 p 9.
14 J.I. Packer *Knowing God* Hodder and Stoughton 1973 p 264.
15 Agnes Sandford *Sealed Orders* Logos 1972 pp 112–114.
16 David Augsburger, *Caring Enough To Hear and Be Heard*, Herald Press, Ontario, 1982, p 25.
17 John Powell, *Will the Real Me Please Stand Up?* Argus 1985 p 113.
18 Ibid. p 142.
19 Ibid p 147.
20 Ibid p 145.
21 Ibid p 162.
22 William Barclay: *The Gospel of Matthew:* vol 2. p 60, St Andrew Press 1975.
23 Michel Quoist *Prayers of Life* Gill and Macmillan.
24 Thomas Merton *Meditations on the Liturgy* Mowbrays 1965, p 105.
25 Jim Wallis *Call to Conversion* Lion 1981 p 5.
26 Martyn Lloyd-Jones quoted by D. Watson *God's Freedom Fighters* Movement Books 1972 p 48.
27 Peter Toon, *Meditating Upon God's Word*, DLT 1988 p 38.

28 Thomas Merton *Contemplative Prayer* DLT 1973 p 15 (italics J.H.).

29 Corrie ten Boom *He Cares, He Comforts*, Lakeland Paperbacks.

30 Richard Foster *Celebration of Discipline*, Hodder, 1978 p 17.

31 William Barclay *The Gospel of Matthew*; St Andrew Press.

32 Margaret Gray *The Donkey's Tale*, Scripture Union 1984.

33 *Lent, Holy Week, Easter*, Church House Publishing p 46.

34 *The Lenten Triodion* p 582.

35 Peter Green *Watchers by the Cross* Longmans, Green and Co Ltd p 15.

36 *Lent, Holy Week, Easter*, Church House Publishing 1986 p 211.

37 Brian Greenway, with Brian Killuck, *Hell's Angel*, Lion 1982, pp 91–92.

38 Caryll Houselander, *The Stations of the Cross*, Sheed & Ward, p 143.

39 Anthony Bloom, *Meditations on a Theme*, Mowbrays, 1971.

40 Gary Collins: *How to be a People Helper* 1985, chapter 3.

41 C.S. Lewis: *The Lion, the Witch and the Wardrobe*; Puffin, 1965, pp 147–149.

42 Anthony Bloom: *Living Prayer* Libra 1976 p 12.

43 David Watson: *Discipleship*, Hodder & Stoughton 1981.

44 J.B. Phillips: *Your God is Too Small*, Wyvern Books, 1960, pp 123–124.

45 Jim Wallis: *Call to Conversion*, Lion 1981, p 108.

46 S.D. Gordon: *Quiet Talks on Power*, Revell pp 41–43.

47 George Sinker; *Jesus Loved Martha*, St Hugh's Press, 1949, p 11.

48 Ibid. p 12.

49 Ibid. p 14.

50 Guy Brinkworth, S.J.: *Thirsting for God*, Mullan Press.

51 George Appleton; *Prayers from a Troubled Heart*, DLT, 1983, p 50.

52 Evelyn Underhill; *Light of Christ*, Longman, Green & Co, 1944, p 27.

53 Richard Foster; *Celebration of Discipline*, Hodder & Stoughton 1980, p 177.

54 C.S. Lewis; *The Screwtape Letters*, Fontana, 1956, p 114.

55 J.I. Packer; *God's Words*, IVP, 1981, p 36.

56 Martin Luther quoted by Donald Coggan; *The Sacrament of the Word*, Fount, 1987, p 23.

57 John Tauler; *The Perfection of Love*, Collins Publishers.

58 J.B. Phillips; *Ring of Truth*, Hodder & Stoughton, 1957, p 18.

59 Richard Foster; *Celebration of Discipline*, Hodder & Stoughton, 1980, p 24.

60 David Augsburger; *Caring Enough to Hear and be Heard*, Herald Press, 1982, p 152.

61 C.S. Lewis; *Mere Christianity*, Collins Fount, 1977, p 172.

62 *Be angry and sin not* Care and Counsel, Pamphlet no 2. 1980.
63 Elizabeth, quoted by David Atkinson in *The Message of Ruth: The Wings of Refuge* (IVP 1983) pp 29–30.
64 Margaret Evening; *Who Walk Alone*, Hodder and Stoughton, 1974, p 38.
65 David Watson *Discipleship*, Hodder & Stoughton, 1981, p 149.
66 John Powell; *Will the Real Me Please Stand Up?*, Harlow, Argus, 1985, p 9.
67 Ibid p 14.
68 Ibid p 16.
69 Monica Furlong; *Christian Uncertainties*, Hodder & Stoughton, 1975, p 15.
70 Lewis Smedes, *Love within limits*, Lion, 1979, p 10.
71 Margery Williams *The Velveteen Rabbit* Heineman, 1977 pp 14–15.
72 Gary Collins; *How to be a People Helper*, Regal Books, 1976, p 58.
73 Michael Jacobs; *Swift to Hear*, SPCK, 1985, pp 124, 125.
74 Michel Quoist; *Prayers of Life* Sheed & Ward, 1963, pp 91, 92.
75 Sheldon Vanauken; *A Severe Mercy*, London, Hodder & Stoughton, 1977, p 36.
76 Quoted by Mark Link; *You* Argus 1976, p 94.
77 Quoted by Carlo Carretto; *Made in Heaven*, DLT 1978, p 57.
78 Kahlil Gibran; *The Prophet*, Heinemann, 1926, p 16.
79 *Reaching Out*, Fount, 1975, p 91.
80 Neville Ward, *Friday Afternoon* (Epworth, undated) p 19.
81 John Powell, *The Secret of Staying in Love* Argus 1974 p 44.
82 Ibid p 44.
83 C.S. Lewis, *A Grief Observed* Faber, 1961, p 18.
84 Keith Miller; *Habitation of Dragons*, Word Books, 1970, pp 185–186.
85 Louis Evely, *Joy*, Burns & Oates, 1968, p 39.
86 Ibid.
87 Margaret Evening. *Who Walk Alone* Hodder & Stoughton 1974 p 220.
88 Ibid pp 200–221.
89 John Stott, *The Cross of Christ*, IVP, 1986, p 183.
90 Judith Pinhey, *The Music of Love*, Collins Fount, 1990, p 142.
91 Julian of Norwich, *Enfolded in Love*, DLT, 1980, p 38.
92 Ibid, p 55.
93 Abbé de Tourville; *Letters of Direction*, Oxford, Mowbrays, 1984.
94 Julian of Norwich, *Enfolded in Love*, DLT, 1980, p 1.
95 Ibid, p 6.
96 Ibid, p 3.
97 Jacqueline Syrup Bergan and S. Marie Schwab; *Love: A Guide for Prayer* from the *Take and Receive Series*, Winona, MN, USA, St Mary's Press, 1986, p 11.

98  Louis Evely; *Joy*, Burns & Oates, 1968.
99  Gerard Hughes' phrase.
100 J.B. Phillips; *Your God is Too Small*, Wyvern Books, 1956, pp 47–8.
101 Jim Packer; *Laid Back Religion*, IVP, 1989, p 52.
102 Charles Elliott; *Praying The Kingdom*, DLT, 1985, p 66.
103 Delia Smith; *Journey into God*, Hodder & Stoughton, 1989.
104 Francis Thompson, *The Hound of Heaven*, Mowbrays, p 4.
105 Dean Eric Milner-White; *The Light of Grace* quoted in *My God, My Glory*, SPCK, 1954, p 158.
106 Tito Colliander.
107 James Houston; *The Transforming Friendship*, Lion, 1989, p 295.
108 Macrina Wiederkehr OSB *A Tree Full of Angels* San Francisco, Harper & Row 1988 pp 49–50.
109 Carlo Carretto; *Summoned by Love*, DLT, London.
110 Inspired by Gerard W. Hughes SJ in a talk in Westminster Abbey, February 1989.
111 Henri J.N. Nouwen; *The Genesee Diary*, Image Books, 1981, p 14.
112 Ibid p 135.
113 Guy Brinkworth SJ; *Thirsting for God*, Mullan Press, p 12.
114 Ibid, p 13.
115 Richard Foster; *Meditative Prayer*, MARC Europe, 1983, pp 23–4.
116 Quoted in *You*, by Mark Link, Argus, 1976, p 53.
117 Sr Margaret Magdalen; *Jesus, Man of Prayer*, Hodder & Stoughton, 1987, p 97.
118 Peter Hocken, *You He Made Alive*, DLT, 1974, p 17.
119 Stephen Verney, *Into the New Age*, Fontana, 1976, pp 91–2.
120 Brother Ramon; *A Guidebook to the Spiritual Life*, edited by Peter Toon, Marshall Pickering, 1988, p 122.
121 Ibid, p 122.
122 Peter Dodson; *Contemplating the Word*, SPCK, 1987.
123 Ibid.
124 Quoted in *Soul Friend*; by Kenneth Leech, Sheldon Press, 1977, p 170.
125 Quoted ibid, p 44.
126 *Pray with . . .*; Bro Kenneth CGA and Sr Geraldine Dss, CSA, C10, 1977, p 15.
127 Thomas Merton; *Contemplative Prayer*, DLT, 1973, p 44.
128 Gerard W. Hughes SJ, *God of Surprises*, DLT, 1985, pp 96, 99.
129 Thelma Hall, *Too Deep For Words*, p 19.
130 John Powell; *He Touched Me*, Harlow: Argus, 1976, pp 53, 54.
131 J.B Phillips' expression.
132 Brian Greeaway; *Inside*, Lion, 1985, pp 9–60.
133 Henri J.M. Nouwen quoted in Robert Durback (Ed); *Seeds of Hope*, DLT, 1989, p 124, 5.

134 Jean Vanier, *The Broken Body*, DLT, London, 1988, p 72.
135 David Watson, *Fear No Evil*, Hodder & Stoughton, 1984, pp 41, 42.
136 Ingrid Trobisch *Learning to Walk Alone* IVP 1985 p 57.
137 See Gary R. Collins, *How to be a People Helper*, Regal Books, 1976, pp 33, 34.
138 Henri J.M. Nouwen, Donald P. McNeill, Douglas A. Morrison; *Compassion*, DLT, 1982, p 27.
139 Ibid p 4.
140 Ibid p 18.
141 Ibid p 4.
142 Ibid p 32.
143 Kallistos Ware; *The Orthodox Way*, Mowbrays, 1979, p 88.
144 Dom Ralph Wright, quoted by Maria Boulding, *The Coming of God*, SPCK, 1982, p 122.
145 Billy Graham; *Angels, God's Secret Agents*, Hodder & Stoughton, 1975, pp 113–114.
146 Ibid pp 12, 13.
147 Henri J.M. Nouwen, Donald P. McNeill, Douglas A. Morrison, *Compassion*, DLT, 1982, p 13
148 Caryll Houselander; *The Reed of God*, Sheed and Ward, London, 1944, p 11.
149 Guy Brinkworth *Thirsting for God* Mullan Press 1970 pp 7–8.
150 Meekness and Majesty; Graham Kendrick 1986 Make Way Music. Administered by Thank you Music.
151 *The Weekday Missal*, Collins Liturgical Publishers.
152 George Appleton; *One Man's Prayers*, SPCK, 1977, p 4.